OUR TIME TO DANCE

A Mother's Journey to Joy

Eva Doherty Gremmert

ISBN 978-1-64559-579-3 (Paperback)
ISBN 978-1-64559-580-9 (Digital)

Covenant Books, Inc.
11661 Hwy 707
Murrells Inlet, SC 29576
www.covenantbooks.com

To my sweet son Nicholas:
You taught me to dance joyfully.
Thank you.

Acknowledgments

Since Nick was born, I knew this book needed to be written. However, I am surprised that this acknowledgment section has been the most difficult part for me to write.

Although this book is dedicated to Nick and I certainly would have had nothing to write about without him in my life, I want to especially thank my sweet husband. Arden, without you this journey would have been endured rather than celebrated. We have walked hand in hand.

I want to thank my friends and family who have read, listened to, and reread the various drafts of this manuscript. We have laughed, loved, and cried together.

Bridget Boland of Modern Muse, I loved your collaborative work style throughout the developmental edit of my manuscript. Your vision of my book's possibilities encouraged me. I am grateful for your insight.

Kim Runciman of Night Vision Editing, you have been amazing. Your vast experience with many different authors and genres was indispensable and your comments were very astute.

The list of people who have helped and supported me on this four-decade journey is extensive. I don't want to hurt anyone by forgetting to mention them, so here is a quote I recently heard watching an award show acceptance speech on television: "There are just too many to thank, you know who you are. Thank you!"

Contents

PART ONE

The Beginning

Chapter One

No mother ever expects to face her child's mortality. It is not the natural course of life. Yet here I was, sitting in a doctor's office in Seattle, Washington in December of 2015, with my husband, my thirty-six-year-old son Nick and his neurologist.

"Look, at this stage, if there is anything you guys really want to do with Nick, just go ahead." Dr. Doherty said, "We have no idea when he won't be with us anymore."

What did he just say? Did I hear him right? Is Nick dying?

I looked over to my husband Arden, whose face reflected the shock I was feeling. Nick was still sitting in his wheelchair, watching his white spinner string going around and around.

Does Nick know he might die? I don't want to do this.

Trying to breathe, my eyes slowly scanning the small exam room, I avoided looking at the doctor's face.

I have to ask but I don't want to. Nick might get upset.

I marshaled my courage and looked intently at the doctor. Carefully I asked, "Is that event imminent?"

"Eva, it is highly likely that when he goes into status epileptic seizures, he won't come out. You guys know that."

"Yes, we do know that, but no one has ever been so blunt about it before."

Gently he said, "Nick has suffered with Lennox-Gastaut Syndrome for his entire life. The seizures are escalating in duration, he is taking five different seizure meds, we did the Vagus Nerve Stimulator surgery a few months ago, and we still do not have good control. Nick's disease has progressed. SUDEP, which is Sudden Unexpected Death in Epilepsy, is a real threat. You have to face the facts. We have done all we can."

I looked at my sweet son, still slowly spinning his string. I looked at Arden, his blue eyes brimming with unshed tears.

Why doesn't he say anything? Why do I have to be the one to talk right now?

Dr. Doherty reached over and patted my hand. "You guys will know what to do. You always have. Just don't put anything off. Now, let's make the follow-up appointment for six months from now to evaluate the VNS. I hope to see you then."

He stood up, signaling that our appointment was over. His eyes showing the compassion he had not expressed. Numbly, I gathered up the files, while Arden unlocked the wheelchair brakes and we followed the doctor out the door.

In the elevator heading to the parking garage, my mind was reeling.

If I look at Arden right now, I will lose it. I have always known that this day would come. What will I do without Nick?

Finally, I glanced at Arden's face. Our eyes met and he quickly looked away.

What will we do without Nick?

As I, too, looked away, I noticed Nick looking straight at me. He usually avoided eye contact, but this time, he had something to say.

"I go to heaven now?"

I glanced at Arden. He wouldn't meet my gaze. It was up to me to respond.

"Nick, you'll go to heaven. I just don't know the day. I hope it's not right now, that's between you and Heavenly Father."

A frown shadowed his face. "You will miss me?"

I heard Arden catch his breath as I reached down to hug our son. "I will miss you so much, but Mommy and Daddy will be okay if you need to go. Right, Daddy?"

I looked at my husband's ashen face. Raising one eyebrow, I gestured my head toward our son. After thirty-eight years of marriage, Arden knew exactly what I was telling him to do.

"Nick, we love you and will always take care of you, but one of these days you'll go live in heaven and yes," pausing, his voice catching, he said, "I will miss you." Looking at me, while speaking to Nick, my gentle husband said, "We will miss you."

On the ride home, no one spoke. The radio filled the silence with country songs as the miles rolled by. As I sightlessly stared out the window trying not to think, I heard the familiar opening chords of Nick's favorite song, Garth Brooks mega-hit titled "The Dance." Nick began singing, "Looking back on the memory of the dance we shared..." The floodgates opened, my mind was filled with memories, as hot tears freely flowed down my cheeks. Nick kept singing. Arden reached over and touched my knee. Our wet eyes met, the comfort we have learned to give each other flowing between us. Simultaneously, we took a deep breath and joined Nick singing, "And now I'm glad I didn't know the way it all would end..."

Chapter Two

Saturday morning, August 18, 1979, a startling familiar pain gripped my belly, waking me up before 7:00 a.m. I was surprised.

This is early. I am not due for another three weeks. I hope everything is okay.

I nudged Arden and waddled to the bathroom. Fourteen months earlier, my labor with Ryan had started at 4:00 a.m. with good strong contractions. It only lasted twelve hours. Second babies usually come even quicker.

I hope this labor is faster. I really wish there was an easier way. As I waited for the second contraction, I gathered my things for the hospital. *Why did I put this off? It's not like I didn't know I was pregnant. I had my bag ready for a month before Ryan came. Oh, wow, another contraction. Fifteen minutes between them, I wonder if I am really in labor.*

Arden was frantically running around the house.

"You can slow down, sweetheart," I said. "This baby doesn't seem to be quite ready to be born. We have time."

He paused. "You sure? We can just run over to the hospital so you can be checked."

Nodding, I replied, "We do need to head over, but we don't need to rush. Go get Ryan up. We can take him to your mother's first."

Arden's parents, LaVern and Darrell, lived a couple of miles away, and Ryan loved being with his Grandma Gremmert.

My contractions were intense.

After the examination, the labor nurse said, "You are in labor, but you'll be more comfortable at home. Come back when the contractions are about five minutes apart."

Leaving, Arden said, "I think that we should go to Mom's. She will help with Ryan and you can rest."

I can't imagine resting at my mother-in-law's, but hopefully, it'll only be a few hours.

Between contractions, I walked around their house. I had heard that it could help.

How will I find room in my life and heart for another child? How will I have enough time to give to both children? Do I even remember how to care for a newborn? What was I thinking?

I experienced the typical worries of a second-time mom. After a couple of hours, I was exhausted and took a nap on the couch. Later, I awoke to Arden whispering with his younger brother, "She'll be fine, it takes hours and hours to have a baby. Don't worry, it won't happen right here."

Interrupting them, I said, "I kinda wish it would happen right here, right now."

A few hours later, we went back up to the hospital, only to be sent home again.

In frustration, I said to Arden, "This labor is already longer than Ryan's. It wasn't that long ago and it seems that my body has forgotten how to deliver a baby."

"The nurses said you're progressing. They believe it's easier for you not to be in a hospital bed for this part."

We got Ryan bedded down at Arden's parents. It was 10:00 p.m. Frustrated, I insisted, "Arden, take me back there, they're going to keep me this time. I want to introduce Ryan to his baby brother or sister in the morning."

I don't remember the next fifteen hours after checking in. It is a blur. Years later, Arden said that they were some of the scariest, loneliest hours of his life. Medical decisions were made to increase the intensity of the contractions and reduce my pain. Sitting by my bedside, holding my hand while I whimpered, he caught the whispered conversations of the nurses in the hall, "She is so exhausted, the baby must be also. We might need to intervene."

Although he never expressed his fear to me, I could read it on his face, when he bravely smiled at me.

Finally, at one o'clock Sunday afternoon, the nineteenth of August, after thirty-one endless exhausting hours of labor, the moment of glory arrived. It's a boy! Arden still looked concerned. I waited anxiously for the small bundle to be laid in my arms. The wait was an eternity, then finally, I held my second son, Nicholas James Gremmert. His sandy-blond hair matched mine.

I hope that Ryan and Nicky grow up to be best friends. They'll be just a year apart in school; they can play together, practice sports together. It will be fun to watch.

He looked so peaceful sleeping in my arms. I was disappointed he wasn't awake, but the nurses counseled me to not compare him to Ryan. (This piece of advice I was to hear often over the next twelve months.) After a short time, they took him to the nursery.

Later, I rang my call button for the nurse. In a few moments, she was at the door. "Yes, Mrs. Gremmert?"

"Could you bring me my baby?"

"Now, Mrs. Gremmert, you know that we have set times to bring baby in. The next scheduled time is in about an hour. He is fast asleep. You rest now and we will see how baby is doing then."

She shut the door, cutting off my response. In the pit of my stomach, an ache was developing, a sense of foreboding and unknown fear. Over time, this feeling grew stronger rather than abating.

The nurses couldn't rouse him from his deep sleep for the four o'clock afternoon feeding, so they didn't bring him in. I was a little concerned, but I did need sleep after such a grueling labor. However, by seven that evening, I was frantic.

My anxious thoughts crowded my mind. *I know there is some-thing wrong, they are just not telling me. I need to see for myself.* Again, I rang the call button. This time the response time was longer.

"Yes, Mrs. Gremmert?"

"Could you bring me my baby? I need to see him."

"Mrs. Gremmert, we told you that baby is fine. Baby is exhausted from the exertion of birth. It was a long labor, was it not? You both need to rest." She turned to leave.

"Please, I must insist that you bring me my son."

Tears of frustration rolled down my cheeks.

"You won't let me get out of bed yet, and I need to see my baby. I haven't seen him for almost six hours. I will just go down to the nursery myself."

Alarmed, she rushed to my bedside. "You mustn't get up yet. Please just lie back down. I will go and see what I can do."

A few minutes later, I heard two women whispering outside my door. "This is most unusual."

"She is a bit unnerved and I hope that this will calm her, she needs to rest."

The door opened and in walked my nurse followed by the nursery room nurse holding my son. They both stood there, not knowing what to do.

"Please give me my son. I will use my call button when I am finished."

Still in control, the nursery nurse mechanically reminded me, "Now, Mrs. Gremmert, don't fall asleep holding baby. You might drop him." My nurse added, "Don't be long, you both need rest. You'll have plenty of time to hold baby when you are back home."

"We will be fine, please close the door," I said as I looked down at the small bundle in my arms.

Cloistered in my hospital room, I sought reassurance that I had fabricated a nightmare in my mind. For a few moments, I just held my new baby. The warmth of his body generated a peaceful feeling throughout mine. I relaxed, comforted for the first time since my labor had started. After a few minutes, I inspected my newborn son. As I unwrapped the blankets that bound him, he stirred and whimpered a bit.

He doesn't have that same lusty cry as Ryan. I won't miss that. This baby is very thin, like a plucked chicken. Ryan was uncommonly large at nine and a half pounds, but Nicky's seven pounds is well within the normal range. His ears do look a little funny, sort of pinched and misshaped. All the baby books mention that a newborn's body needs to be pliable to move through the birth canal. In a few days, his ears should look fine.

Then I gazed into my sweet baby's eyes, searching for a glimmer of life. I found none.

There wasn't anyone looking back at me.

I recalled Ryan's birth fourteen months earlier.

Ryan was so strong, so aware from the moment of birth, eager to make his presence known. The first time I held him in the delivery room, his eyes searched his field of vision, finally resting on my face. Our souls touched as we gazed at one another.

The memory brought tears to my eyes.

The bundle in my arms stirred, bringing me back to the present. I longed for a similar experience with this child and could hardly wait for him to recover from the labor.

A couple of days and he'd be over all this. That's what the nurses said. And after all, he does have ten fingers and ten toes. We'll be fine.

I did feel some relief. I rang the nurse. She came and got the baby, so I could get some rest.

As I drifted on the brink of sleep I thought, *Nicholas James Gremmert. Such a strong name, a dignified name. He will grow into it. The name will look good on a door plaque, whatever his occupation. Nicholas J. Gremmert, Attorney at Law. Dr. Nicholas Gremmert, MD. Nicholas J. Gremmert, Chairman of the Board. For now, he is Nicky to me.*

I felt a deeper exhaustion than I ever felt before. My body was heavy, yet it seemed like I was floating. There was no pain, just a calm serenity.

Then I heard a distinct voice softly call my name. "Eva, do you want to come home, or do you want to stay here?"

I can't die, what about my baby?

In my mind's eye, I saw Nicky sleeping peacefully in the hospital nursery down the hall.

I said to the voice, "I want to stay here."

The voice called my name a second time. "Eva, do you want to come home, or do you want to stay here?"

I can't die, what about Arden and Ryan?

I thought of the two of them at home and what their lives might be like without me. Somehow, I knew that Nicky would go with me; he and I were tied together.

"I want to stay here," I repeated.

The voice asked again, "Eva, do you want to come home, or do you want to stay here?"

I calmly but with full conviction said, "I want to stay here."

Immediately, I fell into a deep, dreamless sleep.

I was awakened in the morning by my mom and Sally, her best friend from college. Both stared at me with startled expressions. A knowing look passed between them.

"Eva, I'll be back in a moment," Mom said. She turned to her friend. "Sally, stay here and visit with her."

Sally sat down next to the bed and rubbed my hand. I'd had a full night's sleep but I was still so exhausted that I dozed off despite the company.

My mother returned with the doctor. She had insisted that he examine me to make sure that there was nothing wrong. He ordered a lot of tests, but nothing explained the black circles under my eyes and my pasty skin tone.

Finally, Dr. Griffith reassured both of them, "She is fine, we will keep an eye on things. Don't worry."

My mom and Sally left and I asked the nurse to bring my baby to me. Nicky had slept most of the night and took a little sugar water around four am. I tried to nurse him, with the same result as before. He was still asleep after about twenty minutes, so I rang the nurse. She asked the usual questions: "How did he nurse?"

"He didn't."

"How responsive was he?"

"He wasn't. He never really woke up."

As she walked out of my room, again, she reassured me, "He's just fine. Just wait and see. A couple of days, he'll come out of this. Some babies are just slower at starting. Just wait."

I knew that I was just fine; Nicky wasn't. My thoughts were in direct conflict with the professional opinions I was receiving. I didn't tell anyone about my experience the previous night until much later because I believed that God had sent me a message for my own knowledge and comfort and I had accepted a divine assignment.

Chapter Three

The final notes died away from Garth's song, "The Dance," and I was brought back to the present with Nick's response, "I love that song. You love that song, Mom?"

"I do love that song, Nick," I replied.

The news today is nothing new. I've faced the same scenario before. My experience in the hospital all those years ago, on Nick's first night set the tone for our journey together. We got this.

"What's next?" asked Nick and we turned our attention to the radio to join in with whatever was playing.

A few weeks later, he began having cluster seizures just after he woke up. These seizures start and stop but occur in groups, one right after another. The doctors warn us that someday in the future, our rescue medication treatment plan won't stop the seizures and Nick will die. We live with that fear daily.

Arden and I are very familiar with the steps to the seizure management dance. Get Nick safe and comfortable, grab the rescue medicine from his bag to start the protocol, begin taking detailed notes of when and what is happening, administer the emergency magnet to the Vagus Nerve Stimulator (VNS) device, call the doctor, sit by his bedside, keeping careful watch for any indication of further seizures. Nick's VNS puts out a regular mild pulse of electrical energy to his brain every five minutes for thirty seconds via the Vagus nerve. The VNS lies under the skin in his upper chest. Placing the magnet over the VNS device for three seconds stops the electrical pulse. Removing the magnet restarts the device at twice the time interval and at an increased milliamperes for an instant cycle.

We repeat these steps until the seizures either stop or we have to call the ambulance and go to the hospital.

I know this sounds rather like a clinical to-do list, just having the routine helps to keep the terror at bay. Often, the cluster seizures will last many hours before they finally stop. Typically, it is only a couple times a year that we need to transport him to the hospital.

This particular day, after the third phone call to the doctor's office, I looked at my sweet husband's concerned face.

"We've given him all the scheduled rescue meds."

"I know" was the quiet reply.

"Are you calling 911, or shall I?"

"Go ahead," he said, returning to his bedside sentry post.

Nick was still seizing. After a few minutes, our quiet vigil was interrupted by the efficiency of four emergency medical technicians from the fire department. We knew them; they had been with us before. We still had to fill out all the paperwork.

As Arden answered the questions, I kept watch.

Jenny, one of the EMTs, came close and put her arm around my shoulders. "We will take care of him, you know."

That opened the floodgates. I had been bracing myself against the build-up of emotions, and I wept. We stood there for several minutes, then Nick seized again. With my protective wall back in place and I stepped forward to monitor and time keep.

When the transport ambulance arrived, the EMTs gently took Nick down the stairs and put him in the ambulance. We had waited to take him downstairs between the cluster seizures, to make it easier. The two transport medics didn't know us.

One said, "Mom and Dad, you can follow to the hospital, just take your time."

"I will be coming with you."

He was a little surprised. "Okay, why don't you sit up front here then?"

"My son needs me in the back with him."

"Ma'am, that is not customary."

I have experienced this same conversation with many others before him and I was firm.

"If one of us is not with him in the back he will be anxious. Anxiety will escalate the seizures. I have been on many ambulance rides and in many hospital emergency rooms."

He relented and I climbed in next to Nick.

Between seizures, Nick was chatty. He loves traveling in the ambulance. With the lights and sirens and all of the attention from the medical team, it is a wonderful experience for him. Except for the seizures.

After we were underway, Nick asked the medic who was taking care of him, "You love the Seahawks?"

A little surprised, he answered, "I do."

"You watch them on TV, like me?"

"I do watch them on TV, Nick,"

"I like number 3, Russell Wil…"

A seizure started. We watched and waited. The medic asked me, "Is this normal?"

"Yes."

A little while later, Nick was back with us and resumed, "I like number 3, Russell Wilson. You like Russell Wilson?"

Laughing a little, the medic, responded, "I do like Russell Wilson, Nick."

The ambulance siren wailed as we flew down the freeway. Glancing at my son Nick I trembled.

Will he survive? We have been here so many times before! Will he come home with me again, or will I go home tomorrow, leaving his cold body in the hospital morgue?

He began to seize again, and habitually, I glanced at my watch, noting the beginning. Looking across the gurney, my eyes met the questioning gaze of the medic.

"I am timing this."

We both looked at Nick. His handsome face, gray, ashen, and grimacing, in the rhythmic dance of a grand mal seizure. I glance at my watch; an eternity of thirty seconds had passed.

I wonder where Arden is, has he left the house yet to follow to the hospital? There isn't much traffic yet. We should get there quicker than last time.

The jerking stopped.

Now comes the hard part. Will he start breathing again?

I mark the time. Thirty seconds, a minute, two minutes, I shut my eyes. Looking at the watch again, two minutes and...

Then I hear it, the deep groan of lungs pulling in air, grasping at life. He lives. This immediate crisis had past.

By the end of the hour-long ride to Seattle, the seizures had stopped and Nick had invited the medic to watch the Hawks play on TV at our house. Though his speech was slurred and apraxic because of the extra seizure meds he had on board, Nick was open and engaged with his newfound friend. He had been seizing for almost five hours when they finally stopped. I was exhausted and deeply relieved.

We experimented with his medication dosages over the next few weeks, trying to get maximum coverage with minimum side effects.

An idea began to germinate.

Nick hadn't met his newest niece Sadie Ann yet. She is Ryan and Tiffany's fifth child and they live in Louisville, Kentucky. We talked to Ryan, who is employed as a commercial airline captain.

"Air travel could potentially make things worse, and if Nick did have seizures while you were in flight that could be problematic for the flight crew. What about driving out here?"

"In a car?"

He laughed. "Think of it as the Nick J's last hurrah trip."

"I do like that idea. We will have more flexibility traveling in a car if something happens."

Although we knew that nothing with Nick goes according to plan, we began mapping our major 2016 road trip.

Chapter Four

Nicky was never very alert during his first few weeks of life. When he was awake, he was drowsily crying. Nothing comforted him—food, warmth, human touch. It wasn't a loud cry, just a constant one. Many times, after hours of rocking and singing to him, in frustration, I put him in his crib, away from me. Suddenly, it was deathly quiet and I'd run to his room, worried that something awful had happened to him. He'd be staring at some point on the ceiling. It was impossible to break his gaze. Arden and I prayed for comfort, we prayed for answers, we prayed for our son.

Nicky completely changed when he was a few months old, and he became an easy baby. He wasn't bothered if he was wet or not, fed or not, held or not. He was happy sitting next to me in the cradle, or rocking in the automatic baby-swing while the days rolled by. But he wasn't growing. At his two-month checkup, he hadn't gained any weight in a month.

The doctor said, "Eva, we call it failure to thrive. Some kids are just slower at getting started. Most of them grow out of it, finally functioning at age level by their first birthday. Don't worry, this is not your fault."

I don't believe him. I feel so guilty that Nicky isn't okay. Ryan had nursed so successfully; he'd known what to do right from the start. With Nicky, every mealtime is a battle as he struggles and cries.

"Doctor, something has to be done. I need a plan."

"I suggest that you stop breastfeeding and begin using formula. There isn't anything wrong with your milk supply or your son. Some babies just have a harder time at the beginning."

But I knew something was wrong. Very, very wrong. My life was busy. Between church and extended family activities, projects around the house, and visiting friends, time to sit down and evaluate Nicky's situation was at a premium. Plus, I really didn't want my worst fears confirmed. It seemed easier to ignore my concerns.

Feeding him remained a challenge. Downing an eight-ounce bottle took him over an hour. I mentally compared that hour to the ten minutes it took to feed other babies. Sometimes Nicky grew so frustrated and agitated while trying to suck the milk from the nipple that he would cry until he fell asleep. When he awoke, the difficult cycle of trying to feed him would begin again.

In October, Arden took a new job as the advertising manager for a Tacoma newspaper. We packed our belongings and bought a cute little three-bedroom house in a neighborhood with sidewalks. There was a fireplace in the living room and hardwood floors throughout. The fenced-in yard was what sold me, however. It contained fruit trees and roses, carnations, and hollyhock, and many beautiful rhododendron bushes. A mature grape arbor bordered the back fence.

Arden had a fantastic salary, and we also bought a brand new 1980 blue four-door Buick Skylark. It was the car of my dreams. I didn't want the black cloud of concern about Nicky to overshadow our new success. Our lives were full with raising an infant and a toddler, and we were on top of the world. At twenty-three years old, we had achieved the American dream. We even bought a dog.

We met a few of the families in the neighborhood, including the Andersons. They were in the middle of remodeling their kitchen and adding a second story. In spite of the mess and confusion they invited us in for a visit. Their daughter Anna was two weeks older than Nicky. We immediately knew we would become friends. They were devout Christians and believed as we did that family should be the center of our lives. We shared many common values.

However, as the weeks turned into months, it was more and more difficult for me to see Anna growing and developing while Nicky just sat there and smiled.

One morning, Leslie Anderson called and invited us to come visit. I got everyone ready and took the boys over.

She greeted me at the door. "Guess what Anna did today! She rolled over, come and see. She may not do it again. Oh, I can't wait to show you. This is so exciting."

With hesitation, I followed her into the front room. There was Anna, on her back on the floor, smiling up at her mom.

Leslie proudly said, "Oh, Anna, you are an amazing baby, look what you did again. Eva, I put her on her belly and see what she did. Isn't it remarkable?"

"Yes, it is," I said weakly.

She seemed surprised by my lackluster response, but I just couldn't engage in her excitement. I didn't notice that I was gripping Nicky too hard until he started to cry.

"Leslie, I need to take Nicky home, he is upset. I will call you and we can reschedule. Sorry about this." I grabbed Ryan by the hand and quickly led him out the front door.

"But, Mommy, I want to play with the toys," Ryan argued.

"We have to get your little brother home, Ryan, we have toys there."

Though I longed for a close relationship with Leslie, I found myself withdrawing from her friendship. It was too hard, too heart-breaking, to see the differences between our two babies.

A few weeks later, Nicky's first Christmas was a real disappointment.

I tried to explain my concerns the next morning to Arden. "He didn't even grasp the idea of opening presents or recognize what was going on. He just wanted to be held. Everything was so different last year with Ryan. At six months old, he was just two months older than Nicky is now, remember how quickly Ryan caught on to the idea of opening presents. He even wanted to open more than his share. Two months can't make that much difference in a child's development, can they?"

Arden tried to comfort me. "The doctors have said that he will be fine. He will grow out of this, right?"

I didn't know, and I didn't want to know. Eighteen-month-old Ryan had been more than willing to open all of Nicky's presents for him, while Nicky was content to sit in his swing, rocking back and forth.

Chapter Five

In January that year, my neighbor Leslie invited Nicky and me to join her and Anna in a twice-weekly mommy-baby swim class at the YMCA.

I hoped that our time in the water would strengthen him. He was so weak that we still needed to support his head like a newborn. Ryan had been so strong from birth. I never needed to cradle his head, even when we were holding him upright on our shoulders. At over four months old, Nicky couldn't hold onto toys or rattles. He didn't reach out and grasp objects. Sometimes his eyes would follow bright colors and loud rattling noises, and sometimes they wouldn't.

One evening, I told Arden, "I feel like I am a failure at being a mom. All these other moms we know have it all together. Their babies are doing everything right on time."

Arden was just as worried as I was but he tried to reassure me. "You are taking Nicky to the swim classes. It's all arranged and hopefully it'll help him."

Instead, the swim classes were a watershed moment for me. The other moms were open and friendly with me at the first class, but a separation soon developed. In the dressing room before class, all their conversations flowed around me.

"How is she doing?"

"Oh, she is pushing herself backward, all around the floor now. The other day, I found her stuck under a chair."

"I tried smashed bananas yesterday for lunch, and he loved them. It was so cute!"

I wasn't able to participate in their discussions about my baby's developmental accomplishments. Even the swim class teacher noticed that Nicky wasn't able to do the same things that the other infants could do. She suggested that I just play with him in the water, while she worked with the other moms.

Every swim class, I went farther out into the pool, conspicuously alone, and let the Nicky float on his back in the water. I supported him on my chest while I manipulated his tiny legs in a kicking motion. I knew that swimming was great therapy for stroke victims, and I hoped that it might be helpful to Nicky. Later, his physical therapists explained to me that the time swimming had strengthened his nervous system and muscles. This development led to him being able to weight bear and eventually walk.

When the eight weeks of class were over, I didn't register for the next session.

I explained, "Arden, even though Nicky loves being in the water, I can't handle it when I am in those classes with all those other babies his age. It's overwhelming to me."

"Don't worry, you don't need to go back. We'll think of something."

As springtime arrived, I began to believe that the physical movement I had done with Nicky in the pool had paid off. Now at seven months old, I could prop him up with a pile of large pillows and he would remain upright. He could finally hold onto a toy if we put it in his hands. Though if it fell out of his grasp, he wouldn't attempt to retrieve it. He would cry until one of us picked it up and put it back into his hands.

At the end of April, Arden's brother Darren came over one evening to visit. After dinner, he cleared his throat and said, "I saw a TV program about children with autism last week and they act a lot like Nicky. I can't stop thinking about it. Do you think that there might be something wrong with him?"

Arden and I looked at one another across the table. I couldn't speak.

Arden said, "Darren, we have been worried about him too. Every time we ask, the medical professionals tell us that there's nothing wrong and not to worry so much. Hopefully they are right."

That topic was over when Ryan ran to the table and demanded that his uncle play with him.

Later after Darren left, I said to Arden, "I have been worried. It seems more real, now that someone else has told us that they believe something is wrong. I don't know if it's autism, or it's something else, but something's not normal with Nicky. I'm going to ask the doctor about it again next week at his appointment."

"I agree, hopefully he'll have an answer for us."

At the appointment, I had my questions prepared for Dr. White.

I began, "I'm really concerned about Nicky's lack of development. In the books that I have read, he should be—"

Interrupting me, he reached over, patted my hand condescendingly, and said, "Mrs. Gremmert, you really need to stop being such an over-anxious mom. It isn't good for you or for your baby."

He stood up to leave the examination room.

Exasperated, I tried to continue, "But he is eight months old and he can't sit up or pick up toys or—"

He interrupted me again, this time, not so gently, "Seriously, Mrs. Gremmert, you must calm yourself. You are completely overreacting. There's nothing wrong with this child. He's gaining skills at his own pace. You need to stop this. Go home and love your son. That's what he needs from you." He spun on his heels and disappeared.

I left the office stunned.

Why can't they see that he is not okay? I know that I am not a crazy mom. I know that he needs help. They just all seem to think that I am nuts.

That night after the boys were asleep, I approached Arden to talk about it.

"Every professional I have seen tells me that I am crazy."

"Now, Eva, they don't say that you are crazy. They're trying to counsel us. They seem to believe that he will grow out of this slow development and catch up."

"I don't know, I still feel like there's something wrong. I just don't know why they aren't concerned."

Hugging me, he said, "We both believe in our hearts that there's something wrong. Let's keep praying about it. Why don't we give it a little more time? Usually when God wants us to do something, He lets us know, right? Remember we both thought that Nicky should be in the swimming lessons and that seemed to help him."

This discussion hardened our resolve to act on any opportunity we discovered to help our son.

Chapter Six

By June, nothing had changed. I am not a patient person, I wanted to take action and I was tired of waiting. I called the local children's hospital and asked for an appointment with a neurologist.

The receptionist said, "You can't see a neurologist until you have a referral from a pediatrician that specialized in neurologic disorders. You must be referred."

"Okay, can I have an appointment with a pediatrician that meets your criteria?"

She made us an appointment for the next week. I spent those days in tortured apprehension. To calm myself, I wrote extensive notes about the concerns I'd had since his birth. It was a vast, depressing list. Then I listed Ryan's developmental achievements from his baby book and compared that with what we had noticed about Nicky.

The day of the appointment arrived. I believed that we would finally get an answer to our concerns. Arden had meetings at work, so I took Nicky to the appointment, alone. Three other moms smiled at me as we entered the small but pleasant waiting room.

The receptionist said, "Here are the registration forms to fill out. Do you need a pen? The nurse would take you both back to see the doctor soon."

Everything seemed so normal.

I sat down, with Nicky on my lap.

The questions began. "How old is your baby?"

"It is a boy or a girl?"

"He's small for his age, isn't he? My kids were all so huge."

"I think this one has an ear infection. What's wrong with your baby?" one asked me innocently.

What's wrong with my baby? How can I tell you, a perfect stranger, the turmoil roiling in my soul?

I checked back my tears and said haltingly, "I don't know."

The other moms looked away, embarrassed, leaving me with my own desperate thoughts.

The wait felt like an eternity. Finally, the nurse called my name. I gathered Nicky and my things and followed her down the hall past the brightly colored animals on the wall, the toy chest and racks of children's books. The nurse began the customary dialogue in the exam room. "What can we do for you today, Mrs. Gremmert?"

It was difficult for me to answer. I merely said, "His father and I are concerned that our son Nicholas isn't developing correctly. He hasn't learned things as quickly as his older brother did. We want him evaluated by this doctor so we can get a referral to a pediatric neurologist."

She looked startled and quickly weighed Nicky and took his vitals. She told me that the doctor would be in shortly. Checking his chart, as she quietly closed the door, she muttered, "That baby isn't much bigger than his birth weight."

Alone and confused, I awaited the doctor. Finally, after twenty minutes, he came in. Without making any introduction he said, "So, you're worried, are you? Well, let's see…"

He didn't ask any questions.

"Here are my notes and questions."

He glanced at me and said perfunctorily, "Just a minute please," as if to keep me from interfering. I watched as he moved Nicky's legs up and down, tried to make him sit up, shone a light into his eyes, and felt the top of his head. The whole examination took about three minutes, during which the doctor didn't say a word to me. He handed Nicky back to me and said, "I'll be back."

I bit back my anger and frustration. He hadn't even looked at the notes I had brought.

When the doctor returned a few minutes later, he stood just inside the door, across the room from me.

Raising one eyebrow, he interrogated me, "How often during the day do you attempt to feed your baby?" His dismissive attitude was palpable and it chilled me.

"Every three hours or so."

He skeptically frowned. "How long are these attempts?"

"About forty-five minutes."

He cocked his head to one side and his eyes narrowed, "How else do you interact with your baby?"

"I try to play with him, but he just doesn't seem interested."

After these few questions, I was feeling defensive.

Does he think that I am neglecting my son?

He didn't say anything for a few moments, then reaching for the door, he disdainfully said, "there is nothing wrong with this infant. His development is completely within normal ranges. I am not making a referral to a pediatric neurologist. It would be a waste of their time."

He looked directly at me, "Mrs. Gremmert, if you don't stop comparing your second son to his older brother, your parenting will prove to handicap him. You need to immediately change your attitude, go home and properly care for your son."

Then he left the room.

I was devastated and confused.

I love my baby and it is so obvious to me that he doesn't have the skills that other babies his age have. I can't understand why these doctors can't see it. Why are they blaming me?

I have since learned that other parents searching for a diagnosis have received a similar deeply offensive reaction from medical personnel.

His incompetent "medical opinion" proved to be totally wrong. However, the damage his dubious diatribe did to me ran deep and was long lasting.

I cried all the way to my girlfriend's house while I drove to pick up Ryan. As she answered the door, she asked, "So what did they say? Is everything okay?"

Slowly I shook my head and said, "He said that Nicky is on the normal scale. I just don't see how that can be."

Putting her hand on my shoulder, she said, "I am sure everything will be all right." But I could tell in her eyes that she wondered if the doctor was right.

When Arden got home from work, he picked Nicky up and asked, "How'd it go?"

I told him about the appointment. He frowned. I waited.

Is he going to think that I am crazy too? Why do I have this nagging horrible feeling about my baby?

With relief I heard him say, "We will find another more competent and experienced doctor. Someone will believe us and see what we see. I should have gone with you for support. I'm very sorry, Eva."

Part of me would have given anything to believe that the doctor's assessment was correct, that I was the problem. But no matter how hard I tried, I just couldn't let go of the gnawing intuitive dread that had begun at Nicky's birth and kept growing steadily as the weeks and months passed.

PART TWO

Preparation

Chapter Seven

Arden and I knew we needed to carefully plan our road trip in 2016, so Nick would survive. One Sunday afternoon in February, the three of us sat down to create a list of what we needed to do.

Arden asked, "Who do you want to visit Nick?"

"Um, let me think."

I laughed and then somberly said, "Who do you want to see again? Remember Dr. Doherty said that this might be your last trip."

Raising his right hand, Nick began listing his requests, one finger at a time. "Grandma in Weiser, Ryan in Kentucky, Cliff and Rebecca in… Where Cliff and Rebecca in?"

"The Robinsons are in Carson City."

Nick continued on the third finger, "Cliff and Rebecca in Carson City, right? Allen and Leonie in Utah, and Emma Robinson. Mom, where Emma?"

"She is in Utah too. I think. I will ask Rebecca," I answered. "We would like to see other people on our road trip, Nick is that okay?"

"Who else?"

"Christina and Matt in Dallas."

"And Shonda Johnson," Nick interrupted.

"Yes, and Shonda Johnson too. We can go to Phoenix and see your aunts, uncles, and cousins there, and we can see aunt Rosie and uncle Darren in Utah. There are lots of people who love you that want to see you."

"Okay, we stay in Best Western?"

Intrigued, I asked, "Why Best Western?"

"They have waffles for breakfast, you know."

I had forgotten that they had a great breakfast included in the price of the stay. Nick looked out the window, spinning his string. He was done talking to us.

Arden asked, "Eva, how long will this road trip be?"

"I don't know, let's see how many miles it is."

We looked at Google Maps and discovered that it would be over eight thousand miles.

"Arden, how many hours do you think we can have him in a car each day?"

"Maybe seven or eight. What do you think?"

"I'm not sure. We might have to play it by ear. But I don't think we can have more than two travel days in a row. We'll need to break it up, so he doesn't get too tired and start seizing."

"You're right about that, I'm also worried about our car, it is fourteen years old with over 318,000 miles on it. I don't think that it is a good idea to drive it."

"You just want to get a new car." I laughed.

Arden does treasure his cars.

"I'm just being practical," he started to say.

"I agree with you, none of our current cars would be safe or comfortable to travel in for that many miles."

Over the next week, I mapped out an itinerary and Arden found us the perfect car. As we researched what would be best and created the schedule for our trip over the next few months, I kept remembering those beginning steps we took to gain an initial diagnosis for Nick.

Chapter Eight

During his first year, at every appointment, I questioned the nurses and doctors about Nicky's development. Each time I was reassured that nothing was wrong with my baby. Awkwardly, family members also expressed concern about Nicky. I felt that some were criticizing our parenting. It hurt.

Sometimes it was uncomfortable because I didn't want to answer any more pointed questions, but holidays are important, so for the Fourth of July, we arranged to spend time with both our parents and siblings. I knew that two-year-old Ryan would love all of the celebration—the parade, the food, and the fireworks. Nicky was quiet most of the day, in his own little world. When he was awake, he was passed around because everyone wanted to hold him and try to make a personal connection with him.

A miracle occurred when the fireworks started. I was worried that the loud noises would frighten him; instead, he was fascinated. His eyes blinked sharply each time the loud noise of the fireworks boomed in his ears, and he smiled the biggest smile I had ever seen him make when the colors burst in the night sky. He was mesmerized. I was astounded. That was a remarkable night for me. The fireworks were spectacular and my baby responded to something. He was obviously pleased. This gave me hope. He still loves fireworks.

A couple of days later, I was cleaning up after the weekend, doing my usual Monday chores. Nicky was napping on my bed and Ryan was playing in their room. I passed the boys' bedroom as I walked down the hall with a basket of laundry to put away. Ryan was sitting on the floor near the door facing the wall. He picked up a few of his favorite trucks and held them out toward the empty space in front of him.

"This one is my favorite, oh, and I like this one too," he said.

"What are you doing?" I asked.

He looked up at me quizzically and asked, "Talking to my baby sister Karen. Mommy, why won't you and daddy let her come and live with us?"

I was stunned, and at the same time, I felt the truth of his words. Fearfully, I thought, *I am barely coping with life right now!*

"I have to talk to your daddy about this."

I went into my room, put the laundry down, and looked at Nicky. *How could I possibly have another child when I don't know what the future holds for you? What is God thinking?*

I was having a crisis of faith. As a child raised in the Roman Catholic church, I had been taught to trust God. This truth was confirmed as I joined the Church of Jesus Christ of Latter-Day Saints when I was nineteen. I found it hard to put into practice, especially when faced with such an overwhelming situation, without a clear path of action. However, I do believe angels can visit us, especially when there is a message to impart.

Is God trying to tell me something? Is this part of His answer for me?

"Heavenly Father, you must be crazy," I prayed out loud as I put away the laundry. "I can't possibly take care of three children right now. Help me know what to do!"

After the boys were in bed that evening, and I had straightened up the kitchen, I realized that I needed to talk to Arden about my conversation with Ryan. He was reading the paper and I sat down next to him on the couch.

For a few moments, I just sat there, and then I cleared my throat, not so much to get his attention, but rather to postpone the inevitable conversation.

He looked up. "Do you need my help?"

"No, I want to talk to you about something and I don't know how to start."

His eyes widened with alarm. "Are you okay?"

I nodded yes.

"The boys then, is everything all right?"

I have got to tell him, he has to know what God is telling us.

Rubbing my forehead and shutting my eyes, I began, "I was walking down the hall this afternoon…"

Quiet and still, he listened intently to the tale of my earlier conversation with Ryan. Looking at me with love in his eyes, he said, "We need to pray about this."

Numbly I nodded.

We knelt down by our bed as we did every night, but tonight seemed more poignant. Arden said the prayer for both of us; he seemed to know that I wasn't up to it. He prayed and wept, feeling the conviction of truth that a little girl was supposed to join our family. I felt nothing. Yet I could tell that Arden knew it was true.

We had a short conversation and I tried to begin to believe. We quit using birth control and Karen was conceived.

A few weeks later, we learned I was pregnant. Arden was thrilled. All I felt was fear.

Arden's job was going through major changes. The owner of the paper had sold it earlier that year without any prior notice. Arden and a friend started a new consulting company called Communications Consortium. The hours were long, as any startup business requires. He was commuting to Burien each day and sometimes he didn't get home until after the boys were in bed. We missed him terribly.

A few days after his first birthday, Nicky spiked a fever of 103 degrees Fahrenheit. We rushed him to the local children's hospital. As the emergency room doctor treated his fever and his pain, he questioned us at great length about our baby's development. I was beginning to feel frustrated; it seemed a repeat of my earlier visit with that other pediatrician a few weeks before.

It was a simple diagnosis, Nicky had an ear infection. We were told no swimming for two weeks, take the antibiotic until it is gone, and see our doctor in ten days for a follow-up. Typical for a year old, except that as the doctor left the room he paused, looked at Nicky with a furrowed brow, shook his head, then slowly closed the door.

My heart stopped. Arden and I looked at each other and then quickly away. We didn't talk. Our fears about our son loomed between us.

We hurriedly packed up our belongings and left the hospital. We drove home in merciful quiet, the radio softly droning out melodies while Nicky slept in the back.

I reached out to hold Arden's hand, seeking some momentary calm amidst the impending storm. My husband is a great man in a crisis. He always seeks to discover the logical solution. Sometimes finding the solution takes too long for my tastes.

We do react differently to disaster, yet we are able to support each other and sense when the other one is about to keel over under the pressure. Later that night, I was the one to fall apart. As I wept in near-hysterics behind our closed bedroom door, I had a fleeting thought of concern about the intensity of my emotional reaction.

Will I ever stop crying?

A few days later, Arden admitted, "I was really afraid the other night. I don't believe I can handle all this if you aren't here beside me. I was worried that you wouldn't be able to pull yourself together. I wanted to comfort you, but nothing helped."

During those early years, Arden and I weathered many such emotional nights as I learned to respond calmly and serenely during a crisis, doing whatever needed to be done. This amazed everyone, including myself. Later, in the quiet restlessness of insomnia, Arden held me for hours as I released all my fears and worries in a deluge of tears. In the morning, I always felt better.

Chapter Nine

Home for a few days over the Labor Day weekend, Arden had been watching Nicky.

"I haven't seen any progress with Nicky for months now. He is almost thirteen months old. What do you think about taking him back up to see Dr. Griffith? We have always trusted him."

Dr. Robert Griffith, a general practice medical doctor, was my doctor since I was eight years old. He had delivered both Ryan and Nicky. An Iowa farm boy, his medical procedures and diagnostic techniques were very conservative. Time proven methods and country doctor treatments were his style.

"That is a great idea. He won't overreact, or over-treat a condition either. He will be straight up honest with me. That's his way."

I called his office the next day. When I arrived for the appointment, the office staff greeted me warmly. I felt comfortable in a way that only years of association can bring. The waiting room was so familiar, from the plastic couches to the Norman Rockwell prints on the walls. There were year-old copies of *Woman's Day* and *Newsweek* casually stacked on the coffee table in the center of the room. It was all the same, all very reassuring.

After only a few minutes, Dr. Griffith's nurse Sally opened the door and said, "I have a room ready for you Eva, come on, you know the way."

Sally was caring and thoughtful. Since my girlhood, I had always thought of her as a kindly loving aunt.

"Your two boys are so cute, Eva. Ryan, you have grown so much, you sure are a big boy."

I could tell he loved that.

"We are here because Mommy thinks there is something wrong with Nicky. He is not getting big like me."

Ryan chatted with Sally all the way around the corner, to the exam rooms. I followed along toting Nicky, the diaper bag and the stroller, attempting to appear composed and self-assured, the epitome of young motherhood.

Once we were in the exam room Sally said, "Ryan says that you're here to get Nicky better. What seems to be the trouble?"

Taking a deep breath, I began, "Arden and I are worried. Nicky just doesn't seem to be learning what he needs to, when he needs to. He is over a year old and can't crawl or even sit up very well. We didn't know what to do, so we came up here."

Sally looked at me tenderly and said, "Doctor will be here soon. We're so glad to see you again."

When Dr. Griffith walked in, he sat on his swivel stool and said with a small grin, "Don't they have doctors in Tacoma?"

I burst into tears, which made him uncomfortable. He reached for the page of questions I was holding.

"Now, now, let's see what you have here," he said soothingly.

While he read, I was able to compose myself. When he was finished, he turned toward us. "Hummm…let me see you, Nicholas."

He gently picked Nicky up, looked in his eyes, listened to his heart and lungs, tested his reflexes on his knees, the front of his ankles and the bottom of his feet. He felt the top of his head and looked into his eyes again. This was the most extensive exam Nicky had received recently. The contrast with the other doctors infuriated me.

"Eva, they call it failure to thrive. When you guys moved, I hoped that if Nicky didn't improve, your new doctor would see what I had feared when he was a newborn. You should visit a pediatric neurologist to get a proper diagnosis. I have heard good things about a new young pediatric neurologist, Dr. Stephen Glass. He has just opened his private practice, and I am impressed with him. He should be able to guide you from here."

He gave me the referral without hesitation and wished me luck. My mother had dropped us off for the appointment. She wasn't back yet and I couldn't wait in the office with all the emotions I was feeling. The weather was mild, so I packed the boys up in the stroller and we headed toward my parents' home, about a mile away. As I walked, I laughed, I cried, I felt fear, and relief.

I'm not crazy, there is something wrong. I don't know if I can do this. I hate not knowing what to expect. I'm not worried about Arden. He is so supportive. I just don't know about me.

Mom pulled up in her car about fifteen minutes later. Sally had told her what had happened. (This was many years before HIPAA.) Mom was worried about me too.

As she got out of the car to help me she asked, "How are you doing, Eva? Are you okay?"

"I'm so relieved Mom, now we can learn what to do."

She hugged me. "That's my girl, you're already formulating a plan. That's my Eva. You'll be just fine. I don't know why I was worried, you always figure out how to handle tough situations."

I didn't believe her then, but it turns out she knew me better than I knew myself. Often, during difficult times, we gain strength from the confidence others have in us, especially when we are doubtful about our own capacities.

Our appointment with Dr. Glass was scheduled for the following week. When the paperwork arrived in the mail a few days prior to the appointment, I let it sit on the sideboard for a couple of hours before opening it. I cried as I completed the health questionnaire. The questions were thorough. Answering them gave a stark picture of how far behind Nicky was compared to other kids his age. I don't have a copy of the questionnaire, but those tear-stained pages are probably filed in some hospital archive somewhere. As soon as the paperwork was completed I put it in the diaper bag to take to the appointment and tried to forget about it.

Arden took off from work to come with me. We arrived at the medical building near the hospital in Renton. We were a little early and made small talk. Neither of us wanted to talk about what was ahead.

Nicky was peaceful and quiet. We had recently discovered that music calmed Nicky. If we played the radio or sang, he wouldn't cry.

That knowledge proved invaluable later as we spent many hours each week in the car traveling to doctor and therapist appointments.

Dr. Glass's bright waiting room, with a large fish tank prominently displayed, was empty. A welcoming voice behind the desk said, "You must be the Gremmert's, and this is Nicholas. Or what do you call him?"

"We call him Nicky."

I watched as the receptionist took a narrow file folder off the shelves behind the desk and wrote on it. There were only two other folders on the shelves.

I had a fleeting thought: *Where are his other patient files? Is this guy experienced enough to help us? Dr. Griffith thinks so, I guess it will be okay.*

Beginning with that first appointment, Dr. Glass always treated us with respect. From the start, his manner was very professional and reassuring. In stark contrast to the other doctors we had seen, he valued my opinions about my son. He asked probing questions and documented our answers in his notes. He felt that since we were the ones caring for Nicky, he could develop a better treatment plan by listening to us.

Dr. Glass examined Nicky very gently, which comforted me. He was thorough and we didn't feel rushed. He kept asking if we had any other questions. He wanted to make sure we could express our concerns and ask questions. What a change from the first pediatric specialist. Finally, we had found someone who understood and respected us as Nicky's parents.

Dr. Glass explained, "We don't know what happened, but based on what he is presenting, it seems that sometime during Nicky's development in utero he had an insult to his brain, possibly from a virus. You couldn't have prevented this and you didn't do anything wrong during pregnancy. This just happened to your baby."

Arden and I looked at one another and I asked the question looming in our minds. "What chance is there that this would happen with another child we have?"

"The same chance you had before."

In that moment, I thought, *One of two kids, that's 50 percent. Not good odds at all.*

I must have had that deer in the headlights look because the doctor said, "Why? Are you expecting another baby?"

Arden and I looked at one another again. "We are, one in two kids doesn't seem like good odds."

He tried to reassure me, "What I meant was that you have the same percentage chance as the general population which is quite low."

I didn't feel much comfort. However, when we left the office about ninety minutes later, we had a diagnosis: developmental delay, static encephalopathy, and Dr. Glass had laid out a plan for us.

Nicky was scheduled to have an Electroencephalogram (EEG) and Computerized Axial Tomography (CT) scan a week later to see what was going on in his brain. These tests gave the doctor more information. The EEG is an electrophysiological monitoring method to record electrical activity of the brain. The test is typically noninvasive, with the electrodes placed on the scalp and usually lasts about forty-five minutes.

Meanwhile, we also had a referral for a physical therapy evaluation. Nicky needed PT sessions to strengthen his muscles so that he could develop. These sessions would jumpstart him to gain the physical skills he needed to ultimately be able to move himself. I was excited. Finally, after thirteen long months, there was something I could do to help my son.

I told Arden when we left the office, "One or two therapy sessions and he'll be on his way. Nicky will be okay."

Arden and I were confident that Dr. Glass could help us, and we are grateful to this day for Dr. Griffith's referral. Every time that Nicholas needed another therapy or treatment, Dr. Glass suggested that we contact a specific person. They were always able to teach us what our son needed next. God placed these people in our life to help Nicky and this has blessed us all.

I requested that Arden and my mother not mention our upcoming appointment with Dr. Glass, until we met with him. I wish I had been more open about what was happening. Because I was afraid of what they would say, we missed out on the support that some of our family and friends would have given to us. Now we could explain what we had learned and what the plan was. Within a few days of our appointment we met with our extended family. Everyone had questions, some we could answer and some we couldn't. It seemed that most everyone was on board.

Chapter Ten

When it was time to drive back to Tacoma after our family meeting, Arden took Nicky into the bathroom to change his diaper. After a few minutes, I heard Arden yell, "Eva, come here, come here quick! Eva, where are you?"

I had never heard such desperation, such fear in my husband's voice. I ran to him from the living room. I looked past Arden's stricken face to my sweet baby thrashing on the floor. His skin tone was gray blue. He was having a grand mal, or tonic clonic, seizure. Whatever the name, they are scary to watch. I recognized it because my great-uncle had epilepsy. He had lived with us for a short while when I was in high school. Also, my younger sister had a febrile seizure as a two-year-old.

Feeling helpless, we watched and waited the couple of minutes for the seizure to stop. It was an eternity. Nicky suddenly relaxed and took a big breath. His skin pinked up and he fell asleep. For a moment, I was afraid he had died. Thankfully he was still breathing.

Dr. Glass had given us his answering service number and said to call if we had any concerns. Boy, did we have concerns.

What if he has seizures as well as developmental problems? How can I possibly handle that?

When the doctor returned our call a short time later, he reassured us that this could happen with any baby; we would only need to worry about it being a problem if it happened again.

That comforted me. After we got off the phone, Arden asked, "Do you think that he has epilepsy too?"

"Although my uncle Bud had epilepsy his whole adult life, Rosie had only the one febrile seizure. This really could be a one-time experience."

The following weekend we stayed overnight at my parents. Sunday morning, we had a quick breakfast and planned to pick up Arden's mom for church.

I don't want to be late. I want to show off the boys to our friends. I do hope that Nicky will sleep through the service. He looks so cute when he is asleep and no one will notice that he has problems.

Arden had gotten our bags in the car and Ryan in his car seat. He ran back inside, "Eva, we got to go, we don't want to be late."

"I know, I am just trying to get Nicky to finish eating. Why is this still so difficult? If I put the food in his mouth too fast, he chokes. It's so runny that there isn't hardly any on the spoon and it runs down his face onto his clothes."

"Just give him another bottle of formula, we have to leave."

"Arden, I want him to have food and not just formula. He is so skinny, he needs more…"

Not responding, my husband headed out the door, back to the car.

All of a sudden, my underwear felt wet. *Something's wrong.*

Immediately, my abdomen started cramping and I ran to the bathroom, yelling, "Mom, please sit with Nicky, and get Arden back in here."

A line of bright red blood slithered down my thigh. *I am losing the baby. Maybe this will be better. Oh, how can I think that? What am I going to do?*

Mom kept the boys while Arden drove me to Highline Hospital. I was put on bed rest to see if the bleeding would stop. It slowed. By evening the flow was no longer bright red.

Dr. Griffith came in the next morning and said that he would take care of me. He was in communication with my OB in Tacoma. They both agreed that I needed an ultrasound to see what was going on. With mixed feelings, I was rolled on a gurney down to the ultrasound room.

The technician turned the screen away from me so that I couldn't watch and muted the sound so that I couldn't even hear my own heartbeat. The imaging was complete and the technician said that the radiologist would come in to explain the results.

I was alone. Arden had an appointment at work, so he wasn't there.

I don't want to think about this situation. I'm not excited about this baby. I feel guilty about that. What should be on the shopping list for Arden so he can stop at the store on his way home? He'll need to get formula and diapers for Nicky. I think we still have some bread at home, but it wouldn't hurt to get another loaf. Will the grapes in the back yard be ripe enough to pick yet? The young women from church can pick them for us if I am not home in a day or two.

I thought about anything except whether the fetus was still alive.

The radiologist came in with a smile. He sat down beside the ultrasound machine and turned everything back on again, including the sound. He rotated the monitor around toward me and said, "Let me show you what we found."

I still was pregnant. I had placenta previa. Part of the placenta was covering my cervix. As my uterus grew, there was some separation in the placenta from the uterine wall, which caused bleeding and tissue loss. He showed me the little peanut, with the heart beating in the middle. That baby was tenacious. I still wasn't sure how I would handle three children, one with developmental problems, but my heart softened a bit. After three days in the hospital, I was allowed to go to my parents', under doctor's orders of complete bedrest.

I stayed there for the rest of the week, while family members and friends cared for the boys. I spent the days doing cross stitch, watching TV, reading and sleeping. I felt so helpless and confused. *If God wants me to have this baby, why was this happening, especially now, when my baby needed so much help?*

One bright spot was that Nicky had pulled himself up to standing, holding on to the furniture, while I was in the hospital. That was encouraging. It seemed that God was giving me hope to hang onto in the midst of the storm.

I was still on bedrest so I couldn't go to Nicky's Physical Therapy (PT) evaluation. I was so disappointed. Arden asked the therapist to phone me and personally report her findings. She was very matter-of-fact, exuding competence and confidence in her professionalism.

"Your son Nicholas has significant delays in all areas of his development. This includes verbal skills, both passive and active, muscle strength, gross and fine motor skills, auditory reaction, and visual reaction."

"Wow!"

To me, that list seemed endless.

"I recommend starting with twice weekly hour-long sessions."

Nicky's condition was more serious than I had thought. "How many sessions will it take?"

"To do what?" she responded with a question of her own.

"For him to reach normal develop levels. How long do you think that it will take?"

"Mrs. Gremmert, he many never overcome some of his delays, but please understand that we will do our best. Nicholas is young. If you and your family are willing to work alongside us, that will give him the best possible chance to gain skills. I will assign exercises following each therapy appointment. It is imperative that someone does these exercises, multiple times a day with Nicholas. This is what I meant by saying you and your family need to be willing to work alongside the medical team. It will be the best for your son."

"We will do whatever it takes."

For someone else the situation might have seemed daunting. However, I had been a competitive figure skater for twelve years and had trained with some of the top coaches in the world. Practicing for hours to achieve physically demanding tasks was something I understood. I had learned to strengthen my body and practice enough, creating the muscle memory to be able to perform the required elements at the various levels to pass all the tests, including the senior level dance tests in two countries. I could do whatever it took to help my son.

After a week, I was finally able to return home. I found that if I stayed in bed the bleeding was minimal. If I didn't follow the doctor's instructions the flow was heavier. The week at my parent's had been long and boring. I was grateful for the help we had received, I just didn't understand why this was happening. I felt useless, and angry at God.

Silently, I yelled toward heaven: *It doesn't make sense that I am on bedrest and not allowed to do my usual chores that other stay-at-home moms are doing. Arden has the increased stress of his startup company. He needs my support. Ryan is only two years old and Nicky has so many appointments. The therapist said it was imperative that we do all of the exercises with him daily. I wonder if it would just be easier if I got up out of my bed and I miscarried.*

My brain kept going 'round and 'round with these silent thoughts.

Over the next five weeks, it seemed that each time I felt really down, I'd bleed a lot. The doctor would order another ultrasound and we would discover that the baby was bigger, growing right on schedule. I then felt guilty for all the negative thoughts and committed to stay positive. That resolve would last for a few days, then the cycle would repeat itself. Gradually I began to believe that I really might be able handle our challenging circumstances.

Nicky began therapy. Arden took the boys with him to Burien on therapy days. Nicky went to our friends the Johnsons. Their daughter took Nicky to his PT appointments. Ryan loved attending Grandma Gremmert's preschool. He was a smart little two-year-old and really enjoyed being around older kids. I hoped that he was doing okay. I worried that he wasn't getting the attention he needed, with everything going on with Nicky and Arden's job situation.

On non-therapy days, our friends in Tacoma helped care for kids. Sometimes Ryan stayed with me, but I couldn't care for Nicky. I missed my little boy. This was such a critical time for him and I wasn't able to help him.

For weeks, I had been having severe cramping, especially when I first woke up and throughout the morning. However, one day I noticed I wasn't cramping anymore. Instead, that morning, all alone in our home, I felt the baby move. I let myself feel the first stirrings of excitement about the new baby.

Somehow, that morning, I knew that things would be okay. It was a pivotal day for me. I learned a major life lesson that shifted my point of view dramatically. For over six weeks, I'd been consumed with thinking that my life was hard and that it wasn't right that these things were happening to us. Once I felt that flutter of life in my womb, I recognized that God was in control and I gained comfort from Him. From that morning, I began to look for the good that comes from difficult situations. The lessons learned from difficult situations are invaluable and my outlook was the key to feeling positive. I began to count my many blessings every day. Learning to do this has made all the difference in my life since.

PART THREE

Initial Steps

Chapter Eleven

We started our epic journey of 2016 on the twenty-fifth of April. The car was packed full, every little nook and cranny. The most challenging thing for us was remembering where everything was in the Altima.

The first week on the road was uneventful. According to Nick, we were "visiting friends and seeing the sites." Following our itinerary and keeping to our schedule, the plan that next day was to leave Las Vegas around noon, and travel the four hours to Surprise, Arizona, arriving for dinner with Arden's family there. We typically stop every few hours to give Nick a bit of a rest. Everything was going according to plan when we stopped at Wickenburg, Arizona to take Nick to the bathroom.

As we pulled into the gas station, I said to Arden, "I am okay, why don't you go ahead and take Nick into the restroom first."

"Are you sure? He is probably just fine for a few minutes, why don't you go ahead?"

"No, you guys go ahead. I think you should take him first. I don't know why."

"Okay, just be sure to keep the windows down, it is hot here."

Arden got Nick out of the back seat and they walked in.

Parked next to us were two Harley motorcycles. Both couples were making slow preparations to get back on the road. They were dressed in the typical biker's leathers.

Those are really very nice bikes. I wonder how long of a trip they are taking? Both couples have a lot of gear with them.

Glancing at the door to the restroom, I thought, *Arden has been gone a long time. I hope that there is nothing wrong. Maybe I should get out of the car and talk to those guys with the bikes. What? What am I thinking? Why should I talk to them?*

I am typically hesitant to start up conversations with strangers. But the impulse was very strong, so I got out of the car.

"You have really beautiful bikes. My son-in-law has one."

"Do you ride?" one of the women asked.

"No, I don't. We are on a cross-country road trip taking our son with disabilities to see friends and family."

"How long do you expect to be gone?"

"Just about six weeks, we…"

My Fitbit vibrated, and I noticed on the display that there was an incoming phone call to my iPhone. It was Arden. I excused myself and opened the car door to answer the call.

I could tell by the way he said "Eva" that he was upset. "Nick's seizing."

Shocked, I asked, "He's seizing?"

"Yes, he fell to the ground in a drop seizure, and a man in here helped me pick him up off the floor."

The woman overheard the conversation and asked, "Your son had a seizure?"

"Just a minute, Arden."

I replied to the woman, "Yes, in the bathroom."

Arden firmly said, "Eva, we need to start the rescue meds and I need the wheelchair."

"Okay, honey, I will get these people parked next to us to help me get all of the stuff to you."

Turning to my new friends, I asked "Can you help us?"

"I just sent my husband into the bathroom to see what he could do, what do you need us to do now?"

"I need to unpack the trunk to get the wheelchair and my son's backpack."

Is this safe? Unpacking all the trunk onto the ground, I am so distracted right now. What if someone steals our stuff? I need to move past my fears and just do what needs to be done.

I unlocked the trunk and the women helped me unload our bags. We got out the wheelchair and Nick's backpack. The second man took the chair and Nick's bag into the bathroom. I waited out by the car not knowing what was happening. It wasn't very many minutes later, and finally, Arden was wheeling him toward the car.

"Arden, let's put him up front, I can care for him better from the back seat and we can recline the front seat."

"That is a great idea. We can also direct the air conditioning onto him."

We knew that temperature changes could bring on seizures. Arden got the car started and I found Nick's pillow from the trunk so he would be more comfortable. Getting into the car, I thanked the people who had helped us. They were standing there, as if they didn't know what to do next. Feeling deeply grateful for their kind service, we waved goodbye. As we pulled away, we noticed that everyone returned to what they were doing before the crisis of seizures interrupted them.

We were underway again. Arden was tense.

Putting my hand on his shoulder I asked, "What happened?"

"We were standing in line. I was watching him closely. You know how hard it is for him to stand for very long. Finally, it was our turn and just as I got him into the stall, he dropped to the floor."

"Were you able to break his fall then?"

"Yes, I had a hold of him, but it was a tight space, someone else was in the disabled stall."

He was silent as if he was recalling the whole incident.

"What did you do then?"

"I opened the stall door and asked the guys in line if they could help me. I told them that my son was having seizures and I needed help getting him up onto the toilet."

Pausing, with tears in his eyes, Arden looked into the rearview mirror at me and said, "Eva it was unbelievable, two guys just immediately jumped forward. Each grabbed a side of Nick to help get him up off the floor. In seconds, he was seated on the toilet. I couldn't have done it myself. Nick then started perseverating with 'I have a seizure, I have a seizure, Dad, I have a seizure…' I was holding onto him so that he could go to the bathroom and that's when I called you. Then it was the weirdest thing; just as I got off the phone with you, one of those guys that were parked next to us, was there asking me what I needed. I told him that I needed the rescue meds in Nick's backpack, but that my wife said that another guy is bringing it in to me. I asked him to help me hold Nick steady so that I could assist with the toileting. Nick kept having the partial seizures while on the toilet."

Arden shook his head slowly. "It all happened so fast, the next thing I knew, the other man was there with the wheelchair and Nick's backpack. He was asking me what I needed out of the bag. I gave Nick the meds and used the VNS magnet. When Nick was finished on the toilet, we got him into his wheelchair and I came out to you. Those four men literally ran to our aid, no questions asked. I am humbled by their selfless service to us as strangers!"

We were about an hour from Arden's brother's house. We were so relieved that the seizures appeared to stop after we got him into the car. Usually it takes more than just the first dose of the rescue meds and using the VNS magnet a couple of times for the seizures to stop.

It was incredible that so many people helped us, perfect strangers quickly stepped forward in our moment of need. That experience reminded me of how many people had helped and supported us from the beginning.

Chapter Twelve

Just before Halloween 1980, I was recovered enough to be released from the six weeks of doctor-imposed bed rest. I took back the reins of caring for my family. The first day, I took Nicky to therapy, vacuumed, did dishes, and ran laundry while the boys were napping. Then I took them grocery shopping, visited friends and had dinner ready for Arden when he got home. I felt like I had my life back.

We settled into a routine: Monday and Wednesday, I packed up the boys and we drove to Renton for Nicky's therapy appointments. I made sure I learned everything that I needed to do to help my baby. Most of the time was spent on strengthening his muscles and improving his balance. The exercises were repetitious but necessary.

Over the next few weeks, I found myself really short on patience, especially with myself. I wanted to do so much and since I was in my fourth month of pregnancy, I was tired. Looking back, I wish that I had cut myself some slack, but that wisdom only comes from experience.

In November, we met with a speech therapist. After evaluating Nicky, she said, "We need to encourage his thought patterns, his inductive and deductive reasoning so that he can develop speech."

"This is very interesting, but how do we do that?"

"He needs to initiate sounds. We need to encourage him to make sounds. You need to mimic or copy any sound that he makes, even if it seems involuntary. He needs to develop this ability to mimic in order to learn. Right now, he doesn't know that he is supposed to copy what others do, so he is not learning as quickly as he could be."

Although we had been trying to encourage him to make sounds, we definitely needed her help and guidance. From that day, any time that Nicky made any sound, a cough, a squeal, a burp, we would copy it. Sometimes, it was hilarious and we laughed at each other.

At first, he didn't seem to notice our sounds, but gradually after a few weeks, he would turn his eyes toward us when we copied him. Later we noticed that he had a little smile on his face, as we copied him. After many months, he finally learned to play the mimic game. We had gained the possibility of speech. Finally, we could model something and he would try to copy us. We have used this teaching technique for many things.

Ten years later, we were sitting around the dinner table one evening when Nicky coughed. Automatically, all five of the rest of us unconsciously coughed in response. With a huge smile on his face, he made a fake burp. We all caught on to his game, and burped back. In a nonverbal game of Simon Says, Nicky did something and we all copied what he did. He put his hand on his head, we all did it. He put his hand on his tummy, and we followed suit. By now everyone was laughing. Nicky was leading us.

By the middle of December 1980, my six weeks of bedrest was a distant memory. One morning, I commented to Arden, "The boys and I have a great routine worked out. I know all of the appointments take a lot of time, but Nicky is really developing physically. Just today, he crawled by himself. This is so crucial for him and I feel like we are beginning to connect while I spend all those hours talking and singing to him in the car."

"You just have to leave so early in the morning and are gone all day. I wish I could help more."

"It is only two and three times a week that we are up to Renton and Burien. It is less than an hour each way. It isn't too bad."

That morning began like all the rest. We got ready and headed north. Nicky was very fussy and uncooperative at therapy.

Driving away from the hospital I thought, *I wonder what was wrong with Nicky today. He is usually so happy and loves being at therapy.*

He made a strange noise in his car seat in the back seat. I looked in my rearview mirror as I stopped at the stop light.

What is wrong with him? Is he breathing? Is he dead?

I spun around to look at him directly.

Okay, he is breathing, barely breathing, but he is breathing. His eyes are blindly staring straight ahead, his body is so still and rigid, his skin tone is gray. I think that this is a seizure. What can I do? He is strapped into his car seat.

I looked ahead at the intersection.

My heart began to race, heavy in my chest, it was hard to breathe. Time slowed down, seconds became minutes, and minutes became hours.

I want to run away. I would love to have a Star Trek transporter right now and be able to say, "Beam me up, Scotty." But that would be selfish and irresponsible. I couldn't just leave. No one is coming to save me. I need to protect and care for my child. I just need to grow up and be responsible. There is a parking lot just past the intersection. I am going there, right now.

I drove through the red light and pulled into the parking lot on the right. Since this was before everyone had cell phones, I couldn't just dial 911.

Why is this happening to me? I have enough to deal with. I am a good person. Bad things are supposed to happen to bad people. I want to run away. What if I just opened the car door and left? I am right by the airport. If I take my purse, I can go get an airline ticket and leave. But where would I go? I can't leave my baby here, even if he wasn't seizing. What would people think when they heard that I just left? What would I think of myself? I hate this.

It was an agonizing eternity until I had released him from the car seat restraints and held him in my arms.

The seizure isn't stopping. It has been more than a couple of minutes. I am so alone. What can I do? Oh, what am I supposed to do? How am I supposed to know what to do? Why do I have to do this? I wish someone else would come and handle this for me. Why me? Come on pull it together. I wish I had Arden's radio telephone in this car with me, I could call for help. Wait, the Johnson's live just down the block, maybe they can help.

I drove there, holding him on my lap. I parked the car and ran frantically carrying my stiff unconscious baby up to the door. Finally, on the doorstep, Nicky's body suddenly went limp. He cried out weakly and immediately fell into a deep sleep. I couldn't rouse him. I was so frightened. I didn't understand what was happening.

Ruth's teenaged son answered the door. "Sister Gremmert, what can..."

Moving through the front door, I said, "I have to use the phone."

He nodded and pointed to the kitchen.

When I reached Dr. Glass's receptionist on the phone her manner calmed me. "Mrs. Gremmert, what you have described is very typical. You don't need to take Nicky to the emergency room. He probably will sleep for three or four hours. I will tell the doctor what has happened. You just need to call back if your son has another seizure today."

I put Nicky back into his car seat, and started for home.

The receptionist didn't seem too concerned. I shouldn't worry. Oh, what am I going to do? Soon I'll have three kids. This seizure was so unexpected, so scary. He could seize at any time. How will I ever get used to that?

Tears were blinding my eyes. I had to pull over again. Rummaging around in my purse, I found tissues. Blowing my nose, I said out loud, "Eva, pull yourself together. You can do this. Nicky needs you and Ryan needs you."

Oh, Ryan, you need a mommy too. I feel bad that I am spending so much of my time and energy helping your little brother. I hope you don't feel neglected. I don't know what else I can do.

Taking a deep breath, I pulled back into the street and drove home.

Nicky did sleep for about four hours, which is typical with epilepsy. Even now, after all these years, his seizures are still frightening to watch. I feel so helpless during them.

Nicky was scheduled for a follow-up EEG and evaluation to check his progress after eight weeks of PT.

After the EEG, we met with Dr. Glass and the three therapists who had been working with Nicky. Even though he was sixteen months old, he tested at twelve months of development. In the first evaluation, the results showed eight months of development. I did the math. Since he gained four months of skills in two months of intense intervention, he should be caught up to age level by the time the baby came in April. I was naively excited.

Dr. Glass was very pleased with Nicky's progress. However, because Nicky recently experienced two seizures, the doctor prescribed Phenobarbital, an anti-seizure medication.

Phenobarbital made Nicky very drowsy. He slept a lot. We were instructed how to manage the seizures. People used to think that you put something in the mouth of the person who was seizing. This is not correct protocol. Dr. Glass explained we should get him down on the floor in a clear space so that he didn't injure himself. If possible, he should be on his side to avoid aspiration, in case he vomited during a seizure. This was great information that we were able to teach our friends and family.

Over the next several weeks, Dr. Glass reviewed the PT evaluation reports, EEG and CT scans. He determined that Nicky had a non-degenerative global brain injury, which meant that while he needed help learning and developing his condition wouldn't worsen. That was comforting.

The EEG showed that he was having clusters of multiple seizures all the time, often without a physical manifestation; there was no way we could know each time he was seizing. Seizures are like electrical storms in the brain. The pathways can become habitual. We needed to interrupt them as much as possible since seizure activity interfered with learning. The meds would help. We were also taught the physical warning signs of overmedication to watch for; things like excessive drowsiness, confusion, rashes, unexplained sores, or sudden behavioral changes. Even increased seizures could mean that the medicine dosage was either too low or too high.

The challenge was to find the delicate balance where Nicky could be seizure free without experiencing the symptoms that accompanied being overmedicated.

Chapter Thirteen

Again, Christmas that year didn't meet my expectations. We didn't have any extra money. Our families knew it and our siblings showered the boys with toys. Nicky wasn't too aware of the presents, but he did like looking at the shiny papers strewn around.

I made the boys homemade teddy bears from fabric left over from other projects. Ryan preferred all the fun toys that he got, although he put his bear on his pillow. Nicky wouldn't hold onto his bear; he let it drop to the floor and crawled over to examine the crinkled wrapping paper. I wanted to be the one that provided the favorite present for Christmas. It made me sad that I couldn't do that for my kids.

A few days later, I took the boys to Goodwill to see what might be on sale after Christmas. Just inside the door I saw two rocking horses. One of our friends had one, and Ryan loved it. Nicky could ride the horse if we held onto him. He loved it.

I wish I could buy those two horses for my boys. I'm sure they are too expensive. We just can't afford any extras right now.

When I turned to walk away, Ryan yelled at me, tugging on my hand, "Mommy, come back, I want it. Mommy, get both. I have one and Nicky have one. Please, Mommy, please!"

I was about to tell him that we couldn't afford it when a clerk walked up.

"They're on sale, ma'am, did you see the price?"

"No, I didn't even look."

"They already have a sale price tag on them and today everything in the store is 50 percent off the lowest price. They are $5 each."

I was stunned. I had $12 in my purse. Just enough. It was a tight squeeze, but we got both rocking horses into the car.

Over time, Nicky gained enough core strength to stay on the horse himself, but at the beginning, I sewed a harness out of canvas to keep him in the saddle. He loved it and would rock for hours if we let him. I didn't know it at the time, but later we learned about Sensory Integration Therapym and we discovered how essential the rocking motion had been to his development.

New Year's Eve 1980 was the fifth one Arden and I celebrated together. That holiday has always been special to us as it marks our anniversary of becoming a couple. We put the boys in bed and began our festivities. We had party snacks, sparkling cider, and chocolate, of course.

"This has been a strange year," Arden began as he poured the drinks. "We have been through so many things."

"I just feel like I'm adrift, going through the motions. I don't feel like I'm accomplishing anything, it's more like I'm putting out fires, and my water bucket is full of holes."

There was an awkward silence, both of us remembering.

Clearing his throat, Arden began, "I feel like we've drifted away from doing some of the basic things that bring us peace and comfort. I don't mean that we're doing anything wrong, more like we're forgetting to do all the things that would help. I think that we should rededicate ourselves to each other and to the Lord."

"Are you thinking of giving me more things to do?" shaking my head.

Arden laughed and reached out to hold my hand, "No, not really, just reminding ourselves to do the things that bring us closer as a couple and closer to the Lord."

"What are you thinking of then, shall I make a list?"

"Well, for starters, let's commit to having prayer as a couple each night before we go to bed. We always have prayers with the boys, and I like it when we pray together too."

"I do like that too. I'd like to support each other in looking for the positive in each situation. I believe that God gives us miracles, we just need to look for them."

"That's a good idea. It seems easier for me to notice the black clouds than see the silver lining. I'd like to change that. I do know that God is in charge and that He has a plan for us. What if we made a list of the good things that have happened?"

I laughed. Then quoting the famous hymn, I sang, "Count your many blessings, see what God hath done."

"That's right. We have a doctor we trust, and I'm working with my friend again. Your pregnancy is finally going great, and…"

"Apart from the pain in my hips, and the difficulty I have moving around," I countered.

Kissing me on the cheek, he said, "I'm grateful that your belly is getting bigger."

"I know, so am I, I do feel better tonight, this has been good."

We recommitted to each other and to God to do the things that we knew we should and then trust God to handle the rest. We both felt the comfort of knowing that we were on the same page with our sights on the Lord. For the first time in many months, I fell quickly asleep, without a tear in my eye.

Just a few days after our New Year's rededication, we got an unexpected impressive offer for a lease/option of our Tacoma home. This contract made it possible to move back north. The next day Nicky walked three steps in therapy without assistance. The following day I had another ultrasound. With the screen turned toward me, the technician said that there was no indication of placenta previa anymore.

As I watched the baby scratch her shoulder with her hand I thought, *I feel like a dark cloud has been lifted, and the sun is brightly shining through. Our house has a lease/option buyer and we are moving, Nicky is walking and this new baby is just fine. Again, I have proof that God works in mysterious ways, His wonders to perform. I am stronger having experienced it all.*

I was grateful for my friends and our siblings. We had three weeks to pack our house and move. Arden was working long hours to build the business, I was six months pregnant, had two boys under three, and was running to multiple therapy appointments weekly. Many people kindly showed up to pack. Every time I traveled north for Nicky's therapy, I took a few boxes with me. We stored them in my parents' basement until we could get into our house.

I was overwhelmed. Normally, I expected that I could do everything that needed to get done, but I wasn't feeling up to this challenge. I made an appointment with our bishop, Larry Judd. I looked upon Bishop Judd as a spiritual father. He always had wise words to share with me at just the right moment.

"Sister Gremmert, this is a particular difficult testing period in your life. You won't be given more than you can handle, if you will call upon the Lord for strength and increase your faith."

This was much-needed counsel.

I have recalled those words many times over the years when I've reached what I thought was the end of my strength. I found that if I remembered to pray, the end of my rope stretched farther than I would have believed possible.

We moved back to Burien, into my childhood home. It was more convenient for Arden's work and for Nicky's therapy and I liked being back near friends and family. I was deeply grateful for all the help.

The week after we moved, I came down with a bad cold. I was miserable and afraid because the baby wasn't moving around very much. I was seven months along. It was the exact same time that Nicky's movements had quieted down. Dr. Glass mentioned that one potential cause of Nicky's brain damage could be that he had an in-utero viral infection around the seventh month of the pregnancy. I worried that it could happen again with this pregnancy. I didn't believe that I could cope with a second child needing therapy. Everyone in our family was adjusting in their own way to Nicky's disability. They had their own concerns and there wasn't anyone I could talk to about my fears.

One morning while unpacking boxes, my negative thoughts consumed me. *My life certainly isn't going along as I anticipated.*

There've been so many changes this past year. I feel off balance. I wonder when my life'll be normal again. Will it ever be normal again?

Later while the boys were napping, I was trying to motivate myself to tackle the mountain of unfolded laundry. The phone rang, it was my friend, the impressive mother of twelve children.

"Hi, Eva, this is Ramona, I thought I'd give you a call. How are you doing?"

"I am fine."

Looking at Mt. Everest on the couch, I thought, *I'm fine, just fine!*

"Can I come over? I'd love to visit with you."

"Ramona, I have so much to do, perhaps we could make it another day?"

"Eva, please let me come over and give you a hand. Many hands make light work, you know."

I looked at my house in shambles, and remembering that she did love me, in spite of the mess, I said yes. She arrived a few minutes later.

Coming in the front door, she laid her coat over the back of the couch and asked, "Where shall we start?"

We sat down on either end of the couch, the mountain range of laundry between us.

As we folded the laundry, I unburdened myself.

"I just feel so overwhelmed, Ramona. I am not sure that I can do all of this."

"Eva, having raised twelve children, I learned for myself that feelings of overwhelm are normal, especially when I was pregnant and had small children. It takes a lot of energy to care for two little boys. In addition, Arden has changed jobs and you guys moved. You also have the extra responsibility of managing Nicky's therapy and treatments. You have been dealing with a lot."

"That is exactly what I mean. The list of our recent experiences is daunting."

"Eva, it's imperative to not let hard situations impact or lessen your self-esteem. Find some time each day that you can use to refill your well. Choose things that buoy you up, things that enliven your spirit and expand your talents. While it's vital to serve others, we need to make sure that we are taking care of ourselves, so that we can serve."

Standing up, she said, "You are almost done here, I want to load up your dishwasher before I go. Is that okay?"

"Sure, that would really help."

While she was in the kitchen, I was left alone with my thoughts as I pondered her counsel. It seemed more than coincidence that I was given this time to think about things.

A short time later, she came around the corner and said, "It's all done in there. I need to get home before my kids get home from school. I've really enjoyed our visit today."

While putting on her coat, she said, "Eva, you're wonderful. You're stronger than you think. You should remember that."

Hugging her tightly, I replied, "Ramona, thank you for coming over today. I really needed it."

Heading toward her car, she said, "You're welcome, sometimes all we need is a sympathetic listening ear."

I was grateful for her kindness and for reaching out to me. Since then I have tried to pass that same compassionate kindness on to others.

PART FOUR

Learning to balance

Chapter Fourteen

We stayed at Arden's sister's home in Phoenix following that long day of seizures on our 2016 epic road trip. It was 10:00 a.m. when I finally rolled out of bed. Arden must have heard me open the bedroom door as he walked over to greet me.

"You were so deeply asleep. I didn't want to wake you." Enveloping me in his arms, his hug soothed me.

"How is the boy?"

Arden laughed. "First thing this morning, I heard him exclaim, 'I am much better. Arden, it's daylight, Heavenly Father make me better. You get me up?' When I brought him out for breakfast, Keva was just leaving for work. I told her that we were planning on resting in the house today."

"That sounds perfect, especially after yesterday's long drive and eventful arrival."

Kissing my forehead, he said, "You get yourself dressed and I'll have your breakfast ready in a few minutes."

We try to give Nick the chance to rest after seizures and we were exhausted. That section of our road trip had been an emotional roller coaster. Over the next few days we recuperated, watched TV, went out to dinner, and visited with friends who had moved to the area. We were on vacation.

After three days of relaxing in our desert oasis, we felt that it was time to head back out on the road.

We packed up and left Arden's sister's house at about 11:00 a.m.

Picking up our GPS, I said, "So where do you want to go today?"

"What do you mean, where do I want to go?" Arden asked as he pulled out from the subdivision.

"Well, have we decided to go home since he had the seizures on Sunday, or are we still heading toward Kentucky?"

Nick joined the discussion, "I go to Kentucky. I see Ryan and his family."

Arden replied, "Nick, we are trying to get you to Kentucky. We just want you to be safe."

"I okay, Arden. I better today."

I patted his arm. "I know you are feeling better today. We have to be careful with you to make sure you stay well. We are worried about the heat and the exertion of traveling. What do you think, Arden, shall we just keep on the planned itinerary and head to Blanding today to visit the Hunts?"

"That sounds like a great idea. We can decide over the next few days if we head east or head home."

"I like that plan. What do you think, Nick? Shall we go to Allen and Leonie's?"

"We go there."

Allen and Leonie Hunt have been our dear friends for over two decades. We purchased their home in Carnation, when they moved to Blanding, Utah in 1992. Driving the four hundred miles from Phoenix to Blanding, Utah would take about six hours.

The drive was uneventful. Leonie had dinner waiting for us. During the meal, we noticed a little seizure activity, so we used the VNS magnet to interrupt the seizures. They never progressed, which was a relief. After dinner, we got Nick settled into bed and then returned upstairs to visit with our friends.

We talked about the book I was writing. Leonie asked if I would read what I had written to her while she cleaned up. We both finished at the same time and she sat down next to me.

"I love it," she said with tears in her eyes.

"Do you really?"

She nodded. "Nick has taught all of us so much. His story needs to be told and you are the perfect choice to tell it. I do love it. I can't wait to read the rest when you are done. It is phenomenal how much he can communicate through music."

"I agree. I believe music was the platform that helped Nick developed speech."

"Really? What do you mean?"

"Nick loves music. He always has. As an infant, we noticed that playing was calming to him. When we were in the car and I didn't play music, he would cry. I experimented with different types of music during the multiple car trips to therapy to see what he liked best. One morning, I sang to him. Although I didn't consider myself a singer, I thought it might soothe him as well as pass the time. I was memorizing a few church hymns, so I thought it would be good practice. I started with some of the simpler ones."

"So how did that go?"

"He was quiet when I would sing and seemed to like it. About a month later, I got a surprising result. I was driving along, my brain swirling around, full of all the thoughts, and ideas of the day. I hadn't begun singing yet, so it was pretty quiet in the car. After a few minutes, I noticed that Nicky was making strange sounds that I hadn't heard before. I looked in the rearview mirror, he seemed to be vocalizing. At first, I couldn't make out what he was doing. Then I began to recognize the pattern. He was attempting to copy the tones of the melody of a favorite children's song titled, "I am a Child of God." I slowly began to quietly sing along with his efforts. He smiled a huge smile and we connected. That was the first time I felt like we related to one another. I broke into tears. I was crying so hard I had to pull over into a parking lot for safety. Leonie, his "words" weren't intelligible that morning, but his intent was. After that, we spent hours singing together in the car. Over time, I learned the hymns and his pronunciation became more and more intelligible. I truly believe that learning to sing gave him the ability to talk."

"That is incredible. But I do believe you. Allen and I love to sing with him."

"I know, and he loves to sing with you guys too."

The next night after dinner, we had our traditional sing along with the Hunts. They are extraordinary musicians and have written many songs. Nick always requests his favorites. After putting Nick to bed, Arden and I sat up quietly talking.

"Eva, I am worried about how hard this trip is on Nick. I don't think we can see all the friends we want to visit."

"What do you think we should do?"

"Let's look at the maps and your proposed schedule to see what our options are."

We spread the maps on the bed and reviewed the timetables I had printed. We still felt unsure of what we should do, so we prayed about it.

We went to bed that night full of faith that in the morning, we'd know whether we should head home or continue toward Louisville.

When we awoke the next morning, we both felt like we should continue on eastward. We decided to go as far as Albuquerque that day and then decide what to do. The morning was spent packing up, working a little, and getting prepared to be back on the road. Arden and I both received priesthood blessings from Alan. In our church, a blessing is a prayer for healing, comfort, or counsel and can be requested from a Melchizedek Priesthood holder. Most of the men in the church hold that priesthood. Blessings are performed by the laying on of hands. Faith, inspiration, and authority are all essential to the giving and receiving of priesthood blessings.

Both our blessings were very inspirational. We always feel more grounded after spending a few days with the Hunts. We have learned over the years how to rely on others to uplift us and help us bear our burdens.

The area we drove through that day is called "the Four Corners." It is the point where Utah, Colorado, Arizona, and New Mexico meet. The road travels through the Ute Mountain Reservation and the Navajo Nation Reservation. The Hopi and Zuni Reservations were nearby. As mile upon mile of new panoramic vistas rolled past, I marveled at all the new adventures we had experienced while traveling along the road of being Nick's parents.

Chapter Fifteen

February 1981 brought another set of trying experiences for me. I had developed a deep trust for the therapists that were working with Nicky. One day I learned that his primary physical therapist (PT), Karen was quitting. A new PT named Irene Banks would be taking over. Karen said that Irene was very qualified. She did seem compassionate as I shook her hand, but I cried all the way home.

I kept looking in the rearview mirror at my sweet son sitting in his car seat oblivious to the tragedy.

I'm devastated. This is horrible. I don't see how changing therapists can possibly work out. It's imperative that Nicky continue to progress as quickly as possible, if he is going to catch up.

Thankfully, I was completely wrong that day. Irene turned out to be an incredible blessing for both Nick and me over the next few years.

Later that same week, I attended the Thursday night women's meeting at church. I felt I should go even though I was exhausted. I usually appreciated an evening with other women. The discussion topic was "Strategies to handle stressful problems." Given our life circumstances it seemed very relevant. I took lots of notes.

The next morning, I discovered how timely that lesson was. Nicky awoke very fussy the next morning around 5:30 a.m. I was able to get him back to sleep, but he woke up again at six fifteen. I stayed in bed, while Arden went to the boy's bedroom to take his turn.

Suddenly Arden screamed, "Eva, come here quick. Eva, he's having a seizure!"

I stumbled out of bed and rushed upstairs. Arden was sitting on the floor next to our tiny thrashing son.

His face stricken with fear, Arden asked, "What are we supposed to do?"

As if I have any idea what we should do.

I fell to the floor next to both of them.

"Why don't you give Nicky a priesthood blessing?"

Typically, two priesthood holders administer the blessing, but when necessary, one man is authorized to do it. I wasn't sure who needed more comfort in this situation, Arden and me, or our seizing son.

Arden laid his hands on our baby's head, calling him by name; he pronounced a blessing of comfort and healing. Just as Arden finished the blessing with "Amen," Nicky stopped seizing. It was a miracle to us.

Nicky didn't immediately fall asleep as he had after the previous seizures. Dr. Glass said to call him if Nicky had any more seizures. When he called us back, he said that the seizure might have occurred because Nicky had been sick. He told us to take him to see Dr. Griffith to be examined. I called and made an appointment for later that morning.

During the examination, Nicky had another seizure. Dr. Griffith and his nurse Sally just stood there, watching.

I asked, "Dr. Griffith what should we do?"

I was in the office of a doctor I trusted. I had looked up to this particular doctor since I was eight years old.

He looked from Nicky to me and said, "I don't have a lot of experience with seizures. You should do whatever Dr. Glass has instructed you to do."

This was really upsetting. I felt so helpless. I thought that Dr. Griffith knew everything, and here he was, saying that I had more specific knowledge in this particular situation than he did.

"I'm supposed to phone him when Nicky has seizures. Can I use the phone, Sally?"

Nicky stopped convulsing, and I gently laid him in the stroller. Sally led us to the office phone and I called Dr. Glass.

"You'll need to increase the Phenobarbital dosage. Please remember that it'll take a while for the medication levels to increase to give Nicky the coverage he needs. He might have more seizures. Please call me back if that happens."

About four hours later, Nicky had a third seizure. Again, I called Dr. Glass. This time he gave me additional instructions concerning if and when we would need to transport Nicky to the emergency room.

Emotionally and physically exhausted, I felt like I was living a nightmare; my life was not at all what I had imagined when Arden and I created the plans of our perfect life together.

Nicky was much better the next morning, just a little tired. Dr. Glass had explained that each seizure episode was akin to Nicky running a marathon, and he had gone through that three times the day before.

Our emotions were up and down like roller coasters. Our schedule was hectic and money was tight. Thankfully friends and family members helped out with the boys, and my parents offered us some financial assistance. Arden changed jobs. The new salary would cover our bills and I hoped Arden would be home more often.

Things evened out for a little while. I drove Nicky to therapy Monday and Wednesdays and did housework the other days. Saturdays Arden and I did chores, and on Sundays we went to church. The weeks rolled by.

One afternoon Nicky spiked a fever of 103 degrees. Ninety minutes later he had another seizure. Dr. Glass increased his medication again. That night in our family prayers, I asked God for the strength to handle everything.

After we put the boys to bed, Arden approached me and asked, "Do you want to talk?"

"Are you sure? You have so much on your plate, you need your sleep and I am probably being silly."

Sitting on the corner of the bed, he reached over to hold my hand and said, "This is serious, I have time. What's wrong?"

"Well, it's just that I can't do it all. Nicky needs so much, and with my due date fast approaching, I don't think I can manage everything. It's not just the time driving Nicky to therapy, it's all the other things too. I'm not keeping up with the house work or the grocery shopping. And I won't even mention the exercises the therapist wants me to do with Nicky. I'm not reading to Ryan every night, and we are supposed to be doing that too. I'm sure that there are other things I'm neglecting as well. I just can't remember right now. But I keep thinking that if I spent more time doing the PT exercises with Nicky, he might progress faster and catch back up to normal. What if I'm not doing enough and Nicky isn't getting everything he needs? What if I fail him?"

Hugging me as I rambled on, my sweet husband tried to comfort me. "You're exhausted. Let's get you settled into bed. You'll feel better in the morning."

"I can't do all of this with two kids. How in the world will I handle another baby?"

Rubbing my forehead to soothe me, Arden gently said, "Heavenly Father knows what we need. We know we were supposed to have this baby. All of this will turn out to be a blessing. Just wait and see. Right now, you need to go to sleep. Everything'll seem more manageable in the morning."

He was right. Somehow each morning, I felt strengthened and had a new resolve to keep moving forward.

Chapter Sixteen

Nicky began attending a preschool program on Friday mornings. Designed for kids with delays, his therapist, Irene, thought that it would be helpful to him. It did mean another day of driving him to another thing, but Arden and I decided it was worth the time and money if it helped him.

Irene had another suggestion. "I think we should cut back on the PT to once a week."

"I don't know, Irene. Nicky has been doing so well working with you. I would like to give it a couple more months before we make a change. I'm afraid if we change anything in his routine, he'll start slipping backward."

"We can wait to cut back. I do think that since he is walking a few steps holding on to hands or the furniture you should get him some tennis shoes."

"That's great news. I'll get that done."

I didn't tell her that we were short on money. I found one of Ryan's old shoes in the dresser but I had to search the entire house before I found the other one. I felt like such a bad housekeeper. I thought that I should be more organized and have both shoes in the same place. I signed up for a program for organizing my house in hopes that it would help.

My pregnancy was progressing, and the baby was more active again. I had the typical complaints of false labor and achy hips. It was painful to sit for long, and sometimes when I walked, I was sure that the baby would fall out. But I knew that the show must go on, and I looked past my own discomfort to get Nicky to where he needed to go.

He was making good progress with his speech therapy. He vocalized a lot although no one was able to make out any words. He said "bye-bye" one day while waving his hand when we were leaving therapy. He wouldn't do it again for Daddy later that night. Arden was disappointed, but I laughed and said, "Of course he isn't going to wave and say bye-bye, he doesn't want you to leave now that you're finally home."

My due date of March 29 passed, and I was still pregnant. After all the trouble at the beginning of the pregnancy, once the baby had gotten a firm hold in there she didn't want to come out. Everybody laughed when I said that, but I was serious. The doctor kept saying that babies come when they come and not to worry. Easy for him to say.

On April 8, with much encouragement from Irene, Nicky stood up by himself in the middle of the room. He was getting closer and closer to walking. He was almost twenty months old. I was so excited. It was easy to forget the difficulties of the past year, watching the huge smile of achievement bloom on my son's face. He could conquer the world. I'd do anything to make it happen.

Karen Marie Gremmert joined our family the next morning. After just three hours of labor, she reassured me immediately by calmly laying in my arms, looking into my eyes. There was the bond that I had missed with Nicky. I knew that she would be okay, and I was grateful. From the beginning, she was a perfectly delightful baby. She only fussed a bit when she needed something and was easily soothed once she was cared for.

We had an idyllic month at home. After that, I was cleared to drive again and we returned to our hectic schedule. That first week was a big adjustment. I took Karen with me to an appointment with Dr. Glass. He had promised that if I was concerned about our new baby after she was born, he would take a look. That had been a great comfort to me but once she arrived, I didn't feel it was necessary. I knew that she was a healthy normal baby.

A couple of weeks later, the unthinkable happened. Nicky got lost in Valley Hospital during his therapy time.

I was sitting in the rest room nursing Karen, when all of a sudden Irene was banging on the door.

"Eva, Eva, come quick."

I yelled through the door, "Irene, what is going on, is Nicky seizing again?"

"No, he's not. No." She paused. "I lost him! I don't know where he is!"

Gathering up Karen and the diaper bag, while buttoning my shirt, I yelled back, "You lost him, you don't know where he is? How did that happen?"

By then, I was through the door and into the hall. Irene was pacing back and forth. She paused, running her hand through her hair, she explained, "I was holding onto his hand right by my desk. I was writing some notes into his file when he let go of my hand. I didn't think anything of it. I thought he was sitting down to play with the ball. You know he can't walk very far yet. It wasn't more than a few seconds, and I looked up. He was out the door and walking across the hall toward the open elevator. I was running toward the elevator and calling his name. He turned around in the elevator and smiled at me. The elevator doors closed just before I got there. I couldn't believe it."

"Irene, run up the stairs to the next floor. I will wait here and push the elevator button to see if I can recall it to this floor."

I stood in front of the elevator, praying that nothing bad had happened to my son. My imagination ran wild. About five minutes later, the doors opened and there stood Irene with a death grip on Nicky's hand.

"Eva, I am so sorry. Nothing like this has even happened to me before. I ran up the stairs to the second floor hoping I could catch him. Luckily it seems that when the elevator doors opened onto that floor, Nicky just walked out. He was standing there, completely calm, in the middle of the hall looking around."

I was so relieved, I handed Karen to Irene to hold, and I scooped up my little explorer. Nicky didn't like being held, so he was impatiently pushing me away. I held on tight, I needed the reassurance that all was well and all of the tragedies I had imagined had been averted.

Dr. Glass and Irene both suggested we enroll Nicky in an early intervention preschool program. The one they recommended was a brand-new program called Birth to Five. They believed that this program had more to offer than the play group he was already attending. The Birth to Five program incorporated physical therapy and speech therapy into their three two-hour sessions each week. It was scheduled to begin in June. When I visited the facility, I noticed that the two other children already enrolled were more delayed than Nicky. I worried whether it was an appropriate placement for him, but he liked it there.

The total tuition was $300 a month, and only the therapy portion was covered by insurance. Arden and I sat down to talk about it.

"Eva, this is a big decision for our family."

"I know, it will take about 20 percent of our monthly income and that doesn't include the transportation costs."

Nodding in agreement, Arden replied, "I don't know if we can afford it. It is a lot of money to spend on just one of the kids. On the other hand, Nicky will be in the public-school system a year from now, and they will provide all of his therapy then. The cost for this program will be temporary."

"Arden, we don't have the money in our budget now to cover even $20 more a month, much less hundreds of dollars."

"I know, I was thinking of ways to make more money. I heard that you can make three to four hundred dollars a month by doing an early morning paper route."

I was astonished. "You already were a paper boy, you didn't make that much when you were twelve."

"This is different, it is called a car route and you drive around throwing papers from the car."

"Well, I could teach some skating lessons again and could do some daycare. That would bring in some more money."

Arden laughed. "That is our family motto. AFM."

"What do you mean?"

"AFM! Anything for Money. That is our family motto."

We decided that it was worth the effort on our part to provide the treatment opportunities that our son needed. AFM is still our family motto.

Nicky kept suffering from ear infections followed by episodes of seizures. It was a horrible cycle. Having ear infections is typical for many children; it was the seizures that were frightening. Both Dr. Glass and Dr. Griffith believed if we could stop the ear infections, we might reduce seizures. In addition, we were concerned about damage to his hearing since chronic infections can cause hearing loss.

Nicky had an audiology test and as expected his hearing was in the very low range of normal. The next day he had a severe series of seizures. We decided to have drainage tubes surgically implanted in each ear.

Nicky handled the surgery really well. It was frightening to learn about all the things that could go wrong from the doctors, but afterward all was well and he did seem a bit more alert. It seemed that he could hear better without the continual fluid behind his ear drums.

Chapter Seventeen

In the midst of all the non-normal things we did: the therapy, doctor's appointments, surgeries, and seizures, we wanted to do something that normal families did. We went camping. We borrowed my parents' truck with a camper and their VW van, loaded up all our things, and set off. We had all three kids with us and away we went, into the wilderness to brave the elements. Okay, it was August and the weather was spectacular. Also, we were only a little more than an hour from home.

Saturday afternoon while I was cooking on the camp stove, I had Karen in a reclining infant seat near me on the ground. Nicky began crawling toward her, which put me on high alert. I wanted to see what he would do as I protected the baby. He sat down next to her. Picking up a few small leaves and twigs, he slowly made a tiny pile on her forehead, while saying, "Baby, baby," over and over.

Arden looked over and asked, "Why does the baby have leaves on her head?"

"Nicky did it, I was watching to make sure she was okay, but I thought that it was too precious to interrupt him."

This was the first time he really interacted with her. He made a sweet connection with his baby sister. I took a picture to remember the joyful moment.

Just before his birthday, I visited Nicky's preschool. This was my first visit, as this program didn't encourage observation. I was concerned whether it was the best placement for him. He gained more skills in the three weeks he was at home following his surgery, than the previous month at school. While I was observing the classroom, I was shocked. The teachers were treating Nicky as if he was non-verbal, with no expectation of speech. I was stunned. By the end of the class time I was very frustrated. I approached the head teacher.

"Why aren't you encouraging Nicky to speak? Why don't you give him opportunity to respond?"

"Mrs. Gremmert, your son can't speak. He is nonverbal. We don't expect that he will ever speak."

"Did you read his enrollment forms or any of the reports I have given you from the speech therapist at Valley Hospital? She obviously has a different opinion than you do, and she is the expert," I said through clenched teeth.

I turned to Nicky, and taking a deep breath to try to calm myself, said, "Nicky, say bye-bye, baby."

He smiled at me and said, "Bye-bye, baby."

I scowled at the teacher. Then I picked up his drink and asked, "What is this, Nicky?"

"Milk."

"Good job, Nicky."

I picked up his toy and asked, "What is this?"

"Truck."

He was right. I gave him a big hug.

I turned back to the teacher. "What do you mean he is nonverbal? Not only can he repeat words when asked, he obviously understands the context of my questions and the meaning of those words. Currently, he has a functional list of about twenty words. How did you not know that?"

Even though Nicky was attending that school three days a week for two and a half months, they didn't know that he could speak.

The head teacher exclaimed, "This is unbelievable. We had no idea. This completely changes how we can work with him."

"You won't be working with him anymore. He is not coming back. I am going to find a competent school that can actually help my child."

We left. I was so disappointed because I had hoped they would be the solution. I talked to Dr. Glass about what happened. He was surprised. He knew the directors as being very experienced professionals and had expected that the school would be exceptional. He had another recommendation.

We enrolled Nicky in Merrywood School, east of Bellevue. They offered both an early intervention preschool program three times a week and an integrated toddler program one day a week. The school was small. They rented two rooms of an old elementary school. I had to drive him to their program. Even though that took more time each week, it also meant I could observe Nicky and be sure the program was actually helping him. For the first time as Nicky's mom, I found a connection with other parents. Peer support was something I didn't know I needed. Rather than just dropping our kids off, most of the moms stayed during the class time. We sat on two couches in a small alcove between the two classrooms.

At first, we talked about our kids; their diagnosis and treatment experiences. Gradually, as we built up trust over a few weeks, the walls began to come down, and we opened up about ourselves. We shared our fears and our hopes. We wept together over the difficulties and the achievements. Although it had begun to sink in that we were all on an arduous journey with our little ones, we felt the strengthening support of our comrades. When each class was over, I felt an increased ability to square my shoulders as I picked up Nicky and walked out of the school, better prepared to slay the next dragon.

We also learned about many community programs and services through being involved at Merrywood. They had a couple of great programs that we joined. Arden started going to the Fathers' Program at the Advocates for Retarded Citizens (ARC) of King County, which met one Saturday a month. I attended the parent-to-parent meetings support group meetings. These programs opened our eyes to what services were available. It was comforting as we got to know other families. We talked to other parents who had been through similar things. We laughed and cried together. I found that I had many things in common with the other moms. Their fortitude encouraged me; their sense of humor gave me perspective. Their stories touched me and their spirituality inspired me. I volunteered on a few of the committees and got to know some moms who had older children.

One afternoon, I went over to a committee member's home to drop off some papers. Two beautiful teenage girls opened the door together. One of them strongly resembled my friend Nancy.

"You must be Jean."

She nodded. A look of confusion crossed her face and she asked, "How did you know that?"

"I am a friend of your mom's. You look like her, so I thought you must be Jean. I have some paperwork for her. Is she here?"

Stepping away from the door and turning completely around, she yelled toward the back of the house, "Mom, Mom, come here. Your friend…"

Turning back toward me, she frowned and asked, "What is your name? I forgot what your name is."

"Jean, my name is Eva."

Turning around again, she yelled, "Mom, her name is Eva. Mom, do we know her?"

Her friend giggled.

Frowning, Jean said, "Stop laughing, Debbie, I'm not supposed to talk to people I don't know. Mom, come here. Mom, do we know Eva?"

While coming to the door, my friend Nancy reassured her daughter that she did know me. I handed her the paperwork and prepared to leave.

"Eva, please come in, if you have time. Can you visit a minute?"

I followed her into the house and we sat in the living room. While Nancy reviewed the paperwork, I watched Jean and Debbie interact.

It's obvious that both girls have developmental delays, but there is so much about their behavior that is like regular teenage girls. I wonder if Nick will have behaviors that are normal. Will he have best friends too? I hope so.

Nancy noticed that I was watching the girls.

"How old is your son now?"

"He's two and a half. He'll start public school in the fall."

Reminiscing, she said, "Oh, those early years are so hectic. Things really calmed down for me after Jean became a teenager."

Laughing, she continued, "Or maybe it was me that calmed down. I'm not sure, but it has been much easier since she has been attending Issaquah High School."

Astonished I interrupted, "She goes to Issaquah High School?"

"Yes, they have an inclusive program that's integrated with the regular classes. Jean and her friends attend the regular education classes when it's the best placement and they are in the special ed classroom when that's better. We really have created the least restrictive environment for Jean. When she was little, we never thought that this type of program was possible. You never know what'll be available for your little guy. Just keep plugging along. You'll be amazed."

That conversation along with many other ones, helped me see the future as something to hope for rather than fear.

At Merrywood, Nicky received his first of many formal evaluations, The Bayley Scales for Infant Development. He was twenty-six months chronologically and scored a functional age of fifteen months, with solid scores at twelve months and a scattering of scores up to nineteen months. These numbers are used as a reference not only to compare a child to typically developing infants, but also for both measuring progress gained over time and creating treatment plans to teach skills that show up as holes in the child's development.

A second Bayley test was administered five weeks later. Nicky scored a functional age of twenty-two months, with solid scores at almost eighteen months and scattered scores to nearly twenty-eight months. He had gained from five to seven months of skills in five weeks, and he had some skills that were up to age level. I was so excited. Even the doctors considered this a miracle. I did the math. I wanted my baby to grow up to be as normal as possible. This progress gave me hope that he would be in regular education classes by kindergarten. I believed that if we all worked hard enough Nicky could successfully overcome this slow developmental start.

PART FIVE

Adding More Steps to our Dance

Chapter Eighteen

After traveling through New Mexico on our epic road trip of 2016, we got to the hotel in Albuquerque around 8:00 pm. We had an appointment to meet with a client for dinner. He was staying at the same hotel, so we had dinner at the Village Inn across the parking lot. Nick loved it and the server was attentive. Afterward my client and I sat with Nick in the lobby while Arden moved all our stuff into the hotel room. We shared stories and got to know one another better.

After our dinner meeting, Nick and Arden went right to sleep, I worked for a few hours answering client emails and preparing reports. I am very grateful for the tax business I inherited from my father. It gives us the flexibility to be able to earn a living while still caring for Nick.

Chapter Nineteen

By 1981, in addition to working full-time at Boeing as a nuclear physicist, my father prepared taxes for about four hundred clients during tax season. He had been struggling to manage the mountain of paperwork, so I offered to help him. I didn't know it at the time that my service to my father was the start of my own highly productive career.

The extra income that Spring helped cover our expenses, especially Nicky's therapy. I scheduled and confirmed appointments, mailed paperwork to clients, checked over my father's calculations, and was the liaison with the computer processing firm that printed the tax forms. It was a great distraction for me, as there was so much going on in our lives that I had no control over. Handling paperwork was something that I could do correctly and accurately. It gave me a sense of accomplishment.

After that first tax season, my dad encouraged me to learn to do income tax preparation. He offered to pay for the training course. Arden and I decided it would be a good way to augment our income. Tax season was only fourteen weeks each year and I could meet with clients in the evenings and on Saturdays, while Arden cared for the kids. I could still be a "stay-at-home" mom and continue to do all that was needed for Nicky. It was a great experience to take a class with other adults and learn new things. I discovered that I had an aptitude for remembering the tax code and applying it to the various examples given during the course.

Chapter Twenty

In the fall of 1982, Nicky experienced some very scary seizures while we were at church.

One Sunday, I met up with Arden in the chapel before church started. He had been at his early morning meetings.

"My jacket is lying on the bench where you like to sit, how was your morning?"

"It was a little stressful," I replied as I ushered the kids into the pew. "Nicky has been fussy this morning, I can't seem to soothe him. I hope he'll be okay."

Arden picked Nicky up from the bench and said, "Come here, little dude, come sit on Daddy. Why did you give your mommy a hard time today?"

Nicky arched himself away from his dad. Arden caught unawares, almost dropped him. Then Nicky started screaming and Arden said, "The meeting hasn't even started and you're already misbehaving."

Nicky's behavior did not improve, and in fact, it was disruptive during most of the main meeting.

When the closing prayer was finished, I looked down the row to check on him. I was excited that he was just sitting still and not screaming.

"Arden, he seems all right now, why don't you take him to his Sunday school class, I'll wait here for you."

Arden returned a few minutes later.

"I told his teacher, Sister Jones, that he was a little unruly. She said that she would watch him. Since she is a physical therapist, I have confidence that she can handle everything."

"I hope so."

About fifteen minutes later, I looked out the window and saw Sister Jones taking Nicky and his whole class on a walk around the building. In our church congregations, we call other adults, Brother and Sister.

"Arden, I am going outside to see if I can help. Nicky's still not very steady walking."

I got Sister Jones's attention as I caught up to the entourage. She was carrying Nicky.

"Sister Jones, I wondered if I could be of some help with your excursion?"

"Sister Gremmert, I am sure we will be okay. Nicky was hitting the other kids in class, so I decided to take them all for a walk. I'm just going to carry him to the grass-yard at the back so he doesn't get too tired."

"Okay, let me know if you need anything."

She and the class disappeared around the corner.

I turned to go back inside the church. Just then I heard an exclamation, "Oh, no!" followed by the sound of feet running on the sidewalk. I waited a few seconds and Nicky's teacher came back around the corner, my unconscious son draped in her arms.

"Oh, Sister Gremmert, I am so glad you're still out here. I set him on his feet in the grass, and almost immediately, he fell to the ground having a grand mal seizure."

Handing him to me, she continued, "I need to get back to the other children, will you be okay?"

Nodding yes, I said, "Don't worry, Brother Gremmert is inside and we're very familiar with what we need to do. Thank you."

I went inside to get Arden so we could go home.

We lived only ten minutes from the church, so by the time we got home, Nicky had been having seizures for about thirty minutes. He was in and out of consciousness. We got in the house and laid him on the carpet, when suddenly he stopped breathing, turned very blue gray, and was convulsing. Dr. Glass had told us that this type of seizure typically lasts about two minutes. After about five minutes of nonstop convulsing, Arden laid his hands on Nicky's head and pronounced a priesthood blessing of healing. Immediately Nicky stopped convulsing and all seizure activity ceased. He just lay there looking up at us. I was so relieved that I burst into tears.

"That was a miracle, he just came right out of it. He is breathing normally and he isn't sleeping. That was so scary, I wonder what the doctor will say. I hope that there hasn't been more brain damage. He was seizing so long today."

"I will call the answering service so we can talk to Dr. Glass. He always is so reassuring."

Dr. Glass told us that we should call 911 if the seizures lasted longer than twenty minutes. We now had a new protocol. That was comforting.

Nicky had another series of severe seizures in early October. One lasted over twenty minutes in the grand mal phase, and we did call the ambulance to transport him to the hospital. Dr. Glass added Dilantin to Nicky's medication protocol in order to help control the seizures. Adding additional medicines can give better coverage than increasing the dosage of the current medication.

The seizures were scary, however, that Fall my biggest concern was Nicky's feeding problems. Following an evaluation by a speech therapist at Children's Orthopedic Hospital (COH), we started feeding therapy sessions. She also ordered a barium swallow test to learn what was happening when he swallowed. She was concerned that low muscle tone was impacting his feeding. He had tongue protrusion when he swallowed and no chewing action when he had food in his mouth. He only ate pureed food, and he couldn't tolerate food resting on or between his teeth without gagging. The gagging often led to vomiting if we were persistent.

The speech pathologist said that I needed to work more with Nicky during meals. I don't think she understood what I was going through. Meal after meal, day after day, we were faced with the fact that he couldn't or wouldn't feed himself. There were days that I was so tired of having to prepare two cups of pureed food three times a day. I wished I didn't have to do it. I just wanted to let Nicky fend for himself. However, he didn't show any interest in food, and he was so skinny. It took a lot of time to prepare and feed him the food, but I couldn't let him alone to feed himself guilt-free.

Feeding therapy added an additional trip twice a week to COH in Seattle, but by the end of the first month, Nicky could feed himself pureed food with a spoon. It was a huge accomplishment and we were very excited.

After Halloween, my friend Dora Mae approached me at church. She had noticed Nicky's progress and wondered what we were doing. A sweet compassionate woman about fifteen years older than my mom, Dora Mae was like a grandmother to me. I wanted to be just like her when I grew up.

Dora Mae had a large family and two of her sons had disabilities. Her oldest son had been oxygen deprived at birth and her youngest son Kay, had Down Syndrome. Kay was a special man. A few years older than Arden and me, he loved my husband and Arden loved him. It was heartwarming.

Dora Mae asked if she could visit Merrywood with me. She had known the five Bellevue-area mothers of children with disabilities who had originally started the program in 1962. Initially called the Eastside Preschool for the Special Child, within a few years, it was incorporated, had gained public funding, gradually replaced volunteers with paid professionals, and changed names to Merrywood School. They now had innovative programming, including support for fathers, foster care, child care and parent education, and had gained status as a neurodevelopmental center. They offered the best of early intervention in our area.

On the way home from the visit, Dora Mae seemed unusually quiet. After about ten minutes, she said, "I really enjoyed coming with you today. Seeing the program that my friends had developed was very moving. There are so many more services available for disabled kids and their families than we had. It really is astonishing."

"We are blessed to have so much available to us. Even with all of this, it seems like a really long road ahead."

"I know, Eva. Your family will learn astounding lessons on this road. I do believe that it truly has been a blessing in my life that I could serve my two sons with disabilities. I didn't understand that with Roland at first. It was after Kay was born that I began to recognize changes in myself that had occurred because of the demands that were placed upon me. I am a different person than I would have been without the experiences of caring for my two sons."

As I drove down the freeway, my view of my current life situation completely turned around 180 degrees. Having a disabled child was not a tragedy. It was a remarkable opportunity, even a blessing. I had never even thought of that possibility.

"Eva, I promise you that the day will come, probably years in the future when you will recognize the changes in yourself. These changes will include your outlook on life and your life goals. Even the things that you feel are of most worth and the activities that you chose to fill your life will be different. I believe that I have gained empathy and greater compassion for others. I also have the ability to be calm in the face of adversity. I was not that way as a young mother."

It was hard to envision, but as she spoke in her kind gentle manner, I could catch a glimpse of what she believed to be true.

Many years later, after she had passed away, I realized that everything she had told me that day had come to pass. I wished that I could phone her up and tell her. Somehow, I knew that she did know and was rejoicing with me. She gave me a profound, life-changing gift that day, wisdom that I have diligently tried to share.

As he got bigger, other people began to notice that he was different. Some were curious, and others felt aversion. I became hesitant to take him to the grocery store. There was something about standing in close proximity in the checkout line that broke down the restraints of common courtesy. People would say the rudest things—blunt questions like, "What is wrong with your baby?" or unsolicited advice like, "You need to take him to a specialist, he has problems." It was as if it was their responsibility and right to set us straight on what would fix our child.

I also noticed how other children treated their peers with disabilities. They were sometimes very cruel. It hurt my heart. Arden and I talked about it.

"What if we took a proactive approach?"

"How would you do that, Arden?"

"Well, we could begin initiating a conversation when we noticed other kids staring at Nicky."

I rolled my eyes, "Like what, 'hey, get your kid to stop staring at my kid.' Is that what you mean?"

Laughing, he said, "No, we could talk to the children directly and say something like, 'He looks a little different, doesn't he?' That might give them the chance to ask us questions."

"Okay, I will try, but it still makes me mad. You might need to take the lead on this."

"I will. I believe this is significant. I think that if we could help educate others, especially children, it could be like dropping a stone into a pond; the ripple effect could help rid the world of some of the xenophobia that seems to grow like a cultural cancer."

We both agreed to try. Sometimes it felt awkward and some parents just whisked their kids away when we initiated conversations, but over all we have had meaningful discussions with both kids and their parents. I believe that it has helped.

Chapter Twenty-One

It felt like I was always running to appointments when Nicky was young. My mom teased me one day that she thought she saw me coming and going at the same time. We were focusing a lot of our time and attention on Nicky's progress. But I felt that I couldn't just stay home with him and hope for the best.

Some of my friends teased me that I was obsessive over organization, rigidly using schedules and planners. What they didn't understand was that organization was a survival skill in the midst of the storm that was my life.

It became difficult for me to watch Nicky in the Friday toddler program at Merrywood. They had typically developing toddlers in class with those with special needs. The stark difference between my child and other children his age was obvious.

One particular Friday, I couldn't do it anymore. I knocked on the open door of the executive director's office and said, "Mimi, I need to withdraw Nicky from the Friday program."

Looking up from her stack of papers, she said, "Oh, hi, Eva, come in a minute, won't you? Please sit down. What seems to be the problem?"

"Mimi, I really do believe in the concept of the program. Today in class, he was the only disabled child with twenty typical children. It's just too hard on me to see the contrast. I leave here every week discouraged and depressed."

"Eva, we don't want that. That's not the goal of the program."

"I know, I wish I was stronger, but I'm not."

"Eva, please don't feel bad. We've noticed a drop-off in attendance for the Friday Toddler Program, but none of the other parents have explained why. I am sure that you are not alone in your feelings. We need to rethink our goals concerning this program."

"Mimi, I do believe in the concept of peer development, but for me, my emotions are too intense. Besides we have a typically developing toddler program in our own home. Ryan is only thirteen months older than Nicky, and Karen just twenty months younger. Between his siblings, their friends, and the kids at church, he is surrounded by typically developing children."

We never attended the Friday program again. It was good for me to have a day off. I did experience some guilt and concern about taking away an opportunity for Nicky, but I believe I was a better mommy without that extra stress.

That Christmas was much more joyful for me than the previous two years had been. We had many fun activities including going to the ARC father's program Christmas party. It was fun to socialize with other parents who were familiar with our experiences. Nicky still loved his rocking horse and would rock away for as long as we would let him. The morning after Christmas I came out from my bedroom to find him on the horse rocking. He had climbed on by himself and was beaming from ear to ear. I really loved it when he learned something new. His face so aptly expressed his feeling of accomplishment, no words were needed.

On Christmas Eve, Ryan came down with chicken pox. Two weeks later both Nicky and Karen followed suit. Ryan and Karen had mild cases which took about five days to heal, but Nicky's case was severe. Covered with pox from head to toe, he was miserable. The only thing that comforted him was rocking him in the rocking chair. For three weeks, he was a very sick little boy. He had no appetite. When he was finally well again, we noticed that he had lost most of his recent developmental progress. He couldn't manage a spoon any more, and could only swallow food if it was blended. He didn't remember how to put on his shirt. It was so disheartening for everyone.

In January, after he recovered, we returned to Merrywood and to feeding therapy at COH. Following an additional five weeks of school and therapy, his teachers administered another Bayley test. It confirmed our fears. At a chronological age of thirty months, Nicky scored a functional age of nineteen and a half months, solid scores to fourteen months with scattered success to twenty-three months. He had lost ground. It took a long time of hard work to make it up again.

It seemed like we had barely taken down the Christmas decorations when tax season was upon us. This was my first year preparing tax returns. I continued managing my dad's clientele and his office, and added ten tax appointments of my own. The income was a great way to help cover Nicky's medical bills. I also took in some ironing to earn a bit more.

Dr. Glass suggested that we participate in a doctoral study. There would be four home visits using various testing mechanisms over eight weeks, followed by a final report.

The doctoral candidate from the University of Washington Department of Psychology, explained that she was studying the things that mothers did with their disabled children that other child researchers believed promoted development in small children.

Questions she posed the first week centered on the child's home environment from the child's point of view. I hadn't considered this before.

What did our home life look like to Nicky? What was my emotional response to him? What language was he exposed to in our home? Were the punishments he received appropriate to the level of his bad behavior? Could he explore his environment and have his behavior corrected in a way that encouraged development?

How organized was our home? Were the toys and play materials appropriate for Nicky's level of development? How involved was I in Nicky's daily life? Did he have a variety of experiences each week?

For the other three visits, she used the Bromwich Parent Behavior Progression. It was developed to guide researchers in observing how mothers engage and play with their small children, as well as discerning the learning play that they do with their children. It evaluates six areas. One evaluated how much I enjoyed playing with Nicky, the second determined if I was sensitive to him and could read his cues. The third measured whether our interaction was satisfying to both of us and provided opportunities for attachment to develop between us. The fourth section determined if I was aware of what was suitable for his current stage of development and the fifth section examined not only how well I initiated new experiences for Nicky, but also how well I followed directions from other professionals.

Finally, she observed us to see if I could independently create new experiences with Nicky as he changed developmentally. It was interesting each time she came to do her observation, although I was a little concerned about what she would write in her report.

In January I had an appointment with the Social Security Administration—we were trying to get benefits for Nicky. I handed in the completed forms.

"You are denied benefits and services for your son."

"Can you tell me why?"

"Your household is above the income threshold by $81 a month."

"But the services he would qualify for cost over $400 a month. We are currently paying for those."

"Ma'am, you are not eligible."

"What if my husband's salary were reduced by $100 a month? Could we reapply and then qualify?"

"You can't do that. You are already in the system with the numbers you have reported. You do not qualify."

It made no sense and was very frustrating to us.

Nicky's gait was still very unsteady. The arches in his feet that were needed to walk hadn't formed properly. Irene suggested we cast his feet for several months. By creating foot bed molds with built up bumps in them, his feet might still form the necessary arches, since his feet were still malleable. Hopefully he could learn to walk rolling his foot from heel to toe, and maybe even run someday.

I was excited and worried. I wanted to do everything possible to help Nicky overcome the problems that were delaying his progress, and I couldn't see how I could take care of him with plaster casts on both of his feet. Not only would I need to carry him everywhere, we also had to bathe him for those several months while wearing the casts.

In February, Nicky was fitted with foot plates for casting. I came away from that appointment devastated. I called Arden.

"He will never catch up developmentally and be normal. He is not just developmentally delayed. Our sweet son is handicapped."

"What is it about these casts that is so hard for you? With everything else that has happened over the previous year and a half, it seems really strange to me that this treatment is causing you such concern."

I couldn't shake my feelings of despair. Perhaps it was the straw that broke the camel's back.

We went back for casting the week after the foot plates had been made. Irene had everything prepared, the long strips of plaster and the water. She was excited in anticipation for the progress that casting would bring. I wanted to be excited too, but the casting process was awful. Nicky was okay during the whole ordeal, until the casts were formed and solid and it was time to remove them. Irene finished cutting the plaster and started on the stocking with a pair of scissors. Perhaps he felt too much pressure on his feet or he was just done, but Nicky began crying and pulling away. I had to restrain him. He was mad. By the time that Irene had finished cutting through both casts, we all were crying. If someone had looked into the therapy room, it would have looked like we were torturing that little boy.

The casts were shaped like basketball high-tops, with Velcro closures where the laces would have been. To me they epitomized the fact that my son was different and would always be different. That weekend Arden's brother Kurt asked if he could paint them. He made them look like Nike tennis shoes; only on the back of the heel, he painted "Nicky's" instead of Nike.

The next week, I had another shock that sent me spiraling further down the despair cycle. I went to a Parent to Parent meeting. These ARC supported meetings were usually uplifting for me. I felt a great sense of community and companionship with other parents of special kids. However, at this particular meeting the speaker mentioned that static encephalopathy was synonymous with cerebral palsy. I didn't know that my son had cerebral palsy, CP, as it is commonly called.

All the way home I could only think of wheelchair-bound non-verbal people. If that was our future, how would I cope as Nicky grew bigger? I called Irene for some comfort and she gave me a vague answer, which I thought was odd. She said that Nicky was too young to receive the diagnosis of CP although many of his symptoms and tendencies did look like CP.

I hung up the phone confused and devastated. The next time I saw her, she explained that she had been evasive on purpose. She hadn't wanted to drop a bombshell like that over the phone. Many people have preconceived ideas about what CP is and the limitations for those diagnosed with it.

Dr. Glass concurred. He believed that using developmental delay or static encephalopathy as a diagnosis rather than cerebral palsy, opened up more opportunities for the variety of therapies, instead of limiting individuals to the standard expectations for projected progress of the disease.

Chapter Twenty-Two

In the springtime, the researcher from the University of Washington phoned and said she was ready to share her report with me. I was worried about her report would say. Discovering that my son was handicapped had sapped my confidence as a mother. I didn't have the same belief in my ability to cope with our situation as I had at the beginning of the year.

As she read the report to me, I realized that she had done a very thorough job of observing my interactions with my son. Her comments were very complimentary. I've saved this report. Whenever I begin to doubt myself, I return to it and reread her incredible comments. It always gives me a boost. Her study also helped refine my understanding of what type of interaction and play was the most helpful for Nicky's development. I was able to teach our children and others how to play with him so that he had the most beneficial social interaction. Without her study, he might not have had those experiences. This has turned out to be another critical part of his learning, as he does model his behavior by observing other children.

Around that time, the Highline School District contacted us. It was registration time for their early intervention program. I visited two other private school programs that spring, but we felt that the free public-school program offered what Nicky needed. I began believing that there was a light at the end of the tunnel. He would still have some outside therapies, but between the administration, the psychologist, the therapists, the teachers and even the aides; we would rely on the professional expertise and experience at the school to educate Nicky. Surely it would lift some of the burden that I felt.

After registering Nicky, we were invited to visit the program at Riverton Heights, the elementary school he would attend in the fall.

Arden, who hadn't been to the private school visits with me, seemed overwhelmed observing all the kids in the program. Many seemed much worse off than Nicky and he didn't see how Nicky would fit in with them.

Nick had a feeding reevaluation in April. He had regained the ability to use a spoon and was able to tolerate food between his teeth. This was crucial as it is the initial step to chew food. Also, he could pick up and eat soft foods such as banana pieces. Nick had feeding therapy with the speech pathologist twice a week for over nine months, then was released to the school district for follow-up treatment. The therapist made many innovative recommendations to reduce his oral sensitivity and was very helpful with this major problem.

However, we vehemently disagreed about his potential ability to learn to talk. After reading her transition report for the school district I requested a meeting to discuss her findings. She set up a phone meeting.

"Mrs. Gremmert, you wanted to talk about my report?"

"Yes, while I appreciate all the work you have done concerning Nicky's feeding issues, I don't agree with you that formal language therapy would be inappropriate for him."

"Mrs. Gremmert, I firmly believe that Nicholas's behavior dramatically interferes with his progress. He doesn't exhibit the beginning base skills needed in order to gain verbal language. I don't think that formal language therapy would be appropriate for your son."

Again, I reiterated my position, "I strongly disagree with your opinion. I am concerned that the district will take your report and restrict the type of therapy that they will offer him. I am not willing to limit his opportunity to talk. Currently he has over fifty words that he uses correctly and some of them he even uses in combination. This is very important to me."

"All right, I don't want to retype the report. I will add a handwritten addendum to the report stating what you have told me his language skills are currently. Will that suffice?"

This concession was crucial. I wanted the school district to give Nicky every type of therapy that could possibly help him develop. I didn't want her professional report to turn into the expert opinion the district could reference as the reason to withhold speech therapy.

Over that summer I kept attending the Parent-to-Parent evening meetings. Some of the discussions grew heated, as many parents used the forum to vent their frustrations. Since I was new to the group, I sat and listened to everyone. I wished that I had the courage to participate. Often, I came home from those meetings wondering if I wanted to go back the next month. Eventually I did stop going.

Arden had been working for a startup newspaper for the previous few months, but hadn't been paid for six weeks. I felt like we were drifting apart from all of the stress of our chaotic life with our three young children. We learned of a nearby weekend conference called "You are the Expert." It was specifically organized for those dealing with disabilities, either for individuals with disabilities or their family members. We left the children with friends who were trained respite care providers. I felt comfortable leaving Nicky.

While driving over the mountains to the event, we popped our current favorite album from the movie *Footloose* in the CD player. There we were, in our twenties, driving my mom's beautiful sports car, laughing and singing. We were still young and desperately needed a break from everything. That afternoon, with the sun was shining and the radio blasting, we certainly felt "footloose and fancy free."

We learned so much that weekend. It was like drinking from the fountain of experience. The presenters were the pioneers of services and programs for special populations. Although we hoped we wouldn't experience the same things that others had faced, Arden and I both knew we could do whatever was needed for our son. The weekend was also an opportunity for some much-needed alone time away from the kids and the responsibility.

It was just what I needed to get out of my downward slide. There were lectures on how to get services from various agencies, including the schools. Other lectures were on legal issues of guardianship and inheritance and the impact on services. These were among many subjects of which we had no idea. We had our eyes opened and we felt changed when we returned home afterward. We had renewed hope and had received empowering information and understanding.

The staff at Merrywood School made sure that Nicky was invited to attend a one-week neurodevelopmental training course just before he started public school. Inviting kids who were in early developmental programs gave the trainees an opportunity to practice on actual clients. It also gave Nicky five days of additional therapy, that didn't cost us anything except the travel time and expense to get him there. It was hectic, transporting him to Bellevue every day, but I was happy to do it. I was always looking for ways to get Nicky more of the services that he needed. The sacrifice was worth it.

Nicky was still having many episodes of intense seizures. Dr. Glass thought we could get better coverage and get rid of the current side effects by putting Nicky on a different seizure medication. Phenobarbital is very sedating and Dilantin had caused so much swelling in his gums that some of his teeth were partially covered with gum tissue which exacerbated his feeding issues.

Changing medications is tricky. You must gradually reduce the old meds over a few weeks as you gradually increase the new one. It's a delicate dance, and we have always followed the neurologist's instructions with exactness.

Dr. Glass switched Nicky to Mebarol. After a couple of weeks, Nicky was measurably more alert and we had great hopes for seizure coverage.

In July, Nicky had four severe seizures in one day. The first one happened in church and we transported him via ambulance to the hospital. Dr. Glass increased the Mebarol and ordered another EEG.

Two weeks later, we had an awesome day. Nicky spontaneously pointed to an airplane in the sky said, "a-pane." He saw a boat on the water and said, "Bo." Although most two-and-a-half year-olds have a much larger vocabulary, achieving these language milestones meant that Arden and I were right. Nicky would be able to speak to communicate. He also fed himself with a spoon. That hadn't happened in seven months.

Two weeks later, he was having seizures again. Our lives were a continuous cycle of exhilarating euphoria followed by deep despair. In addition to reading the scriptures and daily prayer, I wrote in my journal. I could reread the stories of his achievements which helped me gain perspective. The memories buoyed me up when I was discouraged. This restored my optimism and capacity to carry on.

Chapter Twenty-Three

September 1982, Nicky started the Preschool Program at Riverton Heights Elementary. He loved going to school and especially loved his teacher. The bus came at 8:30 a.m. and dropped him back home at 12:15 p.m. For the first time in three years, someone other than me was responsible for Nicky for a portion of the day. I had almost four hours a day, five days a week, without him. I badly needed this. Sometimes I really wanted to be a normal mom, like my friends. Finally, for a portion of each day, I could be.

Ryan had turned four in June, and I committed to give him more attention with my newfound free time. I organized a preschool program with a girlfriend whose son was the same age as Ryan. She took one week, and I did the next. We invited ten other children the same age.

In addition, we joined the local pool and Ryan started swimming lessons. The classes were twice a week in the afternoon. It was awkward corralling Karen and Nicky at the pool during Ryan's lesson time. The other moms sat on the benches poolside and visited with one another. That wasn't possible with my two little ones who could move independently in opposite directions, but I wanted Ryan to know that I was supportive of his activities too, so we did our best.

Swimming gave our family another activity we could do together. We went to the family swim times. Arden and I switched off holding onto the little ones, while Ryan paddled around us. Nicky loved being in the water and wasn't afraid at all. He always headed straight for the pool. With all the water that we had around Seattle, I felt that he needed to learn to swim for safety. After a month of watching Ryan's lessons, I asked the teacher if she would consider doing private lessons with Nicky. This simple request began four years of twice-weekly swimming lessons for him.

In October, we discovered that we were expecting another baby, due the following May. This time I was excited from the start. I had confidence in my abilities to handle raising my kids whatever the situation. I also felt that I needed to learn more about disciplining children and signed up for a month-long class titled, "Behavior Modification Made Simple." Prior to taking this class, my idea of a "time out" was everyone going into to their corner and then coming out fighting. Over the month, I learned the techniques of positive reinforcement, how to observe and record target behavior, and to use reinforcers to reduce negative behavior and increase positive behavior. I learned that it is fundamental to know when to punish, how to set limits and what behavior to inhibit.

Arden and I designated a chair in the living room as the timeout chair. It became known as the black chair. When war broke out in our house, instead of yelling at the instigator, I began picking up the offender and carrying them over to the black chair. I put a kitchen timer on the mantle nearby and told the child to sit there quietly, in time out, until the timer went off. Ryan and Karen both caught on pretty quickly. Nicky, however, would slide out of the chair immediately after I sat him there. It was frustrating as I pondered a solution.

One morning, I awoke with the idea to use one of my kitchen aprons to hold Nicky that could be tied around the back of the chair. That worked for a few days, until he learned to slip his head out and wiggle his body until he was free of the chair. I was concerned that it was a choking hazard also. That afternoon, I sewed a special harness. It was a square piece of cloth with four large straps sewed on the edge. Two at the top corners wrapped around just under his arms to tie around the back of the chair. The other two straps were next to each other at the bottom midpoint of the square. They were placed between Nicky's legs and connected with the other straps under the chair. This worked great. He couldn't get out until I let him out. A similar harness used today as a restraint in child car seats, high chairs, and other equipment. I had never seen one before, back in 1982, those items only had a small plastic lap belt to hold the child.

I was grateful for my increased spiritual practice in my life. I felt comforted as I spent time praying and reading the scriptures. I decided to develop the habit of a daily devotional every morning with my kids before they went to school. We read three scriptures and I tried to keep their attention while I gave a brief explanation. I discovered that three scriptures often didn't contain a complete thought and was sometimes confusing to the kids, so I increased the number of scriptures to be between three and ten each day, trying to find a theme that we could discuss briefly rather than only reading three each day. I was learning to be a little less rigid in my goals and a little more flexible in my expectations. This was to be a life long journey for me.

By March, I was seven months pregnant and by the end of each day, I was exhausted. Some nights, Arden got home from work after I had the kids fed, bathed and ready for bed. He began telling bedtime stories to the kids. I loved it. He took them into their room for the story. I got a much-needed break and he had some time with his kids. He created the stories in his head. Karen loved stories about Jesus. Ryan wanted stories with dirt bikes or the Dukes of Hazzard. Nicky loved it when they were the main characters in the story.

Now Arden tells bedtime stories to our grandchildren. The hero's names have changed but the stories are the same. There are always great cars or other motorized vehicles. All the listeners are characters in the story, portrayed as fully functioning adults. There is always someone who needs help or some vital service that is needed to be organized and implemented. The heroes used to have CB radios to communicate with each other, now they have smart phones and tablets. Some of the content has changed, but the moral of the story has always remained the same: Do your best and help others. Arden really has a storytelling talent and it has blessed our lives.

At the end of the seventh month, I began having early contractions. We were concerned since Dr. Glass said that Nicky's brain injury had probably occurred during the seventh month of pregnancy. I was put on bed rest for a month, which made me more anxious and afraid.

My friend Sharon Dorsey and her daughter Erin were our salvation. They helped with shopping, cleaning, driving, and offered every kind of support imaginable, especially emotional. Sharon had an adult son with disabilities.

One particular morning, she came over to help and I had been crying. She stood by my bed and said, "What can I do for you this morning, my lady?"

Feeling a bit defensive, I said, "What?"

Laughing a little, she explained, "I am your humble servant, my lady, what would you have me do?"

I caught the vision of what she was doing and began to play the part. "Well, Sharon, since I am unwilling to lift a finger here and rise from my bed, I am sure that there are plenty of places that need tidying up and mucking out, so get on with it."

With a deep sigh and a smile on my face, I sent her on her way to do my job. I did feel better. A little later, she came in and sat on the edge of my bed.

"Find the moments each day when you can laugh. If you look, you will find them."

I nodded.

"My son Pat does things each day that are frustrating and things that are hilarious. Sometimes I, too, will cry, but I try to remember the things that are funny. It makes things easier for me. You keep a journal, right?"

Again, I nodded.

"Well, write some of these things down. You can read them later when you need that humorous perspective. It really does help."

"Sharon, you always seem to have a great view of things. I will try to follow your advice."

She showed me her perspective concerning the trying times which gave me hope, and even joy. She had already traveled the long road I was now on.

A few weeks later, the doctor said I could be off bedrest. Sharon kept coming over in the mornings to help get Nicky on the bus. Even though the early contractions had not returned, Dr. Griffith still wanted me to take it easy. During the last two weeks of my pregnancy, my hips were so painful, I had to use a walker to get around. Arden and I agreed that this would be our last baby. For us, four children was the perfect number.

Chapter Twenty-Four

Derek arrived right on his due date, May 5, 1983. Sharon and Erin brought the other kids up to the hospital to meet their little brother. He was such a sweet baby. Everyone was crowded around the bed to see the baby.

"Arden, pick Nicky up and put him here next to me. I don't want him to wander off in all the excitement."

I pulled him in next to me. "What do you think of your new baby?"

"Baby," he repeated.

"That's right, Derek is your baby brother. Do you want to touch his arm?"

He shook his head and pulled away. That surprised me. *I wonder what's wrong.*

"Arden, can you please take the baby, I want to check on something."

I handed Derek to Arden and sat Nicky on my lap.

"Let's take a look at you, big guy."

He's not tapping his lip with his fingers. That's weird. He's always tapping his lip. I wonder if there is something wrong with his hand.

"Hey, Sharon, can you hand me one of Nicky's squeaky toys from the diaper bag?"

As I played with his toy, Nicky's eyes followed, but he made no attempt to grab it.

"Arden, I think something is wrong with Nicky's hand. He is not using it. Can you run him down to the emergency room and get it looked at?"

Arden looked stunned. "Are you kidding me? How am I going to take three kids to the ER?"

Calmly, I responded, "Just take Nicky to the ER. Sharon and Erin can stay here and help me here with the other two. Don't forget to get the insurance card out of my purse. I think he needs an X-ray."

Arden returned about an hour later. Nicky's right arm was in a sling.

"What'd the doctor say?"

"Well, you were right. He has a broken arm."

"A broken what? I thought there was something wrong with his hand. Why is it in a sling and not a cast?"

Arden shook his head. "I don't really know, but this is what the ER doctor said would be the best treatment for the injury. At least this way we can still bathe him. It seems that it's a slight fracture in his upper arm, near the shoulder. They were all surprised that he didn't feel the pain."

"I wonder what that's all about?"

I made a mental note to ask Dr. Glass about this.

Sharon continued coming over to help me in the mornings.

A few weeks later I told her I could finally manage the kids on my own. I was so grateful for her compassionate service to our family.

One morning, I couldn't fall back to sleep when Arden left for work. All the kids, even the baby, were still asleep and although I was exhausted and sleep deprived, I couldn't relax.

The kids finally woke up, and I got everyone bathed, fed, dressed and into the car to take Nicky to therapy. As I got in behind the steering wheel, I breathed a sigh of relief. Getting four kids ready was a chore, but I had done it. I turned the key.

Nothing happened.

I checked the lights to see if the battery was drained. Nothing. I started to cry. The kids were all quietly sitting in their car seats, just looking at me. I thought, I have got to pull myself together. I told them to wait, went inside and called Sharon. She came over and drove us to therapy.

After therapy, Sharon dropped us back at home, I put the kids down for a nap and went for a rest myself.

I was barely asleep when Ryan called out, "Mommy, come quick." I jumped up from my bed a little disoriented. *What's going on? Ryan is yelling for me. Is Nicky having a seizure? Oh, I so don't need this today.*

I ran to the bottom of the stairs.

Ryan was sitting on the top step. He stood up as he saw me. I took the stairs two at a time. He ran down the hall to their bedroom door. He looked in, then covering his mouth with his hand, he giggled.

Why is Ryan laughing, what is wrong?

"Mommy, Nicky's pooped again! Oh Mommy, he's…"

I reached the open doorway.

What is that mess piled up in the middle of Nicky's crib?

I assumed that it was my son. I just couldn't tell.

"Oh no," I whimpered.

Nicky had removed his clothes and dirty diaper and smeared it all over.

It's in his hair, on his face, arms, legs, crib mattress, rails, the wall behind the crib. There is poop everywhere.

I just stood there, stunned.

I gotta go. I can't do this.

I turned and left the room.

Ryan yelled out, "Mommy, where are you going?"

I didn't stop. I yelled back over my shoulder, "Just a minute, kids."

I ran down the stairs to the kitchen and called Sharon.

Finally, she answered, I broke down, sobbing. "I can't do it, Sharon, I just can't do it."

"Do what?"

"Nicky pooped in his bed again and smeared it all over again."

"Where are you?"

"I am in the kitchen, I just ran out of the bedroom and left all the kids in there."

"You will be okay, I am heading over. Just hold on for five more minutes."

"I will leave the front door unlocked, just come on up."

When she arrived, I was sitting at the top of the stairs down the hall from the kids' room.

Pulling on her rubber gloves, she said, "Eva, go downstairs and start the bath water. I will bring Nicky down."

I went downstairs. As I started the water, I heard her coming down the stairs and walking toward the bathroom. She was holding him at arms-length while she talked to him. Her soothing tones with my messy son were comforting to me. After a few moments, I was reenergized.

"Sharon, I can tell that you have this part under control. I am going back upstairs to tackle that mess."

I grabbed the Lysol, a garbage bag and some paper towels. I cleaned and disinfected the crib, the walls, and the floor.

After the clean-up, Sharon and I sat at the dining room table and strategized.

"Eva, this was not the first time Nicky has done this. Although this is a stage that many kids go through, with our kids, these stages seem to last longer."

"Sharon, I need a plan of action. What do you think we could do?"

"There is that small room, next to your bedroom downstairs. What do you use it for now?"

"Well, it is supposed to be the toy room, a place for the kids to play," I commented as I looked at the toys strewn all over the house.

Sharon laughed. "They don't seem to be using it for playing, do they?"

"No, they don't. Why do you ask?"

"Well, I wonder if it would be helpful to move Nicky to a room by himself. You could put washable paint on the walls and install a vinyl floor. That would make days like today much easier."

"That is a great idea, Sharon. I do always feel better when I have a plan. I will talk it over with Arden. I am sure he will agree, we are at our wits end with this one."

As she was leaving, Sharon said, "Someday you will laugh about all this."

"I sure hope so, thank you for everything today. You saved me twice."

I didn't really believe her that day, but she was right about laughing.

A few hours later, I put Nicky in his beautifully clean crib for a nap and went downstairs. I fed the baby and was playing a game with Ryan when Karen went upstairs. I asked if she was going to check on Nicky and she said yes. Although she was just over two years old, she had begun to feel that taking care of her Nicky was her responsibility.

A few minutes later, Karen slowly came down a few stairs and stopped. Looking through the rails, she slowly said, "Mommy?"

I looked up.

"Come."

Terrified, Nicky was seizing again, I climbed the stairs two at a time and ran into the bedroom, straight into a repeating nightmare of the day's disaster. I couldn't fathom where all that poop had come from. This time I was able to keep myself together and clean everything up. I had been strengthened by my friend's service and counsel.

The next day, Arden and I got the supplies and put down the new floor in the downstairs bedroom, painted the walls and moved Nicky into his new room next to ours. From then on, it was much easier for me to clean up the messes, while we worked on changing that behavior.

A few weeks later, we met with a psychologist who specialized in toileting problems. He was very supportive. He recommended we use a star chart for toilet training with both Karen and Nicky. This created a competition with a little incentive for both of them. Karen liked to win and Nicky liked the stars on the chart. The doctor said that it might take a few months to interrupt Nicky's smearing behavior, so as a temporary solution, I sewed some modifications into Nicky's clothes. He couldn't undo them and remove them, so he couldn't create the same mess. We put those clothes on him for about a year whenever we put him to bed.

Chapter Twenty-Five

Nicky kept taking private swimming lessons. After ten months of regular instruction with his teacher, Nicky swam three feet by himself. It was a staggering feat. Progress was being made, we were very excited. I told his teacher that I could envision him swimming in the Special Olympics someday, but she might need to be in the water with him. We both laughed. I really had no idea what to expect with Nicky.

One afternoon in August, I was playing with baby Derek, who was about three months old. He was lying on his back on the floor. I held a squeaky toy above him. He laughed and reached for the toy with his left hand. I noticed that during the exertion of reaching for the toy, his right arm and hand was drawn up tight to his head and shoulder and his right leg was contracted up to his hip. I was horrified. I had seen that same movement pattern with other children who were in therapy with Nicky.

Derek was interested in the toy and kept trying to grab it. I kept moving the toy around so that it was on his right side, encouraging him to reach for it with his right hand. His arm didn't move away from his body. He became very frustrated and started to cry. So did I.

The next day when I took Nicky to therapy, Irene examined Derek. While she couldn't make a formal diagnosis, she confirmed my fears. She believed that Derek had spastic asymmetry. The right side of his body had higher muscle tone than the left.

Dr. Glass corroborated Irene's diagnosis.

Derek started physical therapy the next week. He responded well to the twice-a-week treatments. It was an opportune intervention. Arden and I believe that God showed me at just the right time that Derek needed some additional help over the next three years to move through all the developmental milestones in a timely manner.

My friend Susan Campbell and I took our kids to the Puyallup Fair in September. We had five kids who could walk and two in strollers. It was a big outing.

We got all the kids, strollers, and stuff through the entrance and were standing just inside the gate, trying to decide what to look at first, when I noticed that Nicky wasn't with us. I felt like my heart would jump out of my chest, it was beating so hard. I imagined all sorts of horrible things. Sue and I frantically looked around for probably just a few minutes, but it seemed like an eternity.

Finally, I saw him, standing in the horse barn about fifty feet away, directly behind the backside of the largest horse I'd ever seen. I approached slowly. I didn't want to frighten my son or the beast. I don't think that I took a breath until I scooped up my son and moved out of hoof range. That experience changed the way that I managed my kids on our outings; later they would accuse me of acting like a drill sergeant.

Nicky enjoyed his time at school. His teacher Donna and her classroom aides were very sweet to the kids and encouraged each child to do their best. Donna taught me a great deal about guiding and nurturing while having firm expectations of both behavior and skill development. It was as if she had a soft glove over a firm hand. I learned a lot from her for the two years that she was Nicky's teacher. Most importantly, I gained the ability to implement the behavior modification techniques of replacement and redirection, that I had previously learned.

For Donna's birthday that year, I wrote a poem. It was published in the elementary school newsletter and a local newspaper.

The Child We Share

I give you my son, the light of my life
my child of sunshine, my child of strife.
I love him, I hate him, so mixed are my feelings.
He pushes me past what I think I can bear.

My friend, my advisor, you'll hold my hand.
You're there when I need you, you understand.
Together we'll reach him, beyond all our visions.
We share the frustrations, we share in the joy.
I'm glad that we're teaching my little boy.

We still had grave concerns about Nicky's feeding difficulties. Not only did it take a long time for us to prepare and feed him blended food, he noticed that Karen could feed herself and he wanted to do it too. Sometimes, he would say "by self," then I would lay the spoon next to his bowl. He would look at it and try to pick it up. When he did get a proper grasp on the spoon, he would put it up near his face and then quickly put it back down on the table. Then he would say, "Help," and I would know that he was asking me to feed him.

One afternoon, Nicky's teacher phoned. He had refused all food at school that day and even made crying sounds when he sat at the table with the lunch tray in front of him. I hung up the phone. Feeling helpless, I rested my forehead on the wall next to the phone.

What is going on? He is usually happy all the time. This problem with his eating is so severe. I don't know what to do to help him. Why don't the professionals know what we can do to fix this?

I knew that the school personnel were working hard to help Nicky. They were using various techniques and modalities, including modified spoons, verbal cues and positioning in front of a mirror. But the end of year occupational therapy (OT) report made it apparent that Nicky needed something more. The report was depressing. In one year of school, Nicky had progressed in gross and fine motor age equivalent scores from nineteen months to twenty-two months. He was in the eighth percentile in all subtest areas compared to other children his age. That was significant, but the numbers that were the most disturbing were the feeding scores. At age forty-five months, his chewing was at five to six months' level, his tongue and lip mobility was at six to seven months and his hand use for self-feeding baseline was eighteen months. The OT explained that although his gross motor score had not changed much, Nicky had gained a few very vital skills over the school year, including the ability to catch himself with his hands while falling backward, and the ability to walk backward.

I found it hard to be in those meetings where all of my sweet son's shortcomings were listed in black and white. It seemed none of his strengths were valued in the scoring. Nicky's teachers and therapists understood his strengths, they just weren't part of the standardized tests that were used to evaluate progress.

Nicky was evaluated and placed in a feeding program at Children's Therapy Center (CTC) in Kent. Gay Lloyd Pinder was his speech and language therapist. She is one of my heroes. Gay Lloyd persevered with her chosen profession of speech therapist even after she lost her hearing from an ear infection.

Nicky made progress at CTC but we didn't see any carryover to our home experience of feeding him. As September approached, Gay Lloyd asked if she could have Nicky's therapy sessions in our home before school while he ate his breakfast. She hoped to encourage him to generalize his newfound skills to his home environment. She believed his siblings were superb models for self-feeding and that a home-based program was the best way for him to gain this critical skill.

For the next several years, Gay Lloyd joined our family for breakfast once a week. Through this innovative idea that worked, she became a close friend. More than any other person who worked with Nicky, Gay Lloyd got to know us, as the popular saying goes, "warts and all." It is almost impossible for me to explain the impact this sweet, loving, firm, stubborn, funny, kind, imaginative, creative, and a little unconventional woman had on our entire family.

I tried to have everyone up and bathed and the food prepared before Gay Lloyd arrived. One morning, however, we had been up late the night before and overslept. Gay Lloyd arrived to a dark house. She knocked on the door and peered through the glass but didn't see any movement. When she knocked again, Derek, who had crawled out of his crib, answered the door. She told him to go get Mommy, which he did. Mortified, I pulled on my robe and slippers. I ran past the dining room and asked Gay Lloyd to be seated while I woke Nicky. Rather than sitting down, she went into the kitchen to cook breakfast as I tended to the kids.

Over the years, we tried a variety of things to motivate Nicky to work to overcome the major sensitivities in his mouth. These sensitivities combined with no bite reflex formed the basis of his feeding issues. On weekends, if he didn't feed himself, he didn't get food. Weekdays I did feed him because he needed food with his morning seizure medicines and we had time constraints to catch the bus. Later, we withheld foods that he wanted like pudding or a milk shake until after he had eaten other things that were difficult for him to eat.

Once a few years later, he became particularly resistant to his feeding therapy program. Arden and I talked about it one night.

"I wish I could figure out how to motivate him. He has come so far, yet until he can eat regular food in a restaurant, it still is difficult to feed him when we are out."

"Eva, he's not just lacking motivation, it is physically hard for him to chew. His gag reflex is at the front of his mouth. You can tell by watching him how uncomfortable he is when he is eating."

"I know, but there has got to be something we can do."

"Well, what does he love to do?"

"Arden, he loves swimming but we can't take that away from him. He needs the exercise."

"What if we took away just part of it? Say, he can't jump off of the diving board until he eats something of our choice."

"That would work on the other kids, I just don't know about Nicky, but we can try."

We gathered the kids for a family meeting.

Arden began, "You know that Gay Lloyd has been coming for a few years to help Nicky learn to eat. He is stuck and we have an idea we want to try. We need all your help with this one."

I looked at their concerned faces around the table, they didn't know what to think.

"Arden, I think that you have worried them. You guys are going to like this one, believe me."

Ryan asked, "Mom, what do we have to do?"

"I'll explain. We have an idea to help motivate Nicky to over-come his resistance to chewing. We won't let him jump off the diving board at the pool until he eats a McDonald's cheeseburger. We will keep going to the pool and to McDonald's until he does this."

The kids looked at one another and laughed.

Ryan was the spokesman, "Okay, Mom and Dad, we will sacri-fice this for Nicky."

He missed jumping off the diving board but he resisted eating the cheeseburger for a couple of weeks. The other kids were thrilled that we kept going to McDonald's. The day he finally ate the burger, we immediately drove to pool. When I signed in at the check-in desk, Ryan announced, "He did it, Nicky ate the cheeseburger."

Nicky was beaming.

We quickly changed clothes and headed toward the diving board. All the staff knew about the challenge, and stopped to watch.

Smiling, Nicky kept repeating, "I ate the burger, I jump in the pool," as he climbed the few steps up to the diving board. He walked haltingly to the end of the board, looked at his audience and jumped.

We all watched the pool; he finally surfaced with a huge smile on his face.

He said again, "I ate the burger, I jump in the pool."

Everyone cheered. I was not the only one with tears streaming down my face. We were thrilled at his accomplishment. My other kids were sad that Nicky's great feat stopped the multiple trips to McDonald's.

We are extremely grateful for Gay Lloyd and her persistence while working with Nicky until he was able to self-feed, chew and overcome his reaction to his extreme oral sensitivity. It has given Nicky and our whole family such freedom. Arden often tells others that we wore out three food processors feeding Nicky. He also says that he never knew it was possible to have a whole Thanksgiving din-ner blended into one bowl until we did that for Nicky.

PART SIX

We Stumble, Fall, and Get Back up to Carry On

Chapter Twenty-Six

Not everyone we meet is compassionate and aware of what it takes to care for Nick. After a few days traveling on our epic road trip of 2016, we settled into an efficient pattern. However, not every overnight stay went according to plan. Most days by early afternoon, we would have a good idea of how far we could drive that day and I would research online for accommodations. Sometimes we stayed two nights in the same town for Nick to rest. One particular day, I called ahead to the hotel and reached their front desk.

"I am calling to see if you have a non-smoking air-conditioned room available for tonight and tomorrow night. We have three adults and need a room with two queen beds and a bathtub rather than a shower."

"We do have quite a few two queen rooms available and they are all air-conditioned," the receptionists said.

"I also want to explain our son uses a manual wheelchair, so if your elevator is out of order, we will need a first-floor room. He can't manage stairs."

"I understand. We do have a room that meets your requirements. Let me get your account details."

We finished confirming the reservation. I always get the name of the reservation person I am talking to, in addition to the confirmation number.

We arrived a few hours later and unpacked the car onto the trolley to move into the room. After checking in, we took the elevator to our room. Opening the door to the room, we were hit with a heatwave. While I unpacked our cases, Arden tried to get the air-conditioning going, but it was broken.

Arden called the front desk. They got the manager on the phone.

"Mr. Gremmert, the air-conditioning is broken in that room and I don't have any other rooms available with two queen beds."

"When we made this reservation, your employee assured me that the assigned room would meet our requirements. My son is medically fragile and can't be in a bedroom that is over 80 degrees. You must give us a room that meets the conditions that were promised."

"The only thing that I have available is a room with king-bed and a pull-out. It is not cleaned up yet and won't be ready for another hour."

"We have dinner reservations with family members. We can't wait here for another hour. We will take that room you are offering, but we won't be able to move our things until we return in a few hours."

We didn't take the time to check out the new room, we trusted that it would be okay. We had a lovely dinner with our family. We talked for hours. It was relaxing to have a nice long visit after being in the car for days.

Back at the hotel, we packed up our stuff to move into the new room. It was just down the hall, so it didn't take long. We were very tired and wanted to get Nick settled. Walking into the room, Arden noticed a very strong smoke smell. He called the front desk.

"Mr. Gremmert, I have no other room available."

"This is unacceptable and is not the type of service I expect from your hotel chain. I have stayed in your hotels all across the US and have never been treated like this before."

"Mr. Gremmert, I know that this is truly inconvenient, and I am prepared to comp the room this evening for you because of it. I really have no other room available."

So we made do.

In the morning, I had a bad asthma reaction to the smoke in the room, and we all were congested. I went downstairs to talk to the manager.

"We can't stay a second night in that same room. We need a non-smoking room."

"I am so sorry Mrs. Gremmert. We just took over management of this hotel two weeks ago and are having maintenance problems.

We are working hard to fix this situation. I can give you another room. They just aren't made up yet."

"We are going to a reunion today. We are leaving before 11:00 a.m. and won't be back until about 10:00 p.m. Can we put our stuff into that new room? Can your staff clean around our bags?"

"That will be acceptable. Thank you for being so kind and understanding with all these problems, Mrs. Gremmert. We will take care of this."

After breakfast, we moved all our stuff, again. It was the third room in two days. I had hoped we would have a break by staying in the same place for two days. Instead we had more work than usual.

Arden and I were feeling the stress of all the problems with the hotel and fought on the way to the reunion. We both hate it when we fight. We put our bad feelings aside as we got to my cousin's place. We had so much fun that day. We spent the day relaxing with family then headed back to the hotel.

We arrived about ten and everything was okay. The room was made up and all our stuff was secure. The air conditioning wasn't working very well, but the weather was a little milder and since we were on the second floor, we were able to open the window. The room cooled off quickly. We got ready for bed so that we could have a good rest.

In the morning, the bill for our stay was under the door. It was for two nights. They hadn't credited us anything. Frustrated at the hotel, we decided that Arden would get Nick ready to go down for breakfast and I would go ahead and talk to the manager.

As she came to the front desk I said, "I am very frustrated. I don't feel like being kind or understanding with these problems with you guys anymore."

"What seems to be the problem now, Mrs. Gremmert?"

I showed her the receipt. "We were charged for two nights stay. That first night, you said that you were comp'ing it. Either you lied to me or this is another indication of your incompetence. You said there were lots of problems here since you just took over management, so we have tried to be understanding. Up to this point, we haven't planned on complaining to the hotel corporate offices, but this is ridiculous."

She didn't say anything to me. She turned around and started talking to another woman who came out of the office.

I thought this was rude. I shook my head in disgust and said, "I am going back upstairs to help get my son ready to come down for breakfast. I will come back later. Please redo the receipt so the total is what we agreed to."

Later, as the three of us were eating breakfast, the hotel assistant manager approached our table. She apologized for interrupting and handed me a new receipt. It showed a zero balance, no charge. They had comp'd both nights. We were surprised.

I walked over to the desk and said to the manager, "We are fully prepared to pay for one of the two nights we were here. That is what you offered and what we agreed to. Thank you for comp'ing both, however."

"Mrs. Gremmert, I would have been frustrated too if the same thing had happened to me. I feel that it was the right thing for us to do."

While Arden got Nick cleaned up, I was able to secure a hotel for that night at our next destination. We packed up and got back on the road. Lost in our own thoughts, the miles rolled past.

Finally, Arden broke the silence, "That whole thing at the hotel was very strange. I was thinking about how we have developed conflict resolution skills and what a great team we have become over the years."

Laughing I said, "You mean that when Nick needs something, I can convince other people to do what I think they should do? I believe our kids call it manipulation."

"Yes, that is true, but manipulation is not what I meant. I remember that time in Nick's early years when we challenged the school district. Resolution took over a year and we had to fight them for both a correct diagnosis and classroom placement."

"That was hard, wasn't it? I was worried that we wouldn't do the right thing, and I didn't know exactly what we were supposed to do. We were only twenty-seven years old, but somehow I knew that his teacher and the school psychologist were wrong in their assessment."

Chapter Twenty-Seven

Nicky's two years of preschool were wonderful for him and instructive for us. He loved his teacher and thrived in her classroom. The bus drivers were very kind and he always smiled when he left on the bus in the morning and when he returned home at lunchtime. As school started again in fall of 1984, Nicky was different. I thought the change was because he was at school for the full day. The bus driver even commented that she wondered where her happy Nicky had gone.

After a couple of weeks, he still wasn't happy. I thought that perhaps he was having a hard time adjusting to his new teacher, as he had been in the same classroom for the previous two years. I went to visit the school.

When I arrived at the school office, they were pleasant and welcoming. I was directed to Nicky's new classroom. The door was closed but there was a small window in it so I looked in. Nicky was sitting at his desk with a puzzle on the desktop. He seemed listless and wasn't engaged in the classroom activity. I was concerned that this might be another manifestation of seizures as they can present differently.

The teacher noticed me at the door and opened it slightly. "May I help you?"

"I am Nicky's mom. I am here to observe him in the classroom."

She stepped into the hall and closed the door quickly behind her. I took a step back.

Raising one eyebrow, she began, "Mrs. Gremmert, it is imperative that we have uninterrupted time with the students, especially at the beginning of the year. Your unwillingness to comply will be detrimental to your son's progress. If you have any concerns, please use the notebook that I provided for you. It's in your son's backpack and is intended to be the means of communication between you and me."

I took a breath to begin talking, but she continued, "Now I must get back to the classroom. In the future, please use the proper channels to request a visit and we will do our best to schedule an appropriate time. Thank you."

With that, she opened the door slightly, slid through the small opening, and promptly closed it again.

Stunned, I attempted to look in through the window, but she stood firmly in front of the door, blocking my view. Raising her eyebrows and her hand up at the same time, she shook her head slightly, as if to say, please leave now.

That evening, I told Arden about the encounter.

"I had hoped to have the same collaborative relationship with his new teacher that we have had for the past two years with Donna."

I nodded in agreement. "I also think that we should prepare for our first parent teacher IEP meeting, which is scheduled in a few weeks. I don't imagine it will be fun. I'm afraid that the advocacy training we received a few years ago at the "You are the Expert" weekend in Ellensburg will come in handy."

For two years, the Individual Education Program (IEP) meetings had been completely cooperative working meetings held quarterly with the teachers and staff. Everyone attending was united in the goal of helping our son and we thought that this type of teamwork with the school was normal. Sadly, this is not always the case.

Throughout the coming months, every time we wrote a question in the notebook concerning what Nicky was doing in her classroom, this teacher repeatedly wrote back that she had the training and expertise to educate our son. She continually said that we would be well advised to follow her direction. She never did answer our concerns. It was a difficult school year for Nicky and us. We never developed a working relationship with her. When I sent in the reports from other professionals working with Nicky, I would ask her in the communications notebook whether she had seen them. She wrote back that the paperwork had been put in Nicholas's school file. She didn't read the reports.

Her expectations of Nicholas did not match our own and she appeared unwilling to consider the recommendations of his doctors and non-school district therapists that we forwarded to her throughout the year.

Nicky did not thrive in school that year. He seemed to become himself when he was home on weekends and school holidays, but he didn't like being at school. He continued to have speech, feeding, and physical therapy during that time. He developed some severe behavioral challenges during this school year. His teacher believed that this bad behavior was another manifestation of his disability. We believed it was because he was frustrated at school.

We were very concerned about our son's behavior. He had gotten so disruptive and uncooperative that it was difficult for us to take him out in public. I feared that if this continued, eventually I would have an adult son who couldn't go anywhere outside his home.

In April, we contacted a recommended psychologist to craft an individualized behavior modification program for us to use. The doctor never met with Nick. For the first two meetings, he asked us questions and listened to our answers. Many of his questions concerned how Arden and I each dealt with different situations.

At the third meeting, we thought we would finally be getting some direction from the doctor. Instead of giving us a new behavior management program, he told us that based on our description of our son, he believed that Nicky needed further testing to rule out autism, and that Arden and I needed marriage counseling.

After giving us his opinion, he began again with questions about our relationship. Arden interrupted him and said, "Doctor, we are here to learn what to do to manage Nicky's difficult behavior."

"Mr. Gremmert, unless you are willing to work on your marriage, you will never be able to get a handle on your son's behavior."

Arden and I just looked at one another. We both thought we had a great marriage. We had the typical misunderstandings that most couples did.

Arden then asked, "What specifically do you think that we are doing as a couple that negatively impacts our son's behavior?"

Shaking his head, the doctor said, "You two desperately need marriage counseling. You will never be able to manage your son's behavior until you do."

We were seeking strategies to implement regarding behavior modification and it seemed that again I had found a professional that believed that my child's problems were my fault. We didn't go back.

Nicky was six years old and his school age assessment with the school districts psychologist was scheduled for the end of the school year. These multi-disciplinary testing assessments are done every three years, and the test results direct the student's classroom placement and program for the following three years. Arden and I were deeply concerned about Nicky's lack of development over the previous school year.

We met with the psychologist, in his office, after he had completed his initial evaluation.

"Mr. and Mrs. Gremmert, based on the test scores we now have, your son hasn't progressed at all. He is now more than 50 percent delayed when comparing his age and his developmental scores to typically developing children. In some testing areas, he has even gone backward, compared to the previous test scores. I believe that Nicholas's behavior issues in addition to his general lack of ability are the main barriers hindering his progress."

"Doctor, we've seen a big difference in his behavior in this school year compared to the way he acted during the previous school year. I think that Nicky is frustrated in his current classroom. Could frustration be a factor in his severe behavior change?"

"Mrs. Gremmert, your son is severely impaired. Through testing, I have determined that his diagnosis is severe to profound mental retardation. Behavior issues are part of that disability. It is not frustration on his part. You must accept that. You must learn to be realistic in your expectations."

He stood up to shake our hands. The meeting was obviously over.

In silence, we walked to the car and got in.

I turned to Arden. "It seems that these school personnel have decided that our son is a different person than we know him to be.

140

Are we wrong? We see him do so much more at home with us than they see at school."

"Eva, he is not severe or profound. Children with the severe to profound mentally retarded diagnosis have difficulty communicating. Nick can talk."

Nodding my agreement, I added, "Already at six, Nicky can do more than some of the adults we have met with that diagnosis. Unless he regresses as he gets older, I expect that he will be able to read, write, and do basic math. The individuals that have the same diagnosis the district believes Nick has are unable to work or live alone or care for themselves. Their educational program taught them only life skills and nothing academic. That is not how I envision our son's future life."

"Maybe we need to place him in a private school. You looked at a couple before we decided to try the public-school system. Perhaps they would see Nicky's potential as we do. Why don't you call Dr. Glass and ask him what he recommends?"

I did talk to the doctor and he said to go to the annual IEP meeting to see what the district proposed for Nicky's placement and then let him know.

A week later, I wrote to Nicky's teacher, requesting a copy of her proposed Individual Education Program (IEP) objectives and goals so that we could review them prior the upcoming annual Multi-disciplinary team (MDT) meeting. The MDT typically consists of the student, the parents, the teacher, the school administrator and often other support staff such as school counselors and therapists. Nicky's teacher responded that she was not required by law to present the IEP ahead of the meeting and we would receive them at that time.

That was a surprise. These objectives and goals were her suggestions about the education plan for Nicky for the following year. The annual meeting was designed for the district to present to the parents their proposed program for the child.

I responded back that since there was so much material to go over, Arden and I felt it would be more efficient if we were familiar with her proposed goals and objectives, so that we could prepare our questions and suggestions. We did not get a copy of her IEP until the meeting.

On the day of the meeting, dressed professionally, we arrived at the school ten minutes ahead of the scheduled time. We brought our files containing Nick's previous IEP's as well as the doctors' and therapists' review notes from the various evaluations. Having relevant documentation at the IEP meetings was one of the things we had learned at the "You Are The Expert" conference.

We walked down to Nicky's classroom. The rest of the multi-disciplinary team was assembled and already meeting. We stood in the doorway to the classroom. The teacher stood up and walked toward us. She informed us that they weren't ready for us yet.

We thought that they were meeting concerning another student, so we waited outside the open door in the hall. Instead it was obvious they were reviewing the recommendations for Nicky's IEP ahead of the meeting with us. We were excluded from the discussion that we were legally supposed to be a part of. I felt really awkward standing in the hall.

When Nick's teacher finally invited us into the room, all of the other team members were seated in adult-sized chairs around a table. The remaining two chairs were child-sized and obviously intended for Arden and me. We were also surprised to see the school principal seated there. His name had not been on the original meeting invitation form that we had received. We knew that they were supposed to inform us as to who was going to be at the IEP meeting.

The teacher addressed us by saying, "We need to get started, so please have a seat."

"I am sorry for the delay, but we will need to have two more adult chairs before we can begin."

"Mrs. Gremmert, we only have a half an hour for this scheduled IEP meeting and it is already five after the hour."

"We arrived ten minutes ahead of the scheduled time and have been prepared to begin since our arrival. It is my understanding that IEP meetings are not a specified length. We are prepared to stay as long as needed to complete the task at hand. And we will need adult-sized chairs to sit in because my husband and I are not children."

We stood there waiting. Initially no one moved. Finally, the school principal went across the hall and got the chairs.

It was apparent that this was not a working meeting to co-create an education plan for our son. The teacher had already typed up goals and timelines that she felt were appropriate. At all of the previous IEP meetings we had attended, the proposed goals and objectives had been handwritten in pencil.

She handed each of the professionals a copy of her papers. She had one remaining copy for Arden and me to share.

"Eva and I each need a copy of your proposal so that we can each take notes. Please get us another copy."

The teacher tried to interrupt, but he continued, "Now, I need to write down the names of each of you and your official job title with the district. Let's start to my left."

Startled, the teacher said, "Mr. Gremmert, you will have all of that in our report. We really need to get started."

Calmly, he smiled, "I know that I will receive your report later, and I also know what our rights are as we represent and advocate for our child."

Each person gave him their name and title. One of the therapists in attendance handed her copy of the paperwork over to me. Arden then invited the teacher to continue.

She loudly cleared her throat as she straightened her stack of papers on the table in front of her. "Well, I believe that we are all in agreement that Nicky's diagnosis on his previous IEP was inappropriate and that he should be correctly labeled severely mentally retarded."

Sitting up a little taller, I interrupted. "We are not ALL in agreement. Arden and I don't agree with the diagnosis presented. This is actually something needing further investigation. We don't believe that this meeting is the appropriate time or place to discuss this. We would like to use this time to review your suggested goals and objectives."

"All right, first of all the pre-academic goals you have asked for are not appropriate. It is unrealistic and Nicky will be unsuccessful in meeting them. The appropriate goals that I have outlined for your son are to increase his independent leisure time skills, to work on self-care, personal hygiene, and self-dressing. In addition, he needs to improve his functional communication skills."

"What is your goal for that?"

"It is right here on page four, Nicholas will turn his head with one cue, five out of five times toward the speaker."

"The communication goals should be written by the Communication Disorder Specialist," I countered.

"The CDS has her own goals, they are found in your copy, this goal is our classroom goal."

Arden was taking notes like he always did. I looked over to him. He nodded slightly, encouraging me to go on.

"Well, we do not agree with your proposed goals. We want a goal included in this document to increase his understanding of number concepts up to four. Currently, he correctly names the numbers one to three, so we can increase that to four. We also want a rote counting goal. He can count to fifteen now and we believe that the goal of twenty is plausible. We want a prereading goal of recognizing, matching and naming letters, shapes, as well as colors."

We did not agree with the program that she had outlined for Nicky.

By the end of the meeting, everyone was frustrated.

Arden turned to the school psychologist sitting next to him and said, "We feel that Nicky needed a full assessment at this time."

"Mr. Gremmert, I believe the teacher is correct in her evaluation of the test results."

Looking around the table, Arden said, "Well, in that case, we will not sign the IEP and we will consult with our own team of specialists. After we get their reports, we will request another meeting to present their findings to the multi-disciplinary team."

Arden and I stood up to leave. The teacher was livid. She started to say, "How dare you—" and was quickly silenced by the principal, "The Gremmert's have the right to not sign the IEP and to request further assessments."

I turned to the principal and said, "I am concerned that this woman's attitude will negatively impact my son through the remaining weeks of school."

"I assure you, Mrs. Gremmert, I will make certain the teacher is professional at all times, even if I need to be in the classroom observing myself."

I had my doubts. For the first time, Arden and I left an IEP meeting feeling extremely concerned about Nicky's education.

A week later, we received a letter from the principal recommending that Nicky remain in the same school program with the same teacher for the following year. Now it was I who was livid. To calm myself down, I read through the material they had included, The Parents Guide to Special Education, which included both school district protocols and the Washington Administrative Code, chapter 392–171.

Conforming to their protocol, we mailed a certified letter to the district offices requesting that our son have a different teacher. Then just before the summer break, we received a letter confirming that Nicky would be placed in a different classroom for the upcoming school year in the fall.

Chapter Twenty-Eight

The fight with Nicky's teacher had been stressful. Having that settled made it much easier for me to leave Arden at home for two weeks while I was on my dream trip to Ireland.

The previous summer, we heard about a worldwide Doherty clan reunion to be held in Donegal. My dad invited my two sisters and me to go the birthplace of his parents near Carndonagh, County Donegal.

I was full of mixed emotions. I was excited to go to Ireland and I felt guilty about being gone, leaving Arden to manage the house, the four kids, and Nicky's therapy. And then I felt guilty that I was so excited that I was getting away.

I was twenty-eight years old and it felt like I had the weight of the world on my shoulders. One of my friends told me that it would do me a world of good to be on my own without my family responsibilities. That turned out to be true. It was a cathartic experience for me that happened at the perfect time. We didn't know how easily we would fill our time in Ireland, so we planned one week there and one in England.

That first week in Ireland was magical. We met so many relations and had an instant bond and connection with them. I felt an immediate special closeness with one of my cousins, Margaret Canny, who was the matron of the James Connolly Children's Hospital in Carndonagh. It is the regional residential facility for disabled children. We met at a wedding and spent the evening sharing ideas and experiences. She was intrigued about the programs and services available to us. Margaret was creating innovative plans for community outreach and parent education programs in Carndonagh. I visited with her three times that week. She understood my concerns, and applauded our recent victory with the school district. We spent many hours together sharing thoughts and ideas.

Even while I was away on vacation, my family was always in my thoughts. I was constantly on the lookout for more information and ideas that could help Nicky. I talked to Arden every couple of days. He said that they were doing great, but I could hear the stress in his voice as time went on. This two-week trip of mine was difficult for him. I did appreciate the opportunity that I was given. I marveled that I felt such a strong connection to so many of my relations that I had just met.

When our week was over and we drove away from Carndonagh, everyone was somber, each of us sitting quietly with our own thoughts. Although it was my first time there, and it had only been a few days, my heart broke at leaving; as if I was being torn from my homeland. I didn't think that I would ever have an opportunity to go back again, but from the moment I left, I longed to return to Ireland.

I shared my thoughts with Arden once I got home. We talked about our financial situation and especially our commitment to Nicky, his education and his therapies, all of which utilized a great deal of our resources. We decided to make it a matter of prayer.

One morning about three days later, Arden came upstairs from his home office, into the kitchen, singing an Irish folk song. He declared, "Eva, we need to take the kids to Ireland, let's figure out how make it happen."

I turned from the sink and hugged him, soap suds dripping from my hands, down the back of his shirt.

"Arden, do you really think we can? It's a lot of money. How will we do it with everything else?"

"We have to get the kids to understand it'll be a sacrifice for all of us."

That night, we called the kids together for a family meeting.

After the opening prayer, Arden began the meeting.

"Your mom and I have a proposal to present to our family. We don't want to make this decision without your input. It'll be a sacrifice for everyone."

Ryan looked across the table at Nicky and asked, "Does Nicky need more therapy, is that it?"

"Well, yes, Nicky continues to need more therapy. But no, that is not what we want to discuss. Eva, why don't you tell them what we are thinking about?"

"Dad got the impression today that we should take you guys to Ireland next summer for a family vacation, and…"

I didn't get to finish my thought. Ryan and Karen jumped up and down, screaming, "Yes, yes, yes."

Nicky and Derek joined in with the jumping and the screaming, but I don't think they knew exactly what everyone was excited about.

Arden attempted to regain control. "Kids, kids, sit down, we need to talk about what this means. It'll take a lot of money to take our family there. I want to talk about what we can do to save money for the trip."

"Arden, one thought I have is to put the money into a jar as we choose to save it for our trip. That way we can see it growing."

"What a great idea, so every time we decide to sacrifice something, Mom and I will put the cash we would have spent into the jar. What kind of things can we sacrifice?"

"I looked at all of our closets and I am going to gather up the extra clothes and sell them at the consignment shop."

Karen, who was four, said, "Mommy, I could sell one of my Barbies. I don't need all of them."

Arden looked at me to see what I would say, "Karen, that is very sweet of you. Daddy is making a list so that if we need to sell things, we can remember that you offered. Any other ideas?"

Ryan said, "We could quit going out to eat so much."

Smiling, I said, "Great idea, Ryan. That would save a lot. Daddy and I also talked about spending less money at Christmas and birthdays. How does that sound?"

Two-and-a-half-year-old Derek was very practical, "That's okay, Mommy, Santa and Grandma will take care of us, right, Daddy?"

"That is right, son," Arden said.

We were all excited about our family plan as we began to scrimp and save to make our Irish dream vacation come true.

Chapter Twenty-Nine

In September, we had another setback with the school district. During the summer break, we had shared the teacher's proposed goals and objectives with all the non-district professionals working with Nicky. They all agreed that her suggested plan was not in his best interests. Following the districts' protocol, we formally requested an independent examination by a professional not associated with the school district. While the district believed that the assessment done in the spring of 1985 was appropriate and adequate, they had to comply with our request. They offered to pay the Federal Way School District personnel to do another assessment. Concerned that there would be collusion between the districts, we requested an independent assessment through Children's Orthopedic Hospital in Seattle.

District policies and procedures required that we receive the district's prior approval of the professional we wanted to hire to do the independent assessment. The first name that we proposed was rejected. The district psychologist felt that the individual we asked for didn't have the professional expertise and experience to do a proper school evaluation. I called Dr. Glass, who recommended Dr. Wendy Marlowe, a renowned neurological psychologist in Seattle. He also suggested that we meet with an attorney who specialized in the legal needs of families with disabled children.

The attorney helped us draft a letter to the school district superintendent outlining the historical context of our disagreement with the district personnel as well as our suggested solution to these problems, so that we could, as stated in the letter, "get on with educating Nicholas J. Gremmert." We requested that the district pay for an independent evaluation by Dr. Marlowe. The district denied our request, for no valid reason, as Marlowe was eminently qualified and unassailable.

Arden and I were faced with a huge dilemma. We could fight the district through the courts to force them to change their plan, or we could hire our own expert to do the independent examination and present a different plan to the district. Either course would be costly, and we did not have the available funds to do both. After praying about it, we decided to hire Dr. Marlowe to do an independent assessment.

We were thankful that Nicky was happy with his new teacher, Debi Nicholson. At the beginning of the school year, Debi listened to our concerns, observed Nicky in her classroom and immediately rewrote the goals and objectives for his IEP based on her observation. We agreed with her plan. He worked so hard that semester that Debi called a special meeting in December and asked if she could rewrite his IEP again because Nick had accomplished all the goals from the new September IEP.

Leaving the classroom, I said to Arden, "I am so tempted to march right down this hall to that other teachers' room and wave these papers under her turn-up nose."

"What papers?"

"This copy of the Debi's new September IEP for Nick, containing all of the pre-academic goals we wanted, with all of the signed dates indicating that he has already accomplished all of them."

"I don't think that is a good idea. We are still fighting with the district to correct Nicky's assessment."

We knew that the assessment from the district was not correct. Debi was currently giving Nicky what he needed, but we now understood that we couldn't count on every teacher agreeing with us. We wanted to be certain that our son would have the services he needed and would be educated appropriately for the remainder of his formal schooling. Since the school district's assessment was the legal document labeling Nick's diagnosis and directing his placement as well as his educational plan, it needed to be changed.

Dr. Marlowe met first with Arden and me in January. Then Nicky had six ninety-minute evaluation sessions with her over the following two months. She met with us before and after each evaluation session so that we could discuss her findings and plan the next step. Finally, she presented her report to us.

Dr. Marlowe treated us in the same professional manner as Dr. Glass did, welcoming our questions and listening closely to our observations. She helped us gain understanding when we needed to learn something, without talking down to us. We felt that we were part of a team working to create the optimal learning environment for Nicky. She treated him with the same respect.

After her second meeting with Nicky, Dr. Marlowe requested that we talk to Dr. Glass about prescribing Ritalin. She felt that initially it would have a great benefit and although it might not be a long-term prescriptive protocol, she had seen it enable some students to begin to engage in learning. Dr. Glass agreed that it was a good experiment. The change in Nick's behavior and attentiveness was dramatic. We added Ritalin to his morning medicine. I thought that he seemed more attentive and aware, but receiving a note home from Debi confirmed it. She wrote that within a few days of starting the drug, she noted a reduction in the number of cues Nicky needed to accomplish his tasks. He also had a longer attention span and was less restless. The teachers filled in a daily chart for seven weeks tracking twenty-eight problem behaviors. The chart had four scoring levels for charting the severity of the problem behavior, "very much," "pretty much," "just a little," and "not at all." By week two, Nick was scoring twenty-two "not at all's." He started out with eight. It was remarkable.

In our third meeting, we discussed behavioral modification techniques. Dr. Marlowe reminded us to use techniques such as distraction, replacement, and redirection to help Nicky adjust his behavior. She also suggested we remind Nicky to use his self-soothing strategies to calm himself. She explained that by using the same repetitive phrases that he recognized, his responses would become automatic over time. She emphasized that it takes months to get results. The techniques wouldn't solve our problems in a week. Even if children have the mental capacity of a toddler, they can learn. And just like toddlers they are master manipulators as their brains are acting on instinct-survival mode, fight or flight.

At our final meeting with Dr. Marlowe, Arden and I waited in the lobby. She was running a little late.

Why am I so agitated? I feel a bit nervous.

I looked over, Arden was reading a magazine.

"Are you feeling a little nervous?"

"No, why, are you?"

"I think so, I just feel agitated somehow. I guess it's because it has been over a year of conflict with the district over Nicky's program. I wonder what she will say today and will it make any difference."

"We have to believe that it will make a difference, it will make all the difference."

A few minutes later, Dr. Marlowe called us into her office. She handed us each a copy of her sixteen-page, single-spaced neuropsychological evaluation of Nicholas. We followed along as she began to read.

The first three pages were historical narrative that I had lived through, so I skimmed ahead. Dr. Marlowe noticed and decided to skip to the Evaluation section of the report.

"Nicholas was friendly and cooperative to the best of his abilities throughout the evaluation."

That is one thing I am grateful for. He is usually very friendly and cooperative. When he isn't we know something is wrong. Where is she reading now?

"Nicholas has a large repertoire of stereotypic gestures and utterances. He develops rituals readily. He engages in a high degree of perseveration."

She obviously got to know Nicky. I wonder what her recommendation is.

I flipped through the report pages again.

"Mr. and Mrs. Gremmert, I think it might be a better use of our time, if I share my report with you verbally. You can read the entire report later. To begin with, I believe that Nicholas has been educationally deprived, due to both his seizure disorder and his attention deficit disorder. You will find anecdotal evidence as well as test results to support my findings. He tests in the mildly mentally retarded range for educational purposes."

Astounded I asked, "Can you repeat that, did you say MILD mental retardation?"

"Yes, Mrs. Gremmert, his short attention span has rendered him unavailable for learning. He has been unable to sustain attention long enough to recognize stimuli, comprehend task demands or engage in learning behavior. It is his multiple areas of disability rather than a generalized decrement in learning function which make him a difficult youngster to educate."

"By decrement you mean—"

"It is a reduction in capacity."

That was a huge change from Nicky being labeled severely retarded in the school districts evaluation report.

She supports our position. She sees Nicky as we do. This is huge.

"What do you recommend, Dr. Marlowe?"

"I recommend that Nicky begin sensory integration therapy. This is imperative. I also believe that a typical program for children with developmental delays will not meet his needs. It is essential that Nicholas be placed in a structured "learning to learn" situation, that uses a conceptual teaching model. It will be exceedingly difficult, if not impossible, for the public-school system to meet your son's specific educational needs. He requires a far more systematic approach to learning than a simple developmental model."

The tuition for the private school program she recommended exceeded $4,000 a year. Although our attorney said that we had a good shot at getting the school district to pay for it, the battle would take at least a couple of years. We would be required to pay the tuition up front and we wouldn't be reimbursed until after the court case was settled. We knew that there was no guarantee that the district would change their assessment. However, Arden and I decided we should put our efforts into convincing them to use Dr. Marlowe's assessment, diagnosis and IEP suggestions to create Nicky's program within the district. Then, if this wasn't successful, we would revisit filing a lawsuit.

Dr. Marlowe's evaluation changed the trajectory of our lives. She saw our son as we did. She recognized what was difficult for Nicky. She saw not only his current developmental levels but perceived what he could potentially learn. In addition, she created a pathway for him to get there. Although it might have looked to others as if we were like Don Quixote tilting at windmills, we felt that we had been empowered to fight the school district for that necessary pathway to be implemented. I still cry when I think that he could have so easily been placed in an educational program with much lower expectations.

I'm not saying that the effort was easy. There were times that I wondered if we were being unrealistic. Was I was expecting too much of Nicky, of us? Nicky's happiness mattered most to me. But I thought he also deserved to reach for the highest level of education and skills that was possible for him. Just like all my other children, I wanted Nicky to achieve his potential.

Along the way, most of our friends were supportive. But there were some who thought differently. One morning a woman from church phoned to ask if she could drop by for a few minutes. We agreed on a convenient time.

Later, when I answered the door, she seemed a bit nervous.

"Sister Gremmert, I just wanted to come by and have a short chat with you."

"Come on in, Sister, we can sit right here in my living room."

"Sister Gremmert, I have noticed how busy you are with all of your activities."

"Yes, there is always plenty to do, especially with my four children."

"Well, yes, that is true. However, I was specifically thinking of all of the things that you are doing with your Nicholas."

"He does have a lot of therapy appointments, but we feel that it is critical for us to give him all the opportunity we can."

"I am sure that is true. I know that you were very accomplished in your youth with your ice skating. You must have been very focused and goal oriented to do so well."

I was confused. I didn't know where she was leading this conversation.

"I am sorry to interrupt, but I am not sure what you are getting at."

"I just wanted to talk to you, to counsel with you actually. I can't help but wonder if all of this activity geared toward Nicholas is actually an unmet need for achievement that you have. I mean, is all of this really serving your child? He is already perfect, just the way that God made him. Perhaps you feel that he needs to be different or that he is not good enough? I have been concerned."

I knew that she didn't understand and I recognized that she was sincere in her concerns. Yet I was shocked that she was sitting in my living room, accusing me of thinking that my son was not enough. She believed I was driving the whole therapy thing forward to meet some weird achievement need of mine. It was the first time someone had challenged my intentions toward my son. Even though she was very wrong, it hurt to be judged like that.

Rather than yell at her, I said, "I love my son. I want his life to be rich and full. I want him to experience all that he can, to the best of his abilities."

I invited her to leave.

Chapter Thirty

Nicky could now say his name. He was very proud of himself. The "K" sound is very difficult to enunciate, and often as language develops is pronounced as a "T" sound before the "K" emerges. Even though he could say Nicky, he still was calling his sister Taren when he was trying to say Karen. We were all involved in helping him with correct pronunciation. Two of Ryan's friends approached me one afternoon after school to help.

"Mrs. Gremmert, we would like to help Nicky say his words. What do we do to help him?"

"Well, boys, we are gentle with him, but we correct his pronunciation when we notice that he is not enunciating the sounds correctly. It often helps to separate the syllables too. For instance, let me show you. Nicky, say 'water.' See how he says wa-er, without the T. You can emphasize the T sound, by saying, wa-ter, and that helps him."

Nicky obediently said, "Wa-ter."

"Now Nicky, try to say cup-cake."

"Tup-tate."

"Try again, Nicky, cup-caKe," I enunciated.

"Cup-cake."

Everyone was smiling.

I left the boys in the living room and resumed working on making dinner in the kitchen.

That is so sweet that those two boys want to help Nicky. It warms my heart.

I quickly discovered their game when I heard them laughing. They kept prompting Nicky to say "Kitty" and then burst out in laughter when he made an unsuccessful attempt. I told them to choose a different word.

Derek finished up with his scheduled NDT physical therapy just before his third birthday in May 1986. On the last day, Irene was doing her final evaluation when another therapist came into the treatment room. Irene introduced Derek to her friend, by saying that as an infant he was diagnosed as a classic right-hemi, a term which describes a type of brain damage. The full name is spastic hemiplegic cerebral palsy. This common form of cerebral palsy is a much more severe diagnosis than that of spastic asymmetry, which both Irene and Dr. Glass had mentioned when Derek was an infant. I was glad that I didn't know the full medical diagnosis. It would have been overwhelming to me.

As a family, we had worked alongside Irene for almost three years, doing all of the exercises she gave us as Derek progressed through each of the normal developmental milestones.

For a moment, after I heard Irene's comment to the other therapist, I had an internal meltdown. Then I noticed that the other therapist and Irene were laughing while they watched Derek long jump off the top of the plastic slide that was in the therapy room.

Irene said, "There's a classic example of the benefit of early intervention with regular physical therapy."

Puzzled I asked, "What do you mean?"

"Eva, at three months old, Derek initially presented with a pretty severe spasticity on his right side. Now, after all of this work, no one, especially Derek, will ever know there was a problem. He is a poster child for NDT therapy. The majority of children with a brain injury like Derek's aren't diagnosed until they are much older and often the intervention is not as successful. Your amazing skill of detailed observation caught Derek's challenges at just the right time."

I just know that we're forever grateful that we had a team of specialists already in place to help our youngest son too.

During that horrible year fighting the school district for Nicky, we had the wondrous blessing of anticipating our first family trip to Ireland in the summer. We'd been saving since that family meeting we'd had after my return from Ireland the previous year. We had a large glass jar that was labeled "Ireland 1986." Any coins that we found were put into the jar. Even Nicky would find change and bring it to me to put in the jar. He would say, "Penny, Ireland." Although he didn't know what Ireland was yet, he wanted to help our project.

We decided as a family to forgo eating out and put the money in the Ireland jar instead. Some days I wondered if we were crazy, planning to take four kids ages three to eight to Europe for two weeks. But I felt like we were blessed on every side. When we decided to purchase the plane tickets, there was a special deal that week. Adult tickets were $300 less than the week before and the kids' tickets were a discounted 40 percent off of that. That saved us $2,000. My Irish cousin found us a B&B to stay in and loaned us his car for the time we were there. We traveled light. Each of the kids carried their clothes in a backpack and Arden and I each had a carry-on bag.

The relations in Donegal were so kind, especially to Nicky. No one asked us the usual probing questions, they just gently accepted him. It was such a relief to not have to explain or make excuses. He was still incontinent at night, and wore big diapers. One night the diapers weren't effective, and in the morning, we discovered urine all over the bed. The owner of the B&B was so sweet. I was very embarrassed, but she said it was no bother to clean everything up. It *had* to have been a bother, because although she had an electric clothes washer, she had to dry the washing on the line outside in the damp, cold July weather.

The trip flew by. Each day was an adventure, meeting new people and seeing the local sites. Leaving Carndonagh for the second time was still full of heartache for me, but the pain was not as severe as the year before. Arden had fallen in love with Ireland also and we knew that we would make it a priority to return.

Back from Ireland, we made copies of Dr. Marlowe's report and gave it to the various professionals working with Nicky. We wanted them to understand what he needed to have greater success at learning, and not only at school. We also set the date for the district hearing at the end of August and began preparing for it. We consulted with our attorney to make sure that we had followed all the administrative procedures and protocols. We wanted the hearing to be a success, and for Dr. Marlowe's suggestions to be fully implemented.

The hearing was held in Nicky's classroom. It looked like a typical IEP meeting, although the atmosphere was tense. All the same professionals that usually attend his IEP meetings were there. The one exception was the presence of the district's superintendent of Special Education. This meeting was consequential to both the district and us.

Arden began by asking everyone to spell their names and job title. This attention to detail let each person know that Arden was recording what they specifically said in great detail. Not only does this assure us we have the correct information in our notes, it seems to put the meeting on more of a level playing field. They know that we will hold them accountable for what they say during the meeting.

Next, the district psychologist reviewed all of the reports and documentation that had been submitted prior to the hearing. We had copies of all of the documents, so as he was discussing each one, Arden and I were looking at them too. That took a long time.

Finally, he was finished with all the papers of which we had copies. He took out another two-page report from the folder. I started to say something, but Arden placed his hand gently on my knee, as if to say, "Just wait, let's see what this is about."

The psychologist began to read. "Deliberations regarding the most accurate and appropriate handicap designation for Nicholas have continued since completion of his Summary Analysis report of June 1985. Additional current data in the form of a neuropsychological evaluation by Dr. Wendy Marlowe, dated February 1986 and provided by the parents and subsequent progress reported in the IEP prepared April and May 1986 support the following conclusions."

Here it is, I squeezed Arden's hand. I held my breath.

"The designation of Multi-Handicapped based on (1) Health Impaired, neurological impairment documented by Dr. Stephen Glass and (2) Mild Mental Retardation."

My hand flew to my mouth and I began to cry. The psychologist continued to read the testing instruments and scores that supported the designation, but I didn't hear him.

We did it, we did it. We persevered and truth has prevailed. This legal document will now have a correct diagnosis and placement for Nicky.

We received a signed copy of that report and two additional addendums stipulating the district's acceptance of Dr. Marlowe's report, including her proposed IEP goals and accommodations. It was everything we wanted. We believe that the many factors that influenced their acceptance of our proposal included Dr. Marlowe's professional reputation, the depth and breadth of her evaluation, Dr. Glass's corroborating report, the legal guidance we received as well the progress that Nicky had made when he was in the actual, correct pre-academic program that year.

Nicky's seizures are always unexpected and dramatic. In the fall of 1986, we were attending church one Sunday morning, when we were told that Nicky had a seizure during the children's meeting. Arden grabbed his brother Darren and they headed to the primary room to give Nicky a priesthood blessing.

Later, Darren reported to me, "When we got into the room, everything in it had been moved back along the walls. I mean every-thing, the chairs, tables, podium, and all the children and adults. Well, except for one sister sitting in the middle of the room, on the floor with Nicky. His body was still, breathless, his eyes sightless. It was a stark picture. I stood frozen in place until Arden grabbed me by the lapels and said, 'Come on, we're going to give him a blessing!'"

"We knelt next to his lifeless body. Encouraging me to begin, Arden handed me his vial of consecrated oil. I placed my hands on Nicky's head."

"Brother Nicholas James Gremmert, by the Power of the Holy Priesthood, I anoint your head with this consecrated oil, in the name of Jesus Christ, Amen."

"Removing my hands from Nicky's head, our eyes met. Arden placed both his hands on Nicky's head, and I placed mine on top. I could barely see his face. His skin was the gray blue color of death. I closed my eyes."

"Solemnly, Arden began, 'Brother Nicholas James Gremmert, by the power of the Holy Priesthood, I command you to live, in the name of Jesus Christ, Amen.'"

Tearfully Darren continued, "Everything was in slow motion, his mouth was open but his tongue was at the back of his mouth. Then the end of Nicky's tongue appeared and popped out of his mouth. He took in a huge ragged inhale, the biggest I had ever heard. Immediately, his color changed and he pinked up. He opened his eyes and looked up at me. Our Nicky was back."

It was the first time Darren had assisted with a blessing. It was supremely awe-inspiring. We know that God is all powerful and that He had decided to honor Arden's request and return Nicky to us. Our hearts are full of gratitude for this very personal miracle manifested in our lives.

Nicky had to be transported by ambulance to COH. We kept the blanket that the ambulance crew had given to him for years. Nicky called it his special blanket.

Chapter Thirty-One

Since Ryan's baptism on his eighth birthday in 1986, Nicky seemed enthralled with baptisms. We attended the baptisms of the children we knew, and each time Nicky would say, "I get baptized when I eight."

We would smile and tell him that we would see. In our LDS faith, we believe that children such as Nicky are pure. Since baptism is an ordinance of repentance from sin, according to our doctrine, Nicky didn't need to be baptized. But he still had a huge desire for it. We counseled with our Bishop. He spoke with other church leaders and they all prayed about the question. Soon we learned that Nicky could be baptized.

Our bishop said, "Since we believe that the desire to be baptized is the first requirement for someone to receive the ordinance, we feel it is correct to give authorization for the ordinance of baptism for Nicholas to be performed."

August 19, 1987, on his eighth birthday, we gathered at the church building in the room adjacent to the baptismal font. The service followed the same format as all of the others we had attended. We sang songs, had prayers, heard a talk on baptism and a talk on the Holy Ghost, but this baptismal service was different. For Nicky, it was an unexpected blessing, a cherished ordinance.

On that warm Wednesday evening, Nicholas James Gremmert was baptized a member of the LDS church by his father. He was absolutely radiant as he emerged from the waters of baptism. Immediately, his eyes met mine, and he exclaimed, "I baptized now."

Receiving this ordinance was Nicky's heart's desire. With his limited language, he had communicated his decision to be baptized to all of us. Once the ordinance was complete, Nicky knew that he had accomplished his goal.

That next Sunday, he stood when the bishop acknowledged that he had been baptized. When he sat down, he turned to me and said, "My name is Nick." My baby was expressing self-determination. We started calling him Nick.

Eleven years later, when he was nineteen, Nick was ordained an Elder in the LDS church by his dad. Then Nick went to the temple to receive his endowment. By definition, an endowment is a gift. Adult members of our church are invited to attend the temple and take a course of doctrinal education, receive ordinances, and make covenants with God. It was another milestone in his religious life.

Nick had expressed a strong desire to go to the temple and although it is unusual for mentally disabled individuals to attend, our church leaders felt a confirmation from the Lord that it was something that Nick should do. Again, we were amazed at Nick's abilities to understand things that we could easily assume were beyond his testable intellectual capacity.

In 1988, through the Advocates for Retarded Citizens (the ARC), we learned about a program at the University of Washington called SibShop. Don Meyer had started the program five years before, as an opportunity for siblings of disabled children to connect with one another. Arden and I had heard Don speak and felt that Ryan and Karen might someday benefit from participating in the program. Ryan was almost ten and Karen had just turned seven. I was concerned about the burden that they carried. A large majority of our family's time and money was allocated to caring for Nick and I hoped that they didn't resent it. I also noticed that sometimes they acted embarrassed when Nick became the center of attention in public, either because of the loud noises he made, or the fact others couldn't understand him when he talked, etc.

For example, one Saturday morning, Arden and his brother Darren took Ryan and Nick shopping at Costco. Nick had a long grand mal seizure in the store. A large crowd gathered. It was a huge spectacle. When it was over, Arden and Darren placed him on a flatbed cart to roll him out to the car. A Costco employee had grabbed some decorative pillows and put them under Nick so he would be more comfortable on the flat metal cart. A few weeks later, when Arden took Ryan and Nick to Safeway to get some groceries, Nick had a seizure again.

That spring, we drove Ryan and Karen to an introductory weekend workshop at the university. The SibShop program is typically for older kids, but this workshop is designed to create opportunities for family discussion and Don said they could attend. Ryan didn't say much on the drive home, but Karen talked endlessly about how much fun she had.

The panel discussion that the kids attended introduced topics that we discussed with them over the summer. Attending SibShop opened the communication door with our other children. I learned to ask leading questions such as, "What do you find embarrassing about Nick having seizures in public?" and "Why is it frustrating when others can't understand what Nick is saying?" Being siblings of Nick, from early childhood, my kids faced more situations that required flexibility and problem-solving skills. They received character-building lessons through our tough family experiences. These hard-won characteristics have served them well in their own lives.

Currently, there are over 475 Sibshops in eight countries. Later, Don started SibTeen, Sib20, and SibNet, online communities which allow thousands of siblings of disabled children the opportunity to connect with their peers. Don was also a founder of the SEFAM (Supporting Extended Family Members) program at the University of Washington, which pioneered services for fathers, siblings, and grandparents of children with special needs. We were very blessed to live in the Seattle area, where our family could benefit from these phenomenal programs.

In October, after almost eight years, the tenants in our Tacoma house were finally able to get a mortgage. We were excited for them and it felt good to finally not have the responsibility for that home anymore. We had purchased that home with specific dreams and life plans. While living there, our life path took a huge detour. Being free from that home felt like those old dreams were completely laid to rest. Within our youthful vision of four children, a white picket fence, and flowers gaily swaying in the breeze, we hadn't included some of the realities of life. Not every checkbook balances, not every loaf of bread rises, not every child is born perfect.

We were now able to fully walk the path of our present-day life.

By 1990, Ryan was twelve and attending middle school. Karen and Derek were at the local elementary school and Nick was still at Riverton Heights Elementary, on the other side of the district. I was trying to be active in the Parent-Teacher Student Association (PTSA) in three different schools. I was spread too thin. I couldn't completely track what was happening in any of the schools.

It was time to move Nick to a middle school program. The district recommended that he stay in the self-contained program in the middle school close to his current school. Arden and I wanted him to attend our local middle school. I believed that it would serve our family to have Nick in the same school as his siblings.

During basketball season, when we attended games at our local school, we noticed that the other players and parents didn't know who Nick was and would often stare at him. We were constantly answering the question, "And who is this?" when we were in the bleachers watching the game. No one seemed to remember that Ryan had three siblings, not two.

One afternoon, I took the other kids and traveled across town to watch Ryan's game. It was at the middle school associated with the elementary school that Nick attended. I walked into the gym with my entourage looking for a place to sit. A couple of the parents and kids from the other team said hello and invited us to sit with them. They knew Nick and me, but not my other kids.

"I am here to watch Nick's older brother play. He is on the visiting team over there. I should go and sit with those parents. Thanks for the invite. It was great seeing you."

We walked over to sit with "our" team fans. Even though the parents looked at us approaching, no one said anything welcoming.

During the game, Nick kept making loud noises and yelling Ryan's name. One of Ryan's teammates, said, "Hey, Gremmert, isn't that retard yelling your name?"

Ryan didn't respond. I glared at my son and he turned away from me. I decided that we would talk about it on our way home from the game.

Once we were in the car, I was silent for a while. Ryan was looking away from me, out the window.

I don't know what to say to my son. I am so upset that he didn't defend his brother. I raised him to be better than that. I wonder why he didn't say anything?

"Ryan, why didn't you say anything when that boy called Nick a retard? He is your little brother. You need to protect him."

He looked at me, emotions flooding his face, "I know, Mom. I didn't know what to say. They make fun of me when Nick is moaning and spinning his string. I know Nick does those things. He can't help it, but I don't know what to say."

"Why don't you just tell them that he is your brother? You don't have to say anything else, no other explanation is needed."

The whole thing was deeply awkward for Ryan. That made me so sad.

There was a gap growing in our family, and I didn't like it. We wanted Nick to be a part of our whole community, not someone separate who was only with us when we were at the other kids' ball games. We didn't know if having him at the same school as his siblings would solve the problem, but we believed it would help. The district was required to have Nick in a program that was the least restrictive environment for him and we believed that social integration was as fundamental as educational integration. Finally, the district agreed with our request and Nick was enrolled in our home school, Sylvester Middle School.

Since Ryan already attended Sylvester, we knew many of the teachers and support staff.

During the year that Nick and Ryan both attended Sylvester, Nick's entire program was in the self-contained classroom for disabled students. Although they were at the same school, there wasn't much chance for interaction between the brothers, but they did see one another at lunch and during assemblies. It wasn't the inclusion program that we hoped for, but it was a start.

In February, Nick brought home an application to attend the Special Olympics track and field events. A local team was organized at a nearby middle school. They met twice a week for training and competed in the Track and Field regional events. A couple of the other children in Nick's class were going, and he wanted to join them. Arden and I had supported the other kids when they had the desire to do sports. Since Nick was expressing that desire too, we needed to make it happen.

Nick competed in two events. One was the one-hundred-meter walk and the other was the softball throw. He was so excited to go to his practices. The coaches were very supportive and positively praised even the smallest improvement. He didn't always exactly follow the rules of each event while at practice. He often tried to run part of the "walk" race and he would tease the coaches by throwing the softball at them instead of at the target. Even though he wasn't doing it exactly correct, he had a fabulous time and really looked forward to the practices.

During his races on the meet day, he was very intent on what he was doing and followed the coaches' directions with exactness. He hit the target with the softball and didn't run at all during the walk race. After completing the race each competitor was given a hug by the official huggers waiting at the finish line. He loved that part.

Sitting in the stands at the track, I reflected about all our experiences since Nick's birth.

These twelve years have been nothing like I thought they would be. It was so hectic during those first few years. Now that seems a bit like a bad dream. Caring for him has really become pretty routine. As long as we remember to cut up his food small enough, he doesn't choke. As long as we remember to take him to the toilet routinely, he doesn't have accidents during the day. We still have soiled bedding a few mornings a week, but with a pair of plastic gloves and Lysol spray even that has become a minor inconvenience. Life is pretty good.

I watched his medal ceremonies with tears of pride running down my face. It was a great day for both of us. Nick's medals still hang on our wall.

PART SEVEN

The Dance Steps Are More Complex

Chapter Thirty-Two

After two weeks away from home, Arden and I were still worried about how Nick was dealing with our epic road trip of 2016. That morning in Albuquerque, we prayed about what we should do. We all felt like we should continue traveling toward Kentucky, but at a slower pace. While Arden drove toward Amarillo, Texas, Nick sat in the front seat. His job was to control the music selections on the satellite radio. I sat in the back and worked on my manuscript. Every time I finished writing up a section, I read it out loud to Arden and Nick. Sometimes in the middle of my recitation, Nick would interrupt me to add or correct something in my narrative.

When we were almost to Amarillo, we decided to drive a bit farther. Since it was Saturday night, we searched for a town with a LDS chapel using the LDS app, and found one in Childress, Texas. Again that night, I worked on taxes and some genealogy while they slept.

It was a beautiful Sabbath morning. Nick woke up a little early so we not only had time to get cleaned up; we also got some of the stuff packed before we went to church. It was a small congregation that reminded us of the Foyle Ward in Derry City, Ireland. We were told that they were a little hopeful that we would move there. Even though we had never met any of them before, we did not feel like we were among strangers. We felt right at home. After a few days on our own, we were excited to be on our way to see family in Dallas, Texas.

Chapter Thirty-Three

Arden and I took one of many trips to Ireland in May 1992 without our kids. Our close friends the Hunts came with us. They were moving from Seattle to Utah for work in the summer.

After we developed our photographs, we drove out to their place to trade pictures. Allen and Leonie, along with their children, had hand-built a breathtaking rustic log cabin in the foothills of the Cascade Mountains. After traveling east from Carnation on a narrow two-lane road for about four miles, their home came into view. Surrounded by tall trees, it was so welcoming we couldn't wait to go inside. The horses in the front pasture completed the rural picture.

Leonie prepared a delightful meal, then we visited sitting on the front porch. Arden excused himself; he wanted to walk around the property. The rest of us kept talking while we watched Arden slowly wander through the pastures. After about twenty minutes he came back up on to the porch and said, "I feel like we should buy this property and live here. What do you think Eva?"

When Arden proposed buying the Hunt's home, I was speechless. I hadn't thought about moving to Carnation, but it did feel right.

Rosie and Darren, our siblings who had married each other, had recently sold their home and were trying to decide where they wanted to relocate. The four of us decided to purchase the Hunt's home together. Rosie and Darren had three boys, ages five, four, and almost two. Our kids were fourteen, twelve, eleven, and nine. Our kids didn't want to leave their friends in Burien, but both Arden and I believed that it was the right decision for many reasons. We moved to Carnation the first week of August. We especially hoped that Nick would become part of the community, so that when he was an adult, he would have developed relationships that could continue through his life.

One day, without telling anyone his plans, Darren came home from work with a few boards and some sand and built a sandbox. He leveled out the ground just off of the front porch. I don't know how many bags of sand he used, but it was large enough for thirteen-year-old Nick and his smaller cousins to all sit in and play. Nick loved it. He would sit there for hours, "building his pile," as he called it. He took pieces of wood, and by pouring sand on them, he stacked them at odd angles to each other, higher and higher, until the top of pile was above his head. He'd sit there for a few minutes just looking at what he had built. Then he would knock it over, saying, "Uh-oh, it fell!"

Then he'd start all over again. It was an engineering marvel. How he understood that putting the sand between the pieces of wood would make it possible to create a tall tower, I'll never know. It's just another thing about Nick that's remarkable.

I met with the Riverview school district's special education director as soon as I could get an appointment. When she explained that they didn't have a program in the district that would meet Nick's needs I was so discouraged. They hoped to be able to offer him an in-school placement in two years' time, but for the following school year he would need to attend school on an out-of-district school placement. The special education department of the Lake Washington school district had a good reputation, so we agreed Nick would be transported there.

Nick went to Kamiakin Junior High School in Kirkland on a small school bus, forty-five minutes each way. He really looked forward to Charlotte, the bus driver, coming to get him each morning. He was cooperative with the process of getting ready each day, which was a huge relief.

I got a temporary job testing tax software in Bellevue. It was a great opportunity for me. I learned a lot from my co-workers and my boss Cheryl was very easy to work for. The best thing of all was that when I completed the testing season, I was given the software for free. That was a huge financial benefit.

We had all been through big changes over a few months. Moving house, helping all the kids get settled, me starting a new job and both of our families adjusting to sharing one house had all made those fall months hectic for everyone. We had fall sports, homework assignments, church responsibilities, the holidays to prepare for and I knew that tax season was just around the corner. Every day had more tasks on the schedule than could be reasonably completed. I was running faster and faster.

Then, just a few days before Christmas my Dad died. When he had been diagnosed with lymphoma over three years earlier, he'd been told that his life expectancy was "only a few weeks." He'd rallied so many times we thought the end would never come. Standing with my mother, by his bedside after he had passed, was surreal. It was a shock for all of us. Nick kept asking us where Grandpa Doherty went.

We got through Christmas somehow and then I turned my attention to the tax business. Tax season was horrible for me. I had lost my father *and* my business partner. Now I had to make difficult decisions without his gentle counsel. In the past, whenever I got frazzled, he would calmly remind me that I could handle the situation, after all I was a "gentlewoman and a scholar." I told Arden that he would need to take my dad's place and remind me that I was capable.

The practice was too large for one person to manage, so I sold off half of the client list and hired an assistant to help with appointment scheduling and processing the paperwork.

Focusing on all the changes impacting me, I scarcely noticed what was happening with Nick. I was functioning on autopilot, just trying to get through the days. One morning I forgot to send his lunch with him when he was picked up for school. I noticed it lying on the kitchen counter half an hour later when I was getting Karen and Derek organized to go out the door. Nick wouldn't be able to negotiate purchasing a lunch at the cafeteria, so I had to drive it to the school.

I waited for the other kids to leave on their bus and headed to Kirkland. When I got to the school, I realized I hadn't been there since the day we registered Nick the previous fall. I don't know what else I could have done over those difficult months, but I still felt guilty, like I had neglected my duty.

The secretary in the office was very sweet and reminded me where the Special Ed room was. I walked around the outside of the building to the entrance closest to the classroom. I peeked in the windows as I was walking past. Nick was seated in a desk facing another student. He had a pair of dice on his desk, but he wasn't doing anything, just staring straight ahead.

The classroom assistant came to the door. "May I help you?"

"I am Eva Gremmert, Nick's mom, and came to bring his lunch. I forgot to put it in his bag this morning. Is his teacher available?"

"I'm sorry, Mrs. Gremmert, but she is not here in the classroom."

"Do you know when you expect her to be back? The school receptionist thought that she was here."

"I don't know where she is or when she will be back."

"Oh, okay, well here is Nick's lunch bag. What is it that he is doing?"

"Mrs. Gremmert, they are all playing Yahtzee. It's a dice game."

Under her breath, she added, "That's all they do in here, all day long, every day."

I was stunned.

"Surely, they do other things. Each of these children has an IEP, which clearly designates their education program."

"You are right, Mrs. Gremmert, the students all have IEPs, but this teacher isn't following them. I am left alone with the children here in the classroom for long periods of time with the specific instruction to have them play Yahtzee."

She paused and then said, "I probably shouldn't have said anything."

"I won't do anything to get you in trouble. Thank you for being honest with me."

I drove straight to the Riverview School District offices and requested an appointment with the Superintendent of Special

Education. Miraculously, she was available. I poured out my heart to her, cried a bit, and begged her to help me make sure that my son was getting the education that he needed, the one he deserved. She was very sympathetic and assured me that she would make it happen. The school year was almost over and she would make sure that Nick was placed in our local district for the next school year. That relieved my guilt somewhat yet I felt like I had failed Nick. That entire school year had been a waste of time for him. However, this experience was the catalyst for our school district to create an appropriate program for Nick and other multi-handicapped students like him in the district. That terrible experience did become a great blessing.

One spring morning, without any warning, Nick vomited all over the dining room table during breakfast. He'd never done that before and he didn't understand what was happening.

He kept saying, "What happen to me, I frow up?" and then he would vomit again.

Even though he was thirteen years old, he couldn't tell if and when it was going to happen again.

I sat him down and grabbed some towels to pile around him like a protective bunker. I tried to keep him seated in one place. I thought that would contain the mess but he kept walking around to be with me wherever I was. Throughout the day, he randomly vomited without warning, over and over. After a few hours, I took him upstairs and put him in the shower. He relished being in the water, and the clean-up would be easier there. Or so I thought. He seemed to be feeling better, although he kept talking about "frowing up." All was going well, so I began gathering up some laundry from the adjacent bedroom.

"Mom."

"What, Nick?"

I began to move toward the shower.

His hand appeared at the edge of the shower curtain, drawing it back. His head poked out from the shower stall and he stepped one foot out, just far enough so that as he bent over slightly at the waist and vomited again, he missed the bathroom throw rug completely and hit the carpet in the bedroom. I stood there stunned, with the dirty laundry in my arms.

"Mom, I frow up. Again. Mom, you clean me up."

I couldn't move. Over the course of that morning, he had managed to hit every room in the house. I crumpled to the floor.

Nick walked up and stood over me, dripping wet with both water and vomit.

"I sorry, Mommy, I not do it again. You done being frustrated with me, Mommy?"

He knew I was upset and he wanted me to be happy again.

As I got up from the floor, I laughed. "Believe me, Nick, you will probably do it again. Let's get cleaned up."

We never did find out any real reason that he was so sick that day. Experiences like these did increase my fortitude and ability to keep strong in the face of adversity. I learned to be resilient and be flexible in my expectations. I had a voice in the back of my head, encouraging me to keep on going, to move through the hard time. In the face of overwhelming situations, I learned to keep my emotions in check during the experience. Then later I would process and evaluate each situation. Looking back at that day of vomit experience, it is funny now. It didn't feel very funny then, but that is the wonder of perspective.

That summer, my sister Rosie and her three children came with us to Ireland. At the airport, Rosie had her little ones, I had the tickets and passports, and Arden had our kids and our carryon bags. We were all standing together in a big open area near multiple gates. Some flights had been delayed so it was extra crowded that day.

They called for our flight over the loudspeaker and we all lined up. I stood with the gate agent while she counted our group.

"You have nine, correct?"

"Nine others, and I make ten."

She rifled through the tickets and passports. "There are ten tickets here."

"Yes, there are ten, including me."

"I only see nine people, including you."

We looked around at our little group, counting.

"Arden, where's Nick?"

"He's right here."

He turned around and looked.

Nick was nowhere to be seen.

I ran yelling into the middle of the large crowd.

"Has anyone seen a teenage handicapped blond young man with a red shirt? We've lost our son."

I felt like I was in bad movie. The crowd parted four different times in different directions. Each time revealing a blond young adult disabled man wearing a red shirt. I kept screaming Nick's name over and over while also saying, "No, that's not him. That's not him, either."

After a few agonizing minutes, the crowd parted once more. This time it *was* Nick.

"What, Mommy?"

He had wandered away toward the windows in the bar to watch the airplanes take off and land.

My heart gradually slowed its frantic beating as we moved toward the gate. I still can't believe there were four other disabled young men in red shirts right there in the same gate area. Since then, Arden and I always verbally make sure which of us has responsibility for Nick. Even a short lapse in our attention meant that he could get away and become lost. That thought was a huge source of fear for me.

When he was stressed, it was hard to understand his speech. He knew his name was Nick, but he struggled to know his phone number or where we lived. We had a name bracelet with all that information. Since we had lost him a few times for brief periods, I knew that it was a real possibility, and the awful potential consequences gnawed at me.

PART EIGHT

Dancing on Our Own

Chapter Thirty-Four

On our epic road trip of 2016, Nick wanted to visit Dallas, Texas and three women he considered his sisters. Each one had joined our family through Karen when they were teenagers. Shaunda and Christina were friends from high school and Amy was Karen's college roommate.

Arden and I have become parents to over thirty teenagers that were not born to us. Each one needed somewhere safe to live, be nurtured and loved. We loved each one. Some stayed for a week, some for a year. Many are still part of our family.

Nick was so excited.

On the way to our Texas restaurant reunion, Arden asked, "Eva, do you remember when Lisa moved in."

"Yes, she was our first foster kid. Adding her to our family changed our lives."

One evening in the spring of 1984, my sister Rosie told us that Lisa Hickman, a high school friend, needed someplace to stay. My parents already had my foster brother David living at their house and didn't have another bedroom available. Arden and I said that Lisa could stay with us for a while.

There was something about Lisa that tugged at our heartstrings. She had been in foster care since she was seven. Many of the homes that she had been assigned to were less than ideal.

When her case manager came out to meet us and to see that she was in a safe place, he asked if we were interested in becoming foster parents for Lisa. It felt like the right thing to do. I was concerned at first that it would be hard for a teenager to adjust to living with four little kids, ages five, four, two, and ten months. Life was pretty crazy at our house! The first night Lisa stayed with us, we got her settled into the room across from the kids' bedroom. The next morning, she was awakened by Nicky hitting her on the head with a toy. I guess it was his way of saying hello. She was patient with him and didn't get angry. It made me hope that it would work out.

Lisa's case manager warned me that kids who have been in foster care for a long time have a hard time believing that someone will be there for them even when they're misbehaving.

One particularly difficult day after Lisa had been with us about a month, I was trying to talk to her about something that had happened.

Lisa got angry and yelled, "So are you going to kick me out now?"

She began to pack up her things.

I didn't know what to do. I didn't want her to leave. She had been let down by so many others in her life, that tough exterior was covering a heart that was breaking.

I was frustrated though and yelled back at her. "I am not going to kick you out. You can choose to leave if you want to, but I love you and I want you to be here."

That was the moment that she became my daughter. We ended up crying and hugging. I learned a lot about raising teenagers from Lisa and she learned a lot about being in a family from us.

Our reunion lunch in Dallas was remarkable. I sat there loving the big smile on Nick's face while he fully engaged in the conversation. Amy never lived with us, so Shaunda and Christina were trying to explain to her what it was like at our home back in the day.

Christina explained, "Most of Karen's friends knew that any of us could go to Gremmert's if we needed to. It didn't matter what time of day or night, Arden and Eva would make room."

Shaunda agreed, "It was a safe place to be. You could just walk in and lay down on the couch. If you were hungry, there was food in the frig. You could talk to someone, or not, whatever you wanted to do. It was my refuge."

It was gratifying to hear from these girls, now middle-aged mothers, that we had made a difference in their lives all those years ago.

From Dallas we headed to Louisville, Kentucky. It took us four days to get there and we spent nine days with Ryan and his family. When had we learned about the escalating possibility of Nick passing away, and knowing that he wasn't cleared to fly in an airplane, we had organized the epic road trip to introduce Nick to his newest niece, Ryan and Tiffany's ten-month-old daughter, Sadie Ann. We had been away from home twenty days when that finally happened.

Nick loves little children, especially his nieces and nephews. He was very gentle with Sadie. She wasn't too excited to sit on his lap, but we did get a picture of them. We loved being with them, helping with normal, everyday things like preparing food, shopping, homework, and attending ball games. All the things that families do together.

Louisville was the farthest east we had planned to travel and we did have to make it back west again, so after our sojourn in that oasis, we got on the road again.

That first night back in a hotel, Nick asked us if he would be able to sleep in his bed the next night. His face fell as we explained that it would be another two weeks until we were back home. We were planning on traveling in more of a straight line back to Seattle, than the meandering journey we had out to Louisville.

It was reassuring to know that we were on our way home. I have always been more comfortable when we are working on a plan. It reminded me of the feeling I had back in the fall of 1993 when Nick began attending Tolt Middle School.

Chapter Thirty-Five

It was the first time Nick was attending the same school as Karen. One evening that fall, before school started, we held a family meeting. In addition to the usual scheduling items on our agenda, we wanted to talk to the kids about Nick.

Arden began, "We want Nick to have all the opportunities possible so that his quality of life going forward will be extraordinary. We feel a huge responsibility to make things happen for Nick so that he is happy."

I continued, "Happiness is different things to each of us. Frustration is a great source of motivation to make changes. Remember last year, it was obvious to each of us, that Nick was frustrated. That is why Dad and I have pushed the school district to make this new placement happen."

The kids were nodding with understanding.

Arden added, "Some of your friends may not understand what we are doing as a family. It has always been a balancing game with Nick. On one hand, we help him use his own feelings of frustration to gain skills toward greater independence, while helping him find happiness and joy in living his life, whatever that life looks like."

I concluded the discussion by summarizing, "We haven't always gotten it right, but I do believe we have helped Nick find that balance most of the time."

Even though she was younger, Karen always felt protective of Nick. She was particularly watchful at school especially after the deplorable lack of attention he had experienced at the prior school. She checked in on him every day and would come home with stories of how Nick was doing in each class. It seemed that even if Karen wasn't in a particular class with Nick, she knew someone who was, and they reported back to Karen. We had more information on Nick's school day than we'd had for the eleven previous years since he'd started in public school.

This was very reassuring to me.

Nick thoroughly enjoyed his days at Tolt. The middle school had a resource room where he spent part of the day, but since this was a newly developed program for multi-handicapped kids like Nick, he attended regular classes accompanied by an educational assistant for art, PE, and music. He had friends he sat with during lunch.

Tolt was such a small school that we already knew many of the teachers there through Ryan or Karen. We had approached them to see if they would be willing to try having Nick and his aide in their classrooms. Although inclusion was a big buzzword in special education nationwide, this level of inclusion was a new concept for the district.

Arden and I wanted to have a cooperative relationship with school district personnel. Thankfully most were open to it too. We worked to have Nick included in as many experiences of middle school as possible. We were very creative and most of the teachers were agreeable. It seemed that they caught the vision of possibilities from us. It was an experiment; a successful one.

Through the ARC, we learned about Epilepsy Camp at Easter Seals Camp in Vaughn, Washington on the Olympic Peninsula. Nick was excited to go. I had mixed feelings.

During the ninety-minute drive to the camp, Nick was in the back seat with his spinner string. "I go to camp, I sleep there. I go to camp, I sleep there..."

Trying to interrupt his perseveration, and calm my own anxieties, I said, "Nick, you have your sleeping bag and suitcase of clothes. We will come back on Friday to pick you up. You will have special new friends and do fun stuff."

"What I do there?"

"You will get to swim."

"They have a pool?"

"Yes, they have a pool, and you will do arts and crafts. You love arts and crafts, right?"

"Yes, I eat there?"

"Of course, you will eat there. Now remember, you have to be dry at night for you to stay at camp."

"Okay, Mom. I go to camp, I sleep there. I go to camp, I sleep there…" and he was back into his circular speech.

That is my main concern. Will they send him home if he wets the bed? It is epilepsy camp. Surely, they understand that incontinence is part of seizures. I guess we will find out. It is a growth opportunity for Nick. It is the first time he will be away from home. I am excited for him and I am excited for us. We will have a few days with the other kids without Nick being the central focus. Maybe I shouldn't feel so excited about him being gone. I will miss him.

We arrived at the camp. I sat for a few minutes watching all the commotion. Arden was unloading Nick's gear and I got out to hold on to Nick. A college aged young man approached him with his hand outstretched.

"Hi Nick, I am Jamie. Do you want me to show you around?"

Nick looked at me a little unsure. I nodded encouragingly.

"Okay."

Leading my son away, Jamie said over his shoulder, "Mom and Dad, please bring Nick's things and follow us. Nick, over here is the dining room and that building on the left is where you will sleep. Let's put your things on your bed, okay?"

Nick didn't respond, but he was calmly following along. I was comforted that he wasn't anxious. We put his sleeping bag and pillow on his bed and unpacked his clothes.

"We done, let's go look."

Over the next fifteen minutes we finished the tour and it was time for Arden and I to go.

As we drove away, I had tears in my eyes, "Arden of all the hard things we have done over the years, leaving him here is the hardest for me."

"I thought that you've looked forward to having a week-long break."

"I do want a break. I need a break, and I am excited to go and do summer things with the other kids. It is just weird to have someone else responsible for him. I am sure that he will be okay and they will take good care of him. I just feel sad. And I feel happy at the same time about the chance to put the other kids first for a change."

Arden shook his head and smiled.

"I know, it's complicated."

"Well, for me, I am happy that Nick is going to have a chance to be at camp and experience time away from us and make new friends. I am also happy that our other kids will have a few days of typical summertime activities without worrying about how it will affect Nick's health. It is a good thing as far as I am concerned."

Nick loved being at Camp Easter Seals and I kept myself from worrying for the week by reminding myself that the staff was very caring and very well trained.

Chapter Thirty-Six

Sometimes we underestimate Nick's awareness of life going on around him. One day in the summer of 1995, about a month before his sixteenth birthday, he said, "I be sixteen soon."

"Yes, you'll be sixteen."

I wasn't really paying attention to our conversation and was a little surprised when he followed up with, "Not I drive."

"That's right, you aren't going to drive."

It really stunned me when he added, "Not you get me a car, you get me a hot tub."

Arden laughed when I told him about Nick's request. To Nick it was logical; we had purchased a Jeep CJ7 the previous summer so that Ryan could help with transportation. Since Nick didn't need a car, he wanted a hot tub. We started shopping around and bought a hot tub, a benefit to our whole family.

That fall, Nick and Karen both moved up to the high school. Initially, Arden and I were concerned that Nick wouldn't have the same success that he'd had in middle school. We were wrong. Even though he was the only multi-handicapped student in the school, Cedarcrest High developed a great program for him. He participated in the regular education program. He attended art class and was in the choir, including performances. The PE teacher told us that Nick adored being the exercise leader for the calisthenics—the kids in the class kept asking him to reduce the number of repetitions and he would laugh and then call out for more. He collected the attendance in the mornings from each homeroom and took the papers to the office. He also had the job of cleaning up after lunch with the custodian.

Nick learned to recycle in high school, something he still likes to do. His homeroom teacher said that the UNO card games that the boys played each morning were such serious competitions that it looked like a casino without the smoke. Nick often won.

One Saturday, while sitting in the hot tub relaxing, Nick started singing. At first, we couldn't make it out, but then I recognized that he was singing, *Kyrie Eleison*, which is a Latin transliteration for the Greek phrase meaning, "Lord, have mercy." I recognized it from having attended the Catholic Mass in Latin when I was a young girl. We were shocked and amazed to discover that Nick had learned the song in choir. We came to admire the music instructor at Cedarcrest not only for his treatment of Nick, but also for the magnificent music program, both choir and band, he created for the kids in our community.

For the most part, the other students at the high school treated Nick with great respect and kindness. There were a few who were unkind to him. Whenever his siblings witnessed someone being mean to Nick, they would intervene and we would get a call from the vice-principal.

"Mrs. Gremmert, I have to tell you about an altercation that happened today in school," he would begin. "It seems that another student was making fun of Nick and your son/daughter (depending on the situation) publicly chastised the other student and handled the situation. We hope that your son/daughter could be a little less vocal or explosive in these situations, but we do understand their response and are not giving them any punishment for today."

I would always tell the school administrator that I would not reprimand my kids for defending their brother, and in fact, I expected that they would always look out for him and make sure that he was not abused or mistreated. I would then ask the vice-principal if the perpetrator of the abuse was being punished. I believed that it was the school's responsibility to ensure Nick's safety both physically and emotionally and that they should do their duty to our disabled son. Usually the student who had mistreated Nick did not suffer any consequences, and I never did think that was correct. In spite of the fact that the teachers, staff and administrators told us that Nick was safe at the school, each of his siblings had multiple instances where they felt the need to defend their brother in all sorts of situations.

We had been working to help Nick learn to read for many years. One afternoon in early November, when he was seventeen, Nick and I were grocery shopping. As I put a gallon of milk into the grocery cart, Nick said, "I want eggnog."

He loves that holiday drink. I told him that the holidays were still a few weeks away and we would get some when it came in, but right now there was no eggnog.

"I want eggnog."

"Nick, they don't have eggnog."

"They do have eggnog, see, right there."

I turned and sure enough, there was a quart of eggnog amidst the whipping cream. Later when I told Arden the story, we wondered if Nick had read the words. I knew that he could recognize logos and store brands, such as McDonald's and Pizza Hut, but I hadn't seen any indication of him reading words out of context. Arden told me that the packaging had changed from the previous year, so he thought that perhaps Nick had read the word eggnog on the packaging. He pointed out to me that during the previous holiday season, the eggnog was in a different location in the refrigerator case, than where Nick had seen it that day. But I still wasn't convinced Nick actually had read the words.

The next day, we had lunch with my mom in Burien, at our long-time favorite Chinese restaurant. When Nick and I arrived, Mom was chatting with the owner. I joined the conversation after I got Nick settled.

"Mom, I look at menu."

I handed him one.

"What you have, Mom?"

"I always have the number 2 special."

"I want pizza."

I sighed, "Nick, we are at a Chinese restaurant. They don't have pizza. You should order the sweet and sour chicken like you always do."

He furrowed his brow and said, "I want pizza."

"They don't have pizza in Chinese restaurants."

"They do have pizza, see…right here. I show you."

He opened the menu and pointed. Sure enough, they had pizza in that Chinese restaurant.

"How did you know that they have pizza?"

"I read it."

My mom asked, "Did he really read it? Can he read?"

"I guess so. I guess that he can read."

I just sat there and watched my son, beaming with accomplishment.

He kept repeating, "I read it, right Mom, I read it."

"Yes, you certainly did read it."

It was a miracle. I remembered the fights we had with various teachers along the way, each of them believing that we were unrealistic to insist that they teach him pre-reading and pre-academic skills. I was so grateful that we persevered and gave him the opportunity to learn to read. It is a phenomenal skill and he is so proud of himself.

He has not decided to read for pleasure yet, but he certainly can read.

Ryan graduated from high school in June of 1996. Nick kept saying that he would graduate next year. We explained repeatedly that he got to attend high school until he was twenty-one and was going to graduate after Karen.

He insisted, "I graduate after Ryan, not Karen."

We would explain again and again. This conversation went round and round for weeks.

Finally, Nick stopped talking about it.

Nick attended Easter Seals epilepsy camp for a second summer. He was very excited, especially since he knew what to expect. Arden and I were also excited because we had confidence in the program and it meant that we were going to have a weeklong break too.

We were very surprised on Thursday morning when we received a phone call from the camp director asking us to come and pick Nick up. He'd had a seizure and was recovering but they didn't feel that they could keep him at camp.

Arden and I were quiet most of the ninety-minute drive to the camp.

"Remember last year, how worried I was and nothing happened. Now this year, I was doing great and he had a seizure. I hope that he is okay. I am glad that we will be there soon, but I was really savoring the time off this week."

"Eva, I am concerned about Nick too. He still requires one-on-one monitoring like a small child, and it's disappointing to me that our break was cut short, even by one day. We never know what's going to happen with him; that's part of the stress. I just wish that he didn't have seizures. All of the other stuff we do would be so easy to manage without that."

"I know, I often think the same thing, especially when he's seizing."

"It's like the sword of Damocles is hanging over us, the ever-present symbol of impending doom."

One afternoon, the kids and I were in the grocery store buying milk. (With four adolescents in the house it seemed that I was always buying milk.) We were standing in the checkout line when Derek, aged fourteen, yelled, "Oh shit."

I whirled around to reprimand my youngest son for his language, only to see the two gallons of milk that had been in Derek's hands flying through the air as he gently eased his seizing older brother to the ground. The seizure was a full-blown tonic-clonic, with no forewarning. A crowd gathered as people stopped to watch. As Nick was convulsing, I noticed a puddle of urine growing on the floor near his hips. I was mortified. I had two thoughts, almost simultaneously: *How am I going to clean this mess up?* and *I hope no one recognizes us.*

Just then, I heard a gentle voice. "Mrs. Gremmert…Mrs. Gremmert, can I help you?"

Slowly I looked up. There stood Troy Kerr, a friend of Ryan's from middle school. I was embarrassed that he'd recognized me. Then I remembered that Troy had an older brother with disabilities who had gone to school with Nick. Troy understood our predicament. He worked there and assured me he would clean up the mess while I took care of Nick. It was such a tender mercy that someone who knew us and also had personal experiences like ours was working at the grocery store at exactly the time we needed help.

Chapter Thirty-Seven

Before Nick turned eighteen, we had to apply to be his legal guardians. Arden and I talked about it while we gathered together the paperwork for the application.

"I can't believe it. If we aren't appointed his legal guardians by the courts, we'll have no legal authority over his care, medical treatment, where he lives, or his activities once he's of age. They could take him away from us."

"Eva, according to our state law, he could become someone else's responsibility unless the courts determine that it's in Nick's best interest to remain in our care. If the courts decide that someone else should be his guardians, we'll have no say in what happens to him. I don't believe that'll happen, though."

"I don't like the fact that someone else can decide that we fall short of their expectations and take Nick away from us. I understand that there have been other disabled adults who have been manipulated, neglected and even abused by family members. I also know that it's the court's responsibility to alleviate that injustice, but I have fought so long and hard for Nick, this is hard for me."

A Guardian ad litem was appointed by the court to investigate us and the environment that Nick lived in. They interviewed Arden and me, Nick's doctors, teachers, therapists, a few long-time friends, neighbors and our bishop from church. It was very thorough and felt invasive.

We still have to reapply for guardianship every three years, but we only have to supply a financial report and we are not reinvestigated.

In September, just before Ryan left for his two-year church mission to El Salvador, Ryan, Karen, Nicky and I went to Pizza Hut. We were standing just inside the door, waiting to be seated, when Nick hit the floor, seizing. I told Ryan to give him a blessing and we waited for it to be over. When the seizure was finished, I told the waitress that we wouldn't be staying. Between the three of us, we half-carried, half-dragged Nick out to the Jeep. We had taken the convertible top and the side doors off because it was such a gorgeous day. He is very floppy and barely conscious after a seizure, so we put him in the front passenger seat. I sat behind him, stabilizing him the whole way home to make sure that he didn't fall out.

The next week, our bishop asked Nick if he would give a talk at Ryan's mission farewell at church. It is common for family members to speak when someone is leaving to serve a mission.

"You help me, Mom?"

"Tell me what you want to say and I will type it."

I typed the words for Nick as he dictated them to me. He knew exactly what he wanted to say. During the meeting, he got up and read his three-page talk to the congregation. I stood up with him at the podium in case he needed any help. He didn't need any, which was good. I wouldn't have been any help at all. From the first word of his talk, tears blinded my eyes. I couldn't even see the words on the page. I was so proud of him. He had worked so hard against immeasurable odds. There he stood, reading his talk at his brother's farewell, in front of all those people who loved him.

Nick is really social. He loves engaging with others. At times, he reaches out to others and pulls them toward him to hug and kiss them. He is very strong. It's not appropriate and even in the best cases when he does this with friends, it can be awkward. We began reminding him that he had to ask someone if he could hug them. We told him to reach out his hand to shake hands. Sometimes, when the person didn't want to shake hands, we would explain that he had to accept that they didn't want to. He would often take advantage of the proximity with shaking hands and reach his other hand around the person's neck to draw them into a hug.

We were always watchful to interrupt this behavior. Sometimes our verbal correction was quick and stern. Often people tried to be empathetic and understanding when he grabbed them.

They would say to us, "That's all right, it's okay."

We would explain that we knew they were trying to be understanding; however, it wasn't okay for Nick to touch others without their permission.

Nick had a difficult time understanding that appropriate behavior could be different for different scenarios. We tried to help him avoid these awkward situations by creating certain behavior rules for certain environments. For instance, it was okay to shake hands when greeting people at church, restaurants and at school. We could hug and give kisses when we were at home. We discovered that this rule was not only difficult for Nick to follow; it was hard for the rest of us too. He was so happy and engaging that as others got to know him, they wanted to hug him as much as he wanted to hug them. Our efforts were not effective.

Even the teachers at school who had brought this social situation to our attention needed to be reminded not to be overly physically affectionate with Nick.

Many times when we tried to correct Nick's behavior in public the other individual would say, "But I really do want a hug from Nick."

"See, Mom, it's okay," Nick would tell me.

The problem was that he believed that it was acceptable in all situations and was not able to discern when it wasn't okay. I don't think Nick will ever understand why someone wouldn't want to have a hug.

For the most part, by the time he was eighteen, Nick's grand mal seizures were fairly well controlled. We did see some physical symptoms that could have been seizures but since they didn't happen when he had his EEG test, they were not confirmed seizures. Sometimes for a brief time his speech was garbled. He would almost stutter for several seconds, and then it would dramatically stop, only to repeat in a few minutes. Again this appeared to be seizures, but was not present when he was being tested.

For many years, we took the kids down to San Francisco in March for a St. Patrick's Day party at our cousins' in Vallejo. In 1998, on the trip back home, Nick began having partial seizures in the airport. I took him onboard when they called for preboarding. Just as I got him into his seat on the plane, the grand mal seizure began. The flight attendants came right over and were really concerned.

"Is there anything we can do?"

"No, he has epilepsy, this is normal for him. The seizure will last a couple of minutes and he will be okay. After the seizure finished, he will sleep the rest of the flight. It would help if you get my husband, Arden. He is in the boarding area with my other two kids. He has the medicine I need to give to my son."

I wanted to get his rescue medicines in him as soon as I could. Arden and the kids were on the jet way waiting to board the plane, when he heard the crew calling for "Martin." He somehow realized he was the one that they were paging, since he was always concerned about seizures when I was alone with Nick. By the time he got on the plane and down to our row, the seizure was finished. Arden gave him a blessing, as was our practice, and we followed the rescue medicine protocol prescribed by Nick's neurologist. Everyone around us on the plane was helpful and concerned for our family as well as Nick. This tender outreach from strangers is something we've gratefully experienced throughout Nick's life.

Nick's seizure patterns were changing. Sometimes he had problems with motor planning. He might be picking something up or using his hands in a specific way when he suddenly appeared to lose that function. His arm and hand would shake for a few seconds, after which he was able to resume his previous activity. Since he was taking three different seizure medicines already, Dr. Glass didn't make any changes to his anticonvulsant medications. There was not conclusive evidence that the odd random events were seizures, so Dr. Glass suggested a wait-and-watch approach. He asked us to keep notes to better document the extent and character of the spells and consider further workup should they persist.

In the summer of 1998, we went to Ireland for another visit. While there I decided that I wanted to learn the Irish National anthem "Amhrán na bhFiann." It was originally composed in English as "A Soldier's Song." I had learned it in English, but felt it was more correct to sing in Irish, so I asked a cousin to write the song down phonetically so I could memorize it. During that trip I practiced singing it over and over in the car.

About a week after we got home, we were in the car and Nick said, "Let's sing."

This was not unusual as he knows hundreds of Irish songs, patriotic songs, popular songs, rock and roll classic songs, country songs, and hymns.

"Go ahead."

From the back seat I heard, "Oh, say can you see, by the dawns early light..."

Our national anthem. He knows all four verses. When he finished them, without skipping a beat he launched into "Sinne Fianna Fáil"...

He stopped after the first line and with a huge grin on his face asked, "You sing with me, Mom?"

He was singing the Irish national anthem in Irish. And if that wasn't unbelievable enough, he also recognized that it was similar in meaning to our US national anthem. I was so amazed I started crying. I couldn't sing.

He started over again, "Sinne Fianna Fáil"..., as if to say, *Come on Mom, get it together, let's sing.*

And sing we did.

Chapter Thirty-Eight

After Nick turned eighteen, we began to see a pattern emerging among the professionals working with him. Each person seemed compelled to discuss putting Nick into a group home to live. They all said the same thing: We needed a plan as we aged so that Nick would be prepared for the time when we were no long able to care for him ourselves.

We tried to be polite in our answer, but we reminded each one that since we were just a couple years past forty, we believed we had at least a few years before we needed to worry about that. In addition, Nick's siblings felt a strong sense of responsibility for their brother. Arden and I have never worried about who would care for Nick if we were unable to.

Some of them persisted nonetheless. We told them that since we had at least twenty-five years until retirement, we would consider the question later. I know that they were speaking out of concern for Nick; it just seemed to be invasive to us.

Once Nick turned nineteen, we began having annual assessments from the Department of Social and Health Services (DSHS). Even though Nick needed twenty-four hour care as the report stated, at that time parents were only allowed to bill DSHS for ninety-six hours per month for caregiving time. We received what were essentially minimal payments monthly.

In February 1999, the school district administration realized that they needed to move Nick to the class of 2000 because he was going to be at the high school for another year. We wanted him in school until he was twenty-one to give him the extra year of formalized education and support.

The administration also noticed that Nick was listed in the computer reports as the valedictorian of the class because all of his teachers had given him A's on his report cards. They explained that Nick couldn't be listed as number 1 in the class as it would potentially impact other students receiving scholarships and/or college acceptance. To fix the problem, they were changing how Nick received grades.

When the spring report cards came out, all of the teachers had given Nick a Pass in the grade column. Nick was upset when he saw that.

He kept saying, "Why I no get an A? Why I no get an A?"

He couldn't understand why they had changed his grading system.

The kids at school learned about this and asked that the school administration keep Nick in his place, but they were told it wasn't possible. Nick had been part of the graduating class of 1999 since beginning at Tolt Middle school. Many of the students were disappointed that he wasn't going to go through graduation with them. We kept explaining that he was entitled to be in the school program until he turned twenty-one, so he was eligible for one more year.

When we first moved out to Carnation, back in 1992, Nick was thirteen and he fell in love. That is pretty normal for a teenage boy. To Nick, Emilee Jo Soptich was the most beautiful girl he had met. When he saw her at church each week, he would run over to her, grab her hand and kiss it. You might be thinking, "Such a gentleman!" However, Emilee didn't seem to mind that many times the kiss was very wet. Nick thought it was funny to see how long the string of drool could go from his mouth to the back of her hand. She would laugh at him and say, "Oh, Nick!" as she wiped her hand off on his shirt. Every week he was excited to see Emilee at church. I was always very grateful for her tenderness with my son.

Life got even better for Nick when he was finally enrolled at the local middle school the next year in Carnation. He got to see Emilee every day at school. Later she told me that, for her, the best part of middle school was hanging out with Nick in the resource room.

As the years passed, I would often ask him about Emilee and he would always say, "I love Emilee, she loves me."

Theirs was a special relationship. Nick didn't seem to mind that Emilee and his friend Paul had fallen in love and were dating. He knew that Paul and Emilee were a couple, and he knew that she stilled loved him. I was a little concerned for his feelings. I didn't need to worry. You see, Paul loves Nick as much as Emilee does.

When things followed the natural progression in Paul and Emilee's relationship and they had decided to marry in August 1999, a spectacular, unexpected thing happened. After the traditional talk that Paul had with Emilee's father, he and Em came out to our house to talk with Nick. Nick was very excited to see both of them.

I will always remember that day with great emotion.

Quietly and gently Paul explained, "Nick, Emilee and I are in love and want to get married. I love her very much and I want to know if it is okay with you that we get married."

Nick didn't say anything. And of course, none of us knew what he would say. All of us were looking at one another, wondering what would happen next.

"Nick, Emilee and I are in love and we really want to get married. I love her very much and I really want to know if it is okay with you that I marry Emilee."

Still Nick was silent, looking at both Paul and Emilee.

Paul stated his case a third time. He is an attorney now, so this was good practice.

Still Nick didn't answer him.

Finally, Paul was begging, "Please Nick, Please. I want to marry Emilee. Please."

Nick looked Paul straight in the eye, and taking a deep breath, said, "It's okay, you marry Emilee."

We were all relieved.

Paul and Emilee both hugged Nick, thanking him.

As they drove away, Nick said to me. "I love *both* Paul and Emilee."

I told him that they loved him too. And they still do. A few months later, Nick was pleased to be sitting in the temple with us to witness Emilee's marriage to Paul. He hugged both of them when the ceremony was complete.

When I hear professionals talk about full inclusion in educational and social settings, I wonder if they really understand the beauty of fully including a person with special needs, immersing them in all aspects of life, love and learning. Full inclusion has been my goal for Nick's entire life.

Nick had a new teacher for his last year in school. The administration created a new program and now there were four other students like Nick that would be enrolled. We were excited that the program was increasing since Nick had been a pioneer in the district. They assured us that Nick's program would continue as it had been designed. Sadly, we discovered that this was not the case.

The new teacher decided without consulting anyone, that the Special Education classroom was a self-contained program, rather than a resource room. The students would no longer go to other classrooms during the day. They would receive all their educational program in that classroom. No one told us that anything had changed.

After a few weeks, our youngest son, Derek, mentioned to me that the custodian had stopped him during lunch and asked why Nick wasn't helping clean up after lunch anymore. The custodian wondered if he had done something wrong, because he had received a note that Nick would no longer be there after lunches.

We set up a meeting with the teacher, inviting the school administration and the district superintendent.

Arden began, "We have called this meeting to discuss the changes made to Nick's program that were made without calling a meeting or getting our input. It has come to our attention that Nick is no longer attending PE, Art, Choir, picking up the morning attendance records or cleaning up after lunch. His entire inclusion program has been gutted. Please explain."

The principal turned to the teacher and said, "Please explain what is going on."

"I changed Nick's schedule to protect him and keep him safe. I don't believe that he or students like him are safe physically or socially in fully inclusion-based programs."

The principal was outraged. "He has an IEP, which is a legal document that we as school professionals are duty-bound to follow."

"I rewrote Nick's IEP to be more appropriate."

"You did what? You rewrote his IEP without any input or permission? We will talk about this later, but for now you are to reinstate this student's program in its entirety including the IEP that was signed last spring. I mean immediately. Tomorrow."

The teacher narrowed his eyes, glaring at his boss, but didn't say anything.

Shaking his head, the principal turned to look at us, "I am so sorry that this happened. Starting tomorrow morning Nick's full program will be restored. I will continue to monitor this situation personally and will give you a full report in a couple of weeks. Again, I apologize for this. It was not fair to Nick, everybody loves him here. He is an integral part of our school."

The next day, Nick was happily back leading the gym class exercises, taking the attendance to the office, singing with the choir and helping the custodian with lunch clean-up.

Chapter Thirty-Nine

Christmas morning 2000, Nick had finished opening his presents and was sitting on a chair, watching everyone else. Suddenly he pitched headfirst onto the floor in a grand-mal seizure. We were momentarily stunned, but then everyone moved quickly to clear the space, turn him on his side and wait. Helplessly frozen in place, we watched the seconds tick by while Nick's body writhed and stiffened in his classic seizure's clutches.

Ryan went into the back hallway. In frustration, he hit the wall with his fist. Although as a family we had experienced these seizure episodes for over twenty years, each one was unexpected and traumatic. Every seizure brought the immediate rush of adrenaline, followed by fearful internal scenes of him dying or becoming more disabled as a consequence.

After the seizure was over and Nick was postictal, everything was calm again. I got an ice bag for Ryan's hand. We moved Nick to the couch and while he slept we continued with our traditional Christmas breakfast.

When he woke up a few hours later, the first thing that he asked was, "When we open presents?"

I said, "Just a minute. You go sit in the living room, we will bring them."

With tears of joy and sadness in our eyes, Rosie, Karen and I scooped up his gifts and went into the bedroom to rewrapped them all. Then we all had the pleasure of watching him re-open the presents that he didn't remember opening before his seizure.

Although Nick's IEP had been restored, the classroom teacher wasn't interested in our input at all. It was a frustrating that after all of our work and progress with the district, this happened in Nick's final year at school.

When the second term started at the end of January, I noticed that Nick was not assigned to attend the senior project class even though his IEP specified that he was to complete a project. Nick had watched many of his friends, as well as his siblings Ryan and Karen, work on their senior projects. The semester-long class was required for graduation, with specific time and task requirements.

Nick insisted that he was going to do his own senior project. He titled it, "My Family." The project components were to create a poster, have a product and make a presentation. Nick had told me what he wanted to do for each requirement, but according to the district's policy, the student couldn't start working on their project without prior approval and oversight by the district personnel. Nick asked us about it almost every day. He was, not very patiently, waiting to start his project.

I sent a note to Nick's teacher, mentioning the oversight and asking him to share his timeline for the Senior Project completion with us so that we could support Nick working on it at home. After a couple of weeks with no response, I was so frustrated that I requested a special MDT conference with the school administration. They set a date for the meeting.

The night before the MDT meeting Arden and I talked with Nick.

"Nick, we are going to have a meeting to make sure you get to do your Senior Project."

"Okay."

"You are going to come home with Derek on the bus, he will take care of you."

"Okay. I not go. Okay?"

"Yes, Dad and I will handle the meeting."

"You be frustrated with them, you fix this?"

"Yes, Nick, we will be frustrated with them. We will fix this."

We had decided that Nick would not attend the MDT meeting because he already was upset and we didn't know how strongly we would need to advocate for him to get the district's agreement for him to complete a senior project.

At the meeting, the principal began, "Mr. and Mrs. Gremmert, the school counselor and I are surprised that Nick isn't working on his project. He was on the list for the second semester."

Turning to the teacher he asked, "Can you explain this?"

"Well, first of all, I was not aware that Nick was scheduled to do a senior project. After all, he is not really graduating, so it is not really a requirement."

Arden pulled out a copy of Nick's original IEP and a dated copy of the note that I had sent in Nick's communication folder weeks before and handed them across the table.

"We discussed Nick's IEP with you last September. Remember. You were instructed by your boss to reinstate his entire IEP. If you were truly doing your job correctly, you would know that Nick's participation in the Senior Project program is a big part of his current IEP. I am not convinced that you have even read it. You certainly are not implementing it."

The teacher looked deflated.

I asked the MDT, "We could like to have Katie Hoesel, Nick's prior teacher, assigned as the oversight person for Nick's project. She has always been supportive of Nick and his inclusion program. I have already asked Katie if she had time to help Nick with this project and she told me that she would love to be involved."

The teacher found his voice and said, "In my professional opinion it is not appropriate for district resources to be used in this way. As I said before, the senior project is not a requirement for Nick since he is not graduating. He is only receiving a completion certificate this June."

Arden stood up. Pointing to the teacher, he said, "Nick will be participating in all of the graduation events, even if we as his parents are the assigned assistants. You will not be allowed to take these experiences from my son."

The administrator immediately answered with, "Mr. Gremmert, Nick will be participating, that is not in question."

Arden sat back down.

"Mr. and Mrs. Gremmert, I have two questions. Do you feel that Nick needs to be in the actual Senior Project class and do you know the subject for Nick's project?"

"Nick told us that his project was going to be on Family. With your permission, we would like to be assigned as Nick's volunteer advisors. He doesn't need to attend the class and we will make sure that he meets all of the timetable requirements. As you know, we have been through this program twice before with Ryan and Karen."

It was agreed: Nick would do a senior project on his family with a poster, a scrapbook, and a presentation in front of a Senior Project panel, just like the other students. We were thrilled. It was a big deal to both Nick and us as his parents.

The Saturday after our meeting, Nick and I went to Michael's crafts store to pick up the things he wanted on his poster. I am not a "crafty" sort of person, so the whole poster idea was a stretch for me. He saw some paper doll cutouts and asked for them for the border. That would have been expensive, so I told him I could cut some out and tape them together. He said that would be okay. I was worried that they would look terrible. It took me some time and quite a few pieces of paper, but I was able to recreate what he had wanted from the craft store.

The scrap book took some time to compile. Nick carefully looked through hundreds of photographs, deciding which ones he wanted in the scrapbook. As he placed the ones he wanted in the scrapbook pile, he told me the caption that he wanted below the picture. Scrapbooking was a popular hobby that year, so he found some colorful and appropriate stickers that complemented the themes of his pictures. I typed up the captions and helped him cut them out. He glued the pictures, captions and stickers on the pages. I was so proud of him. He had a huge smile on his face as he was working. He would say over and over, "I do my senior project on my family."

Chapter Forty

Spring brought lots of excitement. Prom plans were the main topic. One night at dinner Nick unexpectedly said, "I got a question."

"Nick what is your question?"

"I go to prom. I get a tux like Derek."

I can't imagine that he means to have me go as his date. I don't know what to say to him. He wants this and I don't know how to make it happen.

"We will figure something out."

"Mom, I could take him," Karen said.

"Are you sure, sweetheart? It will be a big task for just one person. What if he has a seizure?"

Derek interjected, "Daniel and I will be there with Cassie and Mia. Nick will be okay."

Karen agreed, "Besides, I will ask Anjerie if she wants to go with us. Since she went to Ireland with us last summer, she is very familiar with Nick. He loves her and she can help too. Nick will have two dates."

Nick was so excited. "I going to prom! I going to prom with Anjerie and Karen!"

He looked great in his tux. I was very grateful that Karen and Anjerie, both high school graduates, would sacrifice a Saturday night and dress up in formal dresses, to make it possible for Nick to attend his senior prom. Many of the guys at the dance told Nick that they were jealous. He was dancing with two beautiful women and they only got to dance with one. It was a very memorable experience for everyone.

The time was approaching for the senior project presentations. I sent a note to the teacher asking when Nick's time slot was. He wrote back that Nick didn't have a time slot. The teachers who were volunteering to be on the panels were very busy. The note stated that he didn't think it was appropriate for me to expect that they would take their time for this.

Again, I had to call the principal.

I read him the note I had received.

"I am so sorry to have to bother you again. The school has always been so supportive of Nick, and this is just shocking to me that there is such resistance with Nick's current teacher. Do you need a copy of this note sent to you?"

"No, Mrs. Gremmert, I don't need to see the note. I am the one that should apologize. I will take care of this and Nick will have his opportunity to present his project. I am sure that we will have no trouble filling the panel with teachers. I will instruct Nick's teacher to send out a message asking for volunteers for Nick's panel. Thank you."

The response was overwhelming.

I received a phone call from Nick's teacher.

"I am surprised, but there were many more teachers that wanted to be on Nick's panel than we have slots available. A few of them asked if they could be in the room to watch Nick's presentation. Do you think that would be okay?"

I tried to be gracious. "That's great. Nick is loved by many of the teachers. He will benefit from showing all of them his presentation."

Nick loves watching slides, using our slide projector and screen. So for his presentation he picked out slides from our various family trips. We practiced his dialogue describing each slide while he pushed the button on the projector controller. He was so excited that he often got ahead of himself with the slides, rushing forward to the next one before he'd talked about the previous slide.

When I told him that I would have to push the button for him, if he couldn't keep a good pace, he got upset and said, "I push the button. It my senior project."

We kept practicing and gradually he was able to stem his excitement enough to talk about each slide and move to the next one when he was finished.

Just a few days before the assigned panel slot, Nick told Arden that he wanted to sing an Irish song at the end.

"You sing with me? We sing 'Jug of Punch?' Together? After I do my slides?"

Arden agreed to sing with Nick at the end.

When the big day arrived, he was so excited in the morning before school.

"You be there, Mom. After school. I not ride the bus. You bring my poster. Oh, and one more thing, my scrapbook. Oh, and one more thing, don't forget the slide projector. Oh, and one more thing, the slides and the controller."

"Nick, that was more than one thing."

Ignoring me he continued, "Oh, and Mom, don't forget my suit."

The seniors had been instructed to dress up for their presentations.

The day seemed to drag on. I checked the stuff in the car at least three times and kept looking at the clock. I didn't want to be late or forget anything.

Laden with all the stuff, Arden and I went to his classroom after school. Nick looked at us as we came in the door.

"You got it, you not forget."

"Nick, there is no way that I was going to forget. Dad is going to take you to the bathroom to change into your suit and I will set up the projector and screen for you, okay?"

I greeted the teachers for the panel as they arrived, and sat in their designated seats.

"I am so grateful that you would volunteer to help Nick do this. It is so important to him and he is so excited."

Turning to the other teachers and school staff that had arrived I said, "You all have made this high school experience much more successful for Nick than we could have imagined. It is awesome that you are here today to witness his achievement."

One teacher said, "We all wanted to be on the panel, but there wasn't room. Are you sure that Nick won't mind if we watch?"

"He will love it. He loves being the center of attention you know!"

I was on pins and needles but I had nothing to worry about. Nick was in his element. He talked about each slide and what we had done in each of the places he had been in the world.

At the end, he said, "I love Ireland. My dad come up here now. Now we sing Jug of Punch for you."

And boy did he sing. I was so proud of him. The room erupted in applause and I could tell that Nick was pleased with himself too. My son, who wasn't expected to walk or talk, stood there in front of a panel of teachers, made a stunning presentation and sang one of his favorite Irish songs. My baby Nicky had come so far. It really was unbelievable.

There were many tears shed during his presentation that day, as the significance of what we were witnessing touched our hearts. It was proof that inclusion could be an outstanding positive experience for everyone, not just the child with special needs.

Later, his teacher approached me as I was taking down the projector screen.

"I had no idea that Nick was so accomplished."

I held nothing back as I responded, "Well, shame on you then. Each of these other teachers realized Nick's potential and they aren't Special Ed trained."

I turned away so that I wouldn't say more.

Our family celebrated that night at our favorite restaurant, Ixtapa in Carnation. Bill and Gracie, the owners, patiently listened to Nick explain how wonderfully he'd done on his senior project. It was a good day.

Nick's classmates staunchly supported him. We learned about this story later, but it happened during a pregraduation meeting between the administration and the senior class officers. The administration was explaining the traditional order in which people would line up to walk at graduation. One of the students suggested that Nick walk first, at the head of the class. The school officials said that the first spot was reserved for the valedictorian, followed by the salutatorian and then the senior class officers. After that it was customary for the rest of the class to be in alphabetical order. A discussion followed.

The students insisted and prevailed. Nick was assigned to walk first to get his certificate of completion. He was so excited to graduate, especially since he was graduating ahead of his brother Derek, who was in the Class of 2001.

We ordered Nick's cap and gown. Once it arrived Nick tried it on every day.

The principal had asked Nick's prior teacher to assist him during the rehearsals. She called me later that day.

"Mrs. Gremmert, he did really well during the graduation rehearsal today. I think that some of the other graduates could learn a thing or two about appropriate cooperative behavior from Nick."

"Thanks for calling, Katie. Arden and I are worried that if Nick has an outburst during the ceremony, it might spoil the day for the other students and their families. We want the day to be perfect for everyone. I think that he understands how momentous this is, sometimes he just gets excited."

"Cassie will be walking in with him so she can make sure he goes to the right place and doesn't get confused."

"That is a great idea, she is so kind."

"It was her idea, she wants to help."

That was comforting to both Arden and me.

The day finally arrived and we drove over to the large church where the graduation was being held in the sanctuary. We were a little early, so we stood in the foyer with Nick. I felt so proud of my son. He had worked hard since he was three years old to get to this point. Nick's teacher, Katie Hoesel, walked up.

"I'll take Nick back to line up with the other students. I just saw Cassie back there. Let me show you where he'll be seated."

We walked into the auditorium.

"He will walk down this aisle, so perhaps sitting here would be best for you so you can see him."

We took our seats and got ready. I was so full of anticipation. I hoped that everything would be great for all. I was a bit nervous, but even more proud.

It was time. There was a quiet hush as the music started. We all turned around to watch the graduates slowly walk down the aisles toward the raised podium to their seats.

Out in front was Nick, walking with Cassie. He had the biggest smile on his face as he carefully kept pace with the other students. Once in his seat, he sat there so quiet and calm through the speeches and the musical numbers.

I must have looked nervous, because my mom reached over and patted my hand, saying, "It will be all right, don't worry."

All too quickly the program was over. It was time for the graduates to walk across the stage to receive their diploma from the school board president and shake hands with the school administration. The school board president asked everyone to hold their applause until the entire class had walked.

I looked to the side of the stage and there he stood, at the head of the class. He handed his name card to the announcer. "Nicholas James Gremmert." I held my breath, remembering that moment after his birth, in the hospital, when I envisioned his future accomplishments.

Does he know that he is supposed to start walking?

He did know; he walked forward. The school board president called the next name, but the other student didn't move. Nick kept walking.

The next student's name was called again. No one moved.

Suddenly as if by an invisible signal, the entire graduating class of 2000 stood on their feet and gave Nick an ovation. Little by little the entire audience was on their feet, clapping for our Nick. Arden and I weren't the only ones weeping. The ovation continued until Nick received his folder and walked down the stairs.

In that quiet moment, we heard Nick say, "I did it. I graduate."

Immediately after the graduation ceremony, the Senior Class began an all-night party organized at an undisclosed location. A week or so before graduation Nick decided he wanted to go to the Senior Class party. I got permission to go with him as his caregiver.

Again, I was really impressed with those young people. It turned out to be a good experience for both Nick and me. The kids his age were much more accepting, gracious and generous to Nick than some of the adults we encountered. It gave us faith that the rising generation had more compassion and empathy for our son and our situation than many of our own peers. Including Nick in their day-to-day school experience had changed them too.

He had a great time at the graduation party. Many of his class-mates made the effort during that evening to come and sit with Nick and me and talk to him a bit.

"What are you doing after graduation, Nick?"

"I stay at home with Mom and Dad. We go to Ireland. I get a job. What you doing?"

They would explain their plans for after graduation. It was a night of hopeful goals and big dreams.

PART NINE

Dance Like No One Is Watching

Chapter Forty-One

We settled into a regular daily routine during our epic road trip of 2016. In the evening we stopped driving about dinner time. After eating we relaxed in the hotel room watching Nick's favorite TV shows Family Feud, Wheel of Fortune and Jeopardy. In the morning, we took care of Nick's needs, ate breakfast and either packed up to get back on the road, or prepared to go visiting with friends and relations, if we were staying in a city for a few days. We spent many hours listening to the SiriusXM radio and talking about this book. Nick kept asking us if we could talk about his life.

"I go back to school," he announced one day.

"What do you mean? You already graduated."

"Not Cedarcrest, I go to Bridge school."

"Bridge school?"

"You know, that school, they do arts and crafts?"

"You mean the school in Bellevue, Bridge Academy?"

"Yes."

"That is a great idea, Nick, I will send them a text message. They now have a program in Carnation and have new staff. I will talk to them about it."

"I go there, okay?"

"Nick, I said I will check into it.

He had been attending Bridge Academy in 2010. We withdrew him from the program when he got so ill with the seizures and he didn't leave home for a few months. He hadn't talked about the school for the last six years.

He also wanted to add other activities to his weekly schedule too. He asked if we could rejoin the church choir on Sundays and if he could do jobs around the house. It seemed that he was evaluating his current life as he was listening to me read the manuscript of his story.

On another occasion, Arden and I were talking about budgets and expenses when Nick piped up from the back seat, "I want a job."

"You do have a job, Nick. You are shredding papers in our office. Helen is your job coach."

He was quiet and I thought that the topic was concluded. I was wrong.

"Not I get paid."

Arden and I both laughed a little.

"Do you want to get paid?"

"Yes!"

Obviously, we were in full negotiation mode.

"How much do you want to be paid?"

Pausing, he considered the question thoughtfully, then said emphatically, "Twenty dollars."

Arden and I looked at one another and nodded to one another.

"Okay, starting this week, you will get twenty dollars every week you shred with Helen. Is that okay?"

"Yes."

Arden then asked, "What do you want to do with your money after you get paid?"

"Buy stuff."

"What kind of stuff do you want to buy?"

"Christmas presents."

Miraculously, another developmental step had been achieved. He wanted some money of his own. He wanted to work for that money, and he wanted to decide how to spend it.

Despite many bumps in the road, his lifelong journey toward independence was bearing fruit.

Chapter Forty-Two

After Nick's graduation in June of 2000, we approached the Division of Vocational Resources (DVR) to get a job and a job coach for Nick. We were told that although Nick qualified for funding for job coaching, there was no money in the budget for it. We felt that he needed to do something during the day so we asked our friends and everyone we knew to discover what might be possible for Nick. We learned that the senior center in Carnation was looking for a volunteer dish washer.

Nick got the job starting in September 2000. He liked working with Lisa, the cook, who was his direct supervisor. Arden and I took turns being his job coach. Nick learned pretty quickly how to operate the commercial dishwasher and sprayer system with lots of help and cueing from his coaches. It took between one and two hours daily, five days a week to complete the dishwashing after the lunch was served. He learned to be very thorough as he wiped the tables down and cleaned the dishes, pots and pans. Sometimes Lisa left a little in the bottom of the pans so that Nick had the pleasure of really getting after it with the sprayer. After a few weeks, he rarely needed redirection, so we took our laptops up to the kitchen, plugged in and worked on other things. It was a big commitment for us, but it was a good thing for Nick.

After about six months, a case manager from DVR called us to see if he could come evaluate Nick's job and his job coaches. We were confused that they thought they had some oversight of the situation—*we* had gotten Nick the job and *we* were doing the coaching. But we still had some hope of help from that agency so we set up the appointment. The case manager seemed like a pleasant man. However, he never spoke to Nick. He did ask me how many hours we were there each week. He then stepped out to take a call on his phone.

When he returned, he was talking to one of the program directors at the center. They had known each other from previous jobs.

Meanwhile, Nick worked through his pile of dishes and declared, "I done." The case manager didn't notice. I helped Nick out of his apron and told the DVR official that we were leaving.

He said, "I'll send out a report next week," and went back to talking to his friend.

So that was it. Nick and I had our "evaluation" by DVR. The report merely stated the hours that Nick volunteered and that his job coach was proficient in her job. I called him after receiving the report and again requested that we receive job opportunities for Nick and the names of potential job coaches for him. He told me that Nick was doing fine and that there were no funds available to do anything more. It seems to me that the idea of finding meaningful employment for those with special needs is widely accepted as good, however I don't agree with the way the funding is administrated. From that time, Arden and I have created a "daily program" for our son to meet his needs. What his schedule is each day has changed from time to time, greatly dependent on his declining health, but over all these years we know that he is happy.

In September, Ryan introduced us to Tiffany Carter. They had been dating for a while, and although they were not engaged, Ryan had told us that she was really important to him.

Upon meeting her, Nick gave her a big slobbery kiss. We made small talk as we got to know one another. All of a sudden Nick interrupted everyone and started asking Tiffany questions: "Do you love Jesus?"

"Yes."

"Do you listen to the Holy Ghost?"

"Yes."

"Do you sleep in Ryan's bed?"

We all laughed in embarrassment.

She and Ryan looked at one another and both answered, "No!"

It was so awkward, none of us knew what else to say.

Arden reprimanded him.

"Nicholas, that wasn't appropriate."

But Nick just sat there with a big smile on his face. He truly thought they were significant questions and he got his answers.

After they left, Nick turned to me and said, "We love Tiffy, don't we?"

I wasn't so sure what Tiffany thought of us, but she later told me that she felt Nick was saying welcome to the family that day. I have always been grateful for the love and acceptance shown to Nick by the sensational people my kids have married.

Ryan and Tiffany were with us for Thanksgiving and soon afterward Ryan proposed. We organized a bridal shower for her that April. The morning of the shower we were all busy with the final arrangements. Nick looked at me with a questioning look and asked, "We see Tiffany shower?"

"Of course not!" I was horrified.

"She have shower alone?"

It took me a minute. No wonder he was confused. I realized that he didn't understand that as a bride, Tiffany would be showered with gifts. I explained that it was a party for girls.

Just before the shower began, all the men left to go out for the evening. Nick wanted to stay home, but Arden took him anyway. When they returned, Nick looked at the presents, the used wrapping paper, the food, the cake, and the house all decorated.

Clearly, supremely disappointed, he said, "Next time I be at the shower, I not go with Dad."

That's how it's been ever since then.

One day, Nick had a very different seizure. He just dropped to the ground without any warning. The seizure didn't progress into a tonic clonic episode and he didn't fall asleep. The neurologist said they were commonly called drop or atonic seizures. It was strange how his seizures were not only unexpected but also sometimes presented very differently.

About a month later, Nick had another drop seizure at a Blockbuster store. He and Derek were standing in the checkout line when Nick rapidly went down without making any attempt to break his fall. Derek caught Nick's head before it hit the floor. Nick seemed a bit dazed, although, again, the seizure didn't progress to the tonic clonic we were used to.

Whenever Nick had a seizure, Dr. Glass made adjustments in Nick's medication dosage. A few weeks later, we'd take Nick for a blood test to see what the drug levels were.

In June, we had our annual meeting with Dr. Glass, by now a well-known and respected expert in his field. Since Nick was approaching twenty-two and Dr. Glass is a pediatric neurologist, I asked the doctor if he was going to recommend us to an adult neurologist. Arden and I didn't want to change doctors, and we were relieved to hear that Dr. Glass felt that he could continue to help us manage Nick's seizure disorder. We made a videotape of some of the things Nick did that concerned us, such as dropping his head forward whenever he laughed heartily. It would nod in a repetitive, rhythmic, almost convulsive manner. Sometimes he would fall to the floor. These episodes were seizure activity but they never progressed into a tonic-clonic seizure.

It was always good to see Dr. Glass for the annual visit. He had a great overview perspective of Nick's progress over the previous year and it was heartwarming to know that Dr. Glass felt we were doing a good job taking care of our son.

In June 2001, Derek graduated from High School and took a short trip with his friends to Eastern Washington. His plans were to move to Utah, get a job and live in the duplex with Ryan and Karen. We got to spend Fourth of July with him and the next day as he packed himself into the Jeep, prepared to head out the driveway and get on the road to the rest of his life, I kept talking to him.

"Do you have everything you need? Here let me get you some more snacks. Dad gave you some money to tide you over until you get your first paycheck, right?"

He looked up at me but kept on packing.

"I think the tank is full. Check the glove box to make sure you have the insurance card and the registration. What about a tool box? Do you have that?"

"Mom, I gotta go. Ryan, Tiff, and Karen are expecting me to meet them in Twin Falls today. I love you. I will call you when I get there."

Derek hugged me and let me cry as we said goodbye again. Cocking his head to one side, looked me in the eye. He started to speak but I interrupted him.

"I'll be okay. Don't worry about me. I'm excited for you. Drive safe. I love you. Remember who you are!"

Those last three statements were what I always said to my kids when they were leaving. Derek honked as he turned the corner. Arden and I stood on the porch waving until we could no longer see the Jeep.

"Arden, this is such a momentous morning for us. The last of our children, the baby of the family, was leaving the nest."

Arden patted my shoulder. "He will be okay. We will be okay."

I stood there long after Arden went inside.

Derek is so excited to start the rest of his life. The rest of my life is in front of me too. For twenty-three years I have been raising children and foster children, molding my schedule to meet their demands and activities. From here on, Arden and I will only have Nick to care for. It will be quiet. I will miss the noise. It will be clean. I won't miss the mess.

The future loomed before me, I felt deep trepidation.

Chapter Forty-Three

In January of 2002, Nick began to display aggressive behavior, grabbing my arm and pushing me. Arden and I discussed what to do.

"Eva, why do you think that he is all of a sudden being aggressive?"

"I don't know what has caused the change. It could be related to his seizure medication or an emotional response to life after the Christmas holidays. Regardless, I know that he has the ability to learn to self-regulate. Let's be consistent and firm with the techniques we know to modify his behavior and see if that helps."

It didn't. After a few more days, Nick pushed me when I was helping him down the stairs. I fell down a few stairs. I was frightened but unhurt.

Arden and I sat him down and told him that if the behavior continued he would have to live somewhere else.

The aggressive behavior ceased immediately.

For about three days he kept saying, "Sorry, Mommy, I not hurt you. I live here, okay?"

I reassured him that he could live with us if he didn't hurt us.

Later, when we were in Ireland, Arden left to return to work ten days before Nick and me. Nick wanted to go home with Arden, and after his dad left, he started misbehaving. He dropped his dinner on the floor, and threw all the clean clothes out of the clothes basket.

After a couple of days, he said, "You mad at me. I go home now."

That was pretty sophisticated logic on his part, I was impressed.

I said, "Boys with bad behavior can't get on the airplane to go home."

The outbursts stopped.

In the fall of 2002, Nick didn't seem happy working at the senior center anymore either. Most of the people there would say hi to Nick and engage him in conversation, especially when he was clearing the tables. He'd ask them what they did for work and they would all reply that they were retired.

One day, Nick asked Arden, "When I be retired?"

"You will probably work another forty years."

Nick had a stricken look on his face.

Later at dinner, Arden was telling the story to his parents and me. We all were laughing when Nick said, "I quit, I retire."

We didn't understand how serious he was until the next day, when he refused to go to the senior center.

He kept saying, "I retire."

Arden went up and did the dishes that day and told them that Nick wouldn't be coming back. Lisa the cook wanted to see him one more time, but Nick refused to go back into the kitchen. A few days later, we took him up to the senior center to say goodbye, but he wouldn't get out of the car. He really was done.

When Lisa came out to the car all he would say was, "Goodbye Lisa the cook." He wanted nothing to do with working there another forty years.

One of Nick's long time self-calming behaviors is spinning a string or a white shoe lace. He calls it his spinner. He will spin non-stop for a long time. He seems to be mesmerized and will drool, stare blankly at the string, and appear less connected to his surroundings.

Nevertheless, he hears exactly what is going on and often will interrupt the conversation with comments that are completely relevant to the subject being discussed. This always amazes us.

The first time we lost the spinner was tragic. We tried different strings for about three weeks before he accepted the new one. We all became very good at keeping track of where the spinner was but sometimes they wore out and broke. We learned to purchase a large shoelace and cut it in two so that we had a spare available.

Once my mother-in-law took care of Nick while Arden and I went away for a few days. When we picked him up at Grandma's, we found a frantic Nick and a frustrated Grandma. The spinner had broken and the large piece was lost. LaVern had attempted to introduce a couple different strings in hope that they would be accepted but Nick kept saying, "No, I want my spinner. Where is my spinner?"

In desperation, I took one of the new ones that LaVern had already tried, tied a small piece of the previous spinner on the end and asked Nick if it was okay. We all sat there holding our breath, watching Nick look at the tied-together spinner.

Finally, he looked up at me and said, "Thanks, Mommy, for my new spinner."

Tragedy averted!

We saw Dr. Glass again in September of 2002. It had been over a year since Nick had a seizure episode. We were still concerned about the laughing outbreaks, and Nick had started making grimaces in the morning that looked like partial seizures. Dr. Glass ordered a wake/sleep EEG. These are the most difficult EEGs for both the patient and their parents. Nick was expected to be awake for part of the EEG and then to fall asleep, just like taking a nap, for the other portion of the EEG.

Nick is typically very compliant during medical procedures, but when I tried to explain that he needed to take a nap, he kept saying, "Not I tired." It took a while but he finally fell asleep just long enough to complete the test. Based on his findings, Dr. Glass added another anti-seizure medication, Keppra. Nick was already taking Felbatol, Topamax, and Neurontin. Dr. Glass hoped that once Keppra was at a therapeutic level we could taper the Felbatol and eventually Nick could be off it completely. Felbatol is very sedating and causes side effects including aggression, irritability, diarrhea and other digestive problems.

It took a couple of months, but once Nick was off the Felbatol we noticed a big difference. He seemed more awake, more aware of his surroundings. He used more language, including displaying his sense of humor. Nick has a great sense of humor. He often gives appropriate one-liners that show he is following the conversation and understands some nuances of language. This is probably genetic because Arden is well-known for his play on words and puns.

One night, Ryan phoned to tell us that he had gotten his private pilot's license, the first step in his journey to become a commercial pilot.

Nick said, "I talk to Ryan, I got a joke."

We handed Nick the phone.

"Why the pilot not land the airplane?"

He paused for a second and then with a smile on his face said, "He forgot to."

This was a direct slam to his older brother's career choice. We all laughed so hard tears were streaming down our faces and we could hardly breathe.

Taking the phone from Nick, I asked, "Ryan do you remember the time..."

He interrupted me, "When I was 16? Yeah I remember that too."

One night, when the boys were teenagers, Ryan was teasing Nick, as brothers sometime do, by calling him Nicky Baby and Nick a Wuss.

Arden and I had been trying to encourage Ryan to get a job. Nick looked his brother in the eyes and said, "You, Ryan, who can't get no job."

We busted up laughing, but Ryan had nothing to say to his brother. He just walked away shaking his head. We have all learned to not underestimate Nick's ability to communicate.

We've noticed that some people are very willing to serve Nick in ways that make his life a little bit better. Once we went to the Nordstrom Anniversary Sale to purchase a suit for Arden. Arden was talking to Bruce, the salesman he prefers, when Nick asked, "What size I am?"

"A 42 regular."

"Mom, you take me there?"

Nick looked at the rack and said, "Let me see..."

He moved each suit aside until he saw a dark blue pin stripe Joseph Abboud designer suit.

"I want this one."

I was so amazed. It was the first time he had declared that he needed something this sophisticated.

"Let's go see what your dad thinks."

Nick walked purposefully over to Arden. "Dad, I want this one."

Both Bruce and Arden were surprised. But what else could we do? We had him fitted for the suit. Bruce kept commenting on what good taste Nick had. Nick had a huge smile on his face as he watched in the mirror while the alterations were being made. The tailor did a great job. He took care to make sure that the off-the-rack suit fit Nick perfectly.

After the fitting, Nick said, "A tie, a tie."

He picked out the most exquisite purple silk Jerry Garcia (of the Grateful Dead) tie. This was not a color combination that Arden would typically choose. Nick looked great. It complemented his new suit perfectly and he knew it. He wore that tie so often he wore it out.

Chapter Forty-Four

Throughout 2003, Nick had drop-seizure episodes every six weeks or so. We noticed early on that he would often make a strange vocalization—a loud noise—before the attacks. We began staying in very close proximity to him so that we could catch him if he went down. He was a full-grown man and it was harder to catch him but we were able to avoid any injuries throughout this time.

Even though he had made great strides while off of the Felbatol, stopping the drop seizures was the priority. When we put him back on the Felbatol, it seemed like he took two steps back. Within a few weeks, Nick was back to his sedated state. I missed the humor and conversational comments. I missed my son. But the drop seizures stopped. It is the most difficult thing that parents face, weighing the progressive state of the epilepsy disease against the side effects of the various medicines. Each person and their body chemistry is different, so there is not just one answer to handle the seizures. We had made a hard decision, but it was the right decision.

There had been many changes in my life the previous couple of years. Some of my peers were calling this time the transition to being empty nesters. That didn't really apply to me because my nest wasn't empty, and I wasn't sure if it ever would be. At times, I felt lonely and at other times I felt as if I wasn't accomplishing anything.

A dear friend suggested that I find a new hobby, something that would engage my interest, and preferably something I could do with others. It was very good advice. I joined the church choir and begin taking private voice lessons.

I've always loved music, especially vocal music. I got a referral to a vocal coach in Bellevue.

Over the next six years, Phyllis became a teacher, a mentor and a dear friend. The weekly voice lessons with her gave me a much-needed creative outlet where I focused on just me. Finding time to vocalize and practice in the car was easy, and Nick seemed pleased to listen to me. If we were driving somewhere and I hadn't practiced that day, he would remind me. "You need to practice singing, Mom?"

Singing was a beloved point of connection for us.

Nick's seizure pattern changed again in 2004, and he had several grand mal seizures. We also thought he might be having seizures while he was sleeping because he had started wetting the bed again. We noticed that he would have a wet bed every day for a week or so and then a grand mal seizure followed. Nick was twenty-five years old, caring for him was more complicated than taking care of an infant, child or teenager. We were on edge with the unpredictability of it all.

Since Nick experienced the third grand mal seizure in less than a year, Dr. Glass increased his daily Felbatol dosage. As expected, Nick's poor behavior also increased. He became verbally opinionated. Just like a two-hundred-pound two-year-old, he clearly wanted to be in charge, to do things his own way, and was resistant when we tried to prompt him. He was more reactive, difficult and sometimes even contentious, as we tried to balance having better seizure control with decreasing the difficult side effects of the medication.

One particular day by the time Arden got home from work, I was done.

"How was your day, sweetheart?" he asked unknowingly.

"Where will I start? Are you sure you want to hear this?"

"Sure."

"Well, first of all this morning after his bath, he acted as if he had forgotten how to dress himself. He told me I had to do it. Then at the breakfast table, he just sat there not eating."

"What did you do then?"

"Well, I told him that if he didn't eat, I was going to throw it in the garbage."

"Did you?"

"No, because he looked at me and said, 'not I know how.' What was I supposed to do about that? I can't tell if he really can't remember how to do things, or if he is manipulating me."

"You know that Dr. Glass said there might be some regression with the increased seizures."

"I know, but we worked so hard to help him gain these skills, it breaks my heart when he loses them. And I know that he is smart and wants to control things too. I just don't know what to do."

"So did you feed him then?"

"Of course, I did. But that is not all that happened. You know how he will act out in different ways when we have demanded that he do what he was asked to do?"

"Yes, we have seen that for years. What happened today?"

"He made another disgusting mess all over his bathroom after he had a bowel movement. I had gone to answer the phone and I came back to that. I didn't know whether to yell or cry."

"What did you do? You know sometimes his behavior worsens in the days leading up to a big seizure."

"I know, that thought did cross my mind. I try to remember that most of the time he is very sweet and when he isn't, there is probably something wrong. So I didn't yell or cry, I just cleaned everything up."

This pattern meant that our patience was often short and we were reprimanding him more often. We'd feel great frustration, and then he would have a seizure and we'd feel guilty for having been so insistent with him. We couldn't always tell if he was acting out and needed discipline or if the behavior was medicine or seizure related and he couldn't help it. We decided to keep our expectations of his behavior consistent and correct him as needed, while we tried to curb our frustration and not get angry. This was very difficult for Arden and me.

Nick thrived best with a high degree of structure, consistency, and predictability in a supportive and nurturing environment. This can be very difficult to maintain over many years with the changes that happen naturally in a family. Arden travelled for work a great deal and it was challenging to maintain consistent discipline and behavior expectations between us. We both loved Nick and wanted the best for him, but we often had different perspectives on what was the best course of action, especially during times when Nick's behavior was difficult.

I was never one to say, "Wait until your father comes home." I believed that Arden was working hard to support us and he didn't need to be burdened with being the disciplinarian when he returned home each evening from work. Besides, our intrinsic talents were different. Discipline and self-control is what I learned from my years of competitive figure skating and are some of my bedrock values. While Arden exhibits these behaviors, his bedrock values include nurturing and tenderness. We have learned from each other over our many years of marriage and child rearing, but we definitely have very different approaches to the same goals. I don't believe that one way is better than the other. All of our children, especially Nick, have benefitted from exposure to their parents' differences.

One day, we were out shopping and needed lunch.

"Where shall we go?"

"To McDonald's." In chorus, Arden and Nick immediately responded.

"They don't have a lot of healthy choices, Nick. You know that you are supposed to be losing some weight to help your seizure control."

"They have salads there," offered Arden.

"Okay, but we need to be careful with Nick's diet."

Arden ordered the food while I sat with Nick at the table.

"What we got?" Nick asked in anticipation when Arden arrived at our table and began unpacking the paper bag.

"Well, I got you a grilled chicken burger, you know you are allergic to beef. And you and I are going to share a small French fry. Mom has a salad and we are going to drink water."

"What else?"

"What do you mean, Nick?"

"What else we have?" as he grabbed the paper bag.

"Nick, that is all Daddy was going to get us, right, Arden?"

Sheepishly Arden said, "Well…"

"Arden, what else did you get?"

"Not much, I just..."

"Cookies, Mom, Dad got me cookies. Right, Arden!"

"Arden, we are supposed to watch his food intake."

"We are watching his intake. I thought that he needed a treat. He has so many hard things in life to deal with. I think that sometimes having a chocolate chip cookie is a good thing."

Although we don't always agree, Arden and I do balance one another.

In October 2004, Nick and I were visiting Karen in Utah when I got a phone call from Derek. He was very shaken up.

"We were in a bad car accident," he said. "Dad is lying on the side of the road."

Is he saying that Arden is dead?

Karen saw my face. "Mom, what is wrong?"

"Derek said that they were in a bad car accident and your Dad is lying on the side of the road."

I need more information. He'd tell me if Arden was dead. He's probably not dead.

"Was your Dad thrown from the car?"

"No, there was smoke in the car so I ran around and opened his door and got him out."

"Is the car on fire? Is there still smoke?"

"No."

"Is your Dad breathing?"

"I think so. Darren is with him."

"Derek, is your dad okay?"

"He's not okay..."

"Derek, is your dad dead or alive?" I yelled, unable to tolerate not knowing any longer.

"Mom, he's alive but he's hurt."

"How badly?"

Every question he answered created more questions.

"Give the phone to your dad. I need to talk to him."

Hearing my husband's voice calmed me down a little bit.

"Derek and I were hit nearly head-on. Both cars going over fifty miles an hour. The oncoming driver crossed the center line into our lane. We were lucky, our airbags did their job. The ambulance is going to take us to the hospital to get checked out, but we are okay!"

Although Arden and Derek both had soft tissue damage to their legs, backs and necks, it was a miracle that the accident was not a tragedy. Nick and I left Utah early the next day and drove home.

My thoughts rolled around my head as miles rolled by.

What would I do if Arden did die? He says that he's okay and I am grateful, but it could happen. He's such a great support to me. Not just financially. He's a rock and is there for me even if we are not in the same place. I couldn't manage caring for Nick on my own. It would be awful. I sure hope that doesn't happen to me.

Nick was singing songs as we drove along. He was happy we were going home to Arden. I was happy that Arden was at home too.

When we got home, we received a letter from DSHS stating that they would no longer pay for Nick's Neurontin prescription. They insisted that he be put on the generic drug Gabapentin instead. This was a terrible decision. After almost a year with no drop seizures, within a week of being on Gabapentin, Nick began having them again. He had thirteen in one month. In addition, he wet the bed every night, and his speech had rapidly declined so much that only I could understand what he was saying.

Our request to put him back on Neurontin was rejected. Dr. Glass sent DSHS a detailed letter describing Nick's need for the medication and we finally got the prescription authorization we needed.

Within a few days back on the Neurontin, we had our Nicholas back. The bedwetting stopped, and we could understand his speech again.

I do appreciate that Nick has such great medical coverage through Medicaid, but I don't understand why they let a review team who have never seen or evaluated our son make decisions without even consulting his medical doctor. We were grateful that Dr. Glass was so willing to advocate for Nick because DSHS didn't honor the request for the medication until we had the back up support from the neurologist. We believe it is essential to have a great working relationship with Nick's medical team so that we have what is needed in times of crisis.

Chapter Forty-Five

In the fall of 2006, a meeting between the families of disabled individuals and our state Department of Developmental Disability (DDD) leaders was organized to create a communication platform. The room was packed with a few hundred disabled young adults and their parents, and although we had arrived thirty minutes early, Nick and Arden and I were seated near the back. I was impressed with the variety of family groups there, and the commitment and dedication of the other parents around us.

Nick was quietly looking at his spinner during the meeting. As we put Nick in the car after the meeting, he looked intently at me and asked, "What is wrong with those guys?"

"What guys?"

"In the room...the guys by us."

There had been two young men in wheelchairs who were constantly moving in typical cerebral palsy (CP) body movements, sitting across the aisle from Nick. Both wore helmets and spent much of the meeting time striking themselves with their closed fists, while making random loud guttural sounds that can be typical of some individuals with CP.

"Do you mean the guys in the wheelchairs?"

"Yes, those guys, what's wrong with them? They're weird."

It seemed kind of funny that my disabled son found other disabled young men weird.

Nick had not spent much time with others that many might consider his peer group. Since he was seven years old, most of his educational and social interaction had been with the regular population. We had insisted that he be given everything possible to help him achieve the most that he could, and had expended a lot of effort on social integration and teaching him appropriate social behavior.

It had been worthwhile. We were able to take Nick with us everywhere that we wanted to go and he was able to fit in, but I wondered if we had neglected a crucial part of his education. Was he judgmental and critical of others who he considered different? It was a moment of awareness for me. From that evening, I began working with Nick on his ability to accept others even if they seemed different.

It has been a great blessing that our kids feel a special closeness with their brother Nick and that each of them desires to help care for him when they can.

One time when Ryan and Tiffany were visiting, they insisted Arden and I go out alone.

"Mom, you and Dad just go out to dinner tonight."

"That would be fun, Ryan, but what about Nick?"

"We will take care of the Nick J., Karen and Derek are coming over here. I think we all are going to Ixtapa. Nick will love it."

"Are you sure?"

"Mom, you guys need some time that is just the two of you. It will all work out. Besides if something does happen, we can call you on your phone. It's not like we don't know what to do."

He was right; Arden and I did need a break. We appreciated our evening out. We got home in time to complete Nick's bedtime routine.

"How was Ixtapa, Nick? Did you have fun?"

"We all go there. I had chicken burrito. Karen take care of me when you die."

"What?"

"Ryan and Derek help, but I go live with Karen when you die. You die soon?"

"No, Nick, they just want you to know that you will be taken care of all of your life."

"I be okay. I live with you now."

"Yes, go to sleep, you are with Dad and me now."

The kids had all talked over dinner, including Nick, and decided among themselves what their eventual plan would be. It is comforting to Arden and me to know that they feel an equal responsibility for their brother.

Whenever Nick needs someone with a particular expertise to help him, they seem to just show up. When we advertised for a daytime caregiver to help with Nick, we were lucky to hire Susan Alling, a friend from church who had a doctorate in psychology. She came to our home four mornings a week for several months. Nick responded well to her cues and even did things differently than we expected.

Susan felt Nick had an obsessive-compulsive disorder and anxiety. She taught us to recognize when he was anxious and how to implement relaxation activities including cueing him to stop, shut his eyes and breathe deeply. We would try to refocus him on thoughts that were relaxing rather than anxiety-provoking. Susan gave us statements we were to ask him repeat, such as: I am okay, I am safe, Mom/Dad will take care of me. These new techniques really helped all of us. Susan felt that when Nick misbehaved, he was probably feeling overwhelmed and needed assistance to remember self-calming and refocusing techniques.

Susan also worked on Nick's sight reading and comprehension skills. He would handwrite papers retelling the stories she read to him and then he would read them to us. She also did thematic studies using subjects he was interested in to enhance his cognitive abilities. It really was enlightening. Nick's ability to be engaged in meaningful conversation increased, and we recognized a remarkable decrease in his anxiety.

Because Nick was so obsessive about things, we had begun to keep secrets concerning upcoming plans. We found that if we waited to tell him that something was going to happen, until the actual day, it was easier.

Of course, he was pretty smart and he did listen to the conversations going on around him, so there were times that he did figure out what was happening. Then the questions would start. "When they coming?" "What time they be here?" "When they going?" and again, and again.

He also would keep himself awake through the night with excitement. This was not good. Often, just when Arden and I were almost asleep, Nick would call loudly from his room, "When they coming?"

We would take turns, as one of us went in to quiet him, so that we could all sleep. Then after about an hour of quiet, we would be awakened by "When they coming?"

It was easier on all of us if we just kept him in the dark until the actual day. We have tried to explain this to other family members. Some are better than others at not talking in front of Nick about upcoming events.

It seemed to us that Nick was maturing in his understanding of social situations. We noticed that he sometimes was embarrassed, especially in unfamiliar situations. He was more opinionated about what clothes he wore, and how his hair looked. Not that he was vain, it just started to matter. These are normal responses for a person to have, and we were thrilled. He also was very resistant to things that were new or that he didn't think he would enjoy. We learned to be a little more persuasive when we were asking him to do things.

Other times, when he said to me, "I not go, I not want to," I would feel frustrated and just tell him that I didn't care what he wanted. He had to come with me and he would be happy about it. I was still the mom!

Nick wanted to attend the Coomer's Second Annual Summer Fun Fair. The day finally arrived and the weather was beautiful. As I drove toward Duvall, I began to feel a terrible sense of dread.

I don't know what's happening. As far as I know nothing's wrong. Nick's happy. I just need to snap out of it.

We got there, signed him in, then he got his t-shirt and his list of activities. I knew most of the volunteers and many of the campers. Everyone was united to provide an impressive two-day experience for individuals with developmental disabilities and their families.

Yet I felt like I had a dark cloud hovering above me. My friend Sally Coomer noticed something was up. Even though she was hosting the event at her home, she came over to me.

"Eva, why don't you go inside my house for a break. Nick is doing great. He has two attentive high school girls assisting him, as well as his cousin Jacob. Just go into the living room and relax for a bit."

I went in, but I couldn't settle down. I tried to sit on the couch, I got a drink of water, I looked out the window and saw Nick. He was laughing with Jacob. I tried to sit on the couch again.

Sally came in. "What's going on, Eva?"

"I don't know."

"You wanna talk about it?"

"Sal, you have a couple hundred people out there. I'm sure you're needed for something more urgent outside."

"Everything's going really well out there. Why don't we sit down?"

I burst into tears, which surprised me. I don't think it surprised Sally.

"Tell me what you're thinking."

"Well, you know Nick is older than most of the other campers. Last year, I sat with the other mothers for the two days of camp and visited with them. They were so full of hope for their children's future. It was so sad to me. I hadn't the heart to tell them that in my personal experience, not all of their dreams would come true. I just sat and listened to them. I didn't disclose anything about our experiences with Nick as he grew up and transitioned from school. I feel I wasn't truthful with them. That burden has weighed heavily on me, although I wasn't even aware of it. Today, driving here I was overwhelmed with a deep feeling of dread."

Sally was so sweet. She gave me some Kleenex.

"Eva, you know that hope sustains us through the dark days we experience."

"I never want anyone else to go through it, and it makes me sad to realize what was ahead for some of them."

"Yes, but it's those very experiences that have made us who we are."

Her comment reminded me of the conversation that I had with Dora Mae on the way home from visiting Merrywood School when Nick was first in a daily program. She had told me that she was grateful she had her two sons with disabilities because of how those experiences had changed her.

I told Sally about Dora Mae and what she had taught me when I was a young mom.

I laughed and said, "I guess I'm not to the grateful part yet. I must have a bit more to go through."

I was beginning to feel better.

"Why don't you rest inside for a little longer."

When I finally went back out, the sun was shining and I didn't feel that black cloud hanging over me anymore. Besides, Nick was having a great time. He was happy and I wanted to be happy with him.

Nick's seizure pattern changed again. Sitting helpless by his bed we would time the events to relay the data to the doctor. The facial grimaces would progress to partial seizures with hand flips, and then drop seizures began that would continue for a couple of hours until he had a grand mal seizure.

Are we done? It has been seven minutes since the last drop seizure. Oh no, there it is again. Seven minutes and ten seconds. Was that two drops in a row? I think it was. Okay, now we wait again.

"Nick, you just had another seizure. You will be okay. Mommy and Daddy are here with you."

"Heavenly Father, make me well."

"Yes, Nicky, they will stop, hopefully soon. Just rest."

"I not better yet. You call the doctor."

"I know, honey. We did talk to the doctor. We are here with you."

What if this time this becomes Status Epilepticus. Dr. Glass said it can happen any time with intractable epilepsy. The seizures become continuous and don't stop with any type of intervention until finally, the body shuts down. I don't think I can cope with this. Oh wait, there is another one. Four minutes and fifteen seconds.

Dr. Glass made a couple of increases to the seizure medicines which finally stopped that pattern.

Chapter Forty-Six

Nick's seizures seemed to be in control, so we felt that we had the right balance of medicines. However, he started waking up a few times during the night and calling out to us. This made him tired in the afternoon and he'd fall asleep for a couple of hours. If we tried to wake him early, he would be irritable and say, "Why you do this to me?"

At bedtime, it took a long time for him to fall asleep and the pattern repeated. I was grateful that he was not as sedated as before, but I was sleep deprived. Arden was traveling a lot for work and sometimes life was very hectic.

We had some help each week, and Arden shared the responsibility for caring for Nick when he was home, but the weeks he was traveling, I had the responsibility to toilet, bathe and do other personal hygiene, manage his medicine, as well as shop, prepare and feed him his food. I was approaching fifty years old and still working full time, so sleep deprivation was an additional stress on me.

In April, we took a trip to Kentucky to visit Ryan's family. Nick loved being there with his niece and nephew. We toured around, and played in the water parks. At twenty-seven years old, Nick was becoming more interested in playing with younger kids. His communication skills were still a problem with most adults, but with the kids he played Legos, Uno, or marble games, talking all the while. Kids don't seem to worry whether they completely understand what he is saying. Nick is always gentle with children and really enjoys watching them play.

Arden and I hired a company to install closet organizers in our bedroom. When our friend and sales rep Becca came to measure and create the plan for our closets, Nick walked in the room and told Becca that he wanted one too.

I asked him why and he said, "For my brochures. They a mess."

He loves to collect any and all travel brochures. We bring them back from everywhere we travel and he stacks and sorts them. They were piled up on his dresser and in boxes on his bedroom floor so we were thrilled that he wanted to organize them.

Becca designed the closet without a door and built in a large open shelf in the middle of one section. It's just the right height so Nick can sit on a chair facing the closet while he sorts and stacks his brochures. He loves it. He says that he is working.

A few years later, Nick was in my office. Watching me at my desk he said, "You work like me, Mom?"

I realized that my job of tax accounting, moving papers around my desk, probably looked just like his sorting and stacking his brochures.

We have known since Nick's diagnosis that epilepsy is a progressive disease. The seizures increase in complexity and frequency, often causing death at an early age. In the beginning Nick experienced only grand mal seizures. These occurred periodically and the doctor would adjust the seizure medication, either by increasing or adding new ones. Later Nick began having Absence seizures and partial seizures, both simple and complex ones. In 2006, Nick started having what Dr. Glass called "cluster seizures." These seizures occurred every few minutes and lasted from two to fifteen seconds with periods of consciousness in between. With Nick, the cluster seizures continue for several hours, culminating in a grand mal seizure lasting around five minutes. He cries after the seizure is over until he falls asleep for three or four hours. It is heartbreaking, since it is the only time he cries. Each time the seizures begin, we worry if this time will be the end. We know that the seizure pattern becomes habitual electrical pathways in the brain.

Dr. Glass introduced the idea of creating a rescue medicine protocol. It is specific medicines to use only when Nick is actively seizing. We keep them in a plastic bag separate from his other meds with an instruction sheet. That way, in the stress of the moment we have something to reference. Others can use it too. When the seizures begin, we call Dr. Glass immediately. He phones back with the dosage of extra medicine we are to give Nick to try ward off the grand mal seizure.

Karen became engaged to Troy Linn in May and they planned a wedding in August on the beach at sunset in Maui, Hawaii. Time change, sleep deprivation and hot temperatures can bring on seizures but we knew that Arden, Nick and I needed to be at that wedding. We booked our trip with great faith, putting it into the Lord's hands.

Nick had an excellent time. He loves Hawaii—the beautiful scenery, the food, and the music. He even learned to use a snorkel on the surface with a helper right by his side. He could find turtles when the rest of us hadn't noticed. He would lift his head, and yell, "Turtle!" through his snorkel and the rest of us would swim over to see what he had found.

We had to sit him in the shade to keep him cool, but the tropical breezes helped. He kept falling, however. Most of the time he just got bruises, but one of the falls required a few stitches by his ear.

We didn't know if these were drop seizures or if he was stumbling because of the seizure medicine. In any case, we felt compelled to keep him as safe as possible. We closely monitored his movements by holding on to him when he was up and moving. He didn't like being restricted. Sometimes we would have a battle of wills, or at other times, he would try and sneak away if he noticed that our attention was on something else.

Arden and my brother-in-law Jeff wanted to check off another adventure from their bucket list, so they organized a dive trip to Ambergris Caye in Belize, one of the best dive spots in the Caribbean. We booked an all-inclusive resort and Nick came along with us. It had become difficult to find caregivers to stay with Nick overnight, so Arden and I decided to bring him when we traveled rather than all of us staying home. Nick, my sister Ann and I were used to hanging out on the beaches swimming or shopping in the small towns while the guys went diving. We all anticipated a great trip.

It was a beautiful clear day when we arrived into the San Pedro airport. Our flight was a couple of hours late, but the resort staff was waiting for us. They loaded us into Jeeps and drove along dirt roads through the small town until we reached a dock. We had been told that it was a short boat ride to the resort. I don't know what we were expecting; perhaps we thought the boat would be like the ferries used on Puget Sound back home in Seattle. That's not what was tied up to the dock. The craft was about twenty-five feet long, and sat low in the water with two 125 horsepower Mercury outboards. Benches ran along the gunwales. I must have looked nervous because Arden put his hand on my shoulder and said, "The boat is called a launch."

I don't know what he means by a launch, but I don't see how we are going to get Nick safely to the resort in that. How will we even get him onboard? I don't want Nick to know I'm nervous, but I certainly will need help getting him on that boat.

They sat Nick and me at the very front of the boat. There were no life jackets. Arden sat in the back with all of our bags, so I was on my own with Nick.

Finally, everyone was on board. It was getting dark. In the tropics, when the sun drops below the horizon, night is immediate. We couldn't even see past the beach to the buildings of the town.

"Nick, hang on tight to the hand rail."

I put one of my arms around him, grasping the hand rail on either side of him so that he wouldn't be able to let go. The captain slowly pulled away from the dock.

This isn't too bad.

Then the engines roared, and with increasing speed, the boat planed and we hurtled over the sea, bouncing along the tops of the rough waves.

We are bouncing so hard on the waves; I don't think I'm strong enough to hold on to Nick and the boat rail. My hands are slipping. What's going to happen now?

I flashed back on those early days when Nick was just a baby and I'd floated him on his back in swim class.

He knows how to swim, but I don't think he'd survive being in the water in the darkness. If we fell overboard, I don't think we could tell which way the surface was. He'd just become disoriented and drown.

Nick was wide-eyed.

"Keep holding on, Nick, everything is all right."

I feel like I'm lying to my son. Everything is not all right. It's so cold. We are wet from the sea spray. It's so dark that I can't anything around us. I can't tell where the shore is. There are no lights. How does the boat pilot even know where we are? Are we lost?

After what seemed an eternity, the boat slowed and turned to the left. We saw lights on a few buildings ahead. We had arrived at the resort. As the crewman tied up at the dock, loudly Nick asked, "I not dead yet?"

Everyone laughed nervously. We were all shaken up and relieved to be back on land. Arden and I found each other in the chaos of unpacking the luggage and hugged like long lost lovers.

The resort staff was very accommodating and the condo was comfortable. Arden and Jeff went on quite a few dive trips. Nick seemed to relish the week. He was content sitting in the soft breeze on the deck, looking at the ocean and spinning his spinner. He kept saying to Ann and me, "I love this. You love this, Mom?"

Ann and I would look at one another and shake our heads. In politeness, I agreed that I loved being with him. However, because the initial boat trip had been so awful, Ann and I didn't want to go anywhere. The boat was the only transport from the resort, so we stayed there the entire week. We started calling it the compound because it felt like we were in a prison and the looming return boat trip required to get back to the airport filled us with dread.

Luckily, the boat ride back was pleasant. The sea was calm and it was daylight, as we watched the scenery glide by.

When we got back from Belize, Nick began tripping more often, especially going upstairs. I called Dr. Glass about it.

"Eva, I don't think it is seizure activity. How long has it been since Nick had new orthotics?"

"He hasn't worn them for years. When he outgrew those that Irene made, we put them in a box. That was probably fifteen years ago. I didn't know he should have new ones."

"I am surprised that the physical therapists at school haven't mentioned it."

I felt really bad, like I had let Nick down. I didn't realize that the orthotics were supposed to be a lifelong physical assistance for Nick. I thought that they were a one-off need. Somehow this information had fallen through the cracks, and I felt I hadn't provided something for Nick that he needed. I thought that the medical professionals would tell me when he needed something and no one had said a word.

I made an appointment with Children's Therapy Center in Kent. The physical therapist there remembered Nick and our family and was willing to make him some new orthotics. As I watched her create the forms for the footbeds, I couldn't help but think back to all those years ago, when I watched Irene do the same thing for Nick's first casting. I had been so overwhelmed that day. The future had seemed so dark, looming full of fear and uncertainty.

Looking back, I felt so much compassion for the young mother I had been. She was a lot stronger than she knew. She had unknown abilities and talents that had emerged and developed because of her life experiences. It was a marvelous feeling to sit in the casting room, listening to Nick and the therapist carry on a conversation. I did feel confident that I had done the best that I could being Nick's mother and that we were both blessed.

Nick had a really bad cluster seizure series one day. He was sitting at the breakfast table when his spoon went flying across the dining room.

"What happened, Nick? Did you have a seizure?"

"I don't know."

Again, his left hand flipped up toward his head, jerking twice.

"Yes, baby, you are having seizures. Let me get you over to the couch so you can lie down."

"Arden, Nick is seizing, let's get him upstairs."

Between the seizures, we had a few minutes break so we carefully took him upstairs to his bedroom. With the partial and drop seizures his whole body loses muscle control momentarily. If they occur on the stairs, we gently assist him down. As soon as he regains his strength, we begin again to move him to his room.

"There, baby, you are in bed, oh another hand flip. Let me write that down."

"You call Dr. Glass? You tell him, I having seizures? You tell him?"

"Yes, I will call him. Daddy has your rescue medicine. Now take it before the next one."

He suffered from these partial and drop seizures for over three hours before the grand mal seizure happened. For Nick, a grand mal involves his complete body. His skin tone is gray, his eyes twitch side to side, his head is drawn up and back to the left. Often his left arm is up over his head. His whole body is writhing and twitching in a strange rhythmic pattern.

This time, the grand mal lasted over five minutes, and afterward he couldn't seem to regulate his breathing. It was very scary. It took another ten minutes before he was breathing normally again. We just kept hugging him and talking to him, hoping that the experience would soon be over.

Nick's seizures still frighten me, even after watching him go through them countless times. Throughout his entire life, Arden or I have somehow managed to be there for almost every episode. That's a miracle.

Chapter Forty-Seven

Coordinating the O'Dochartaigh reunion of 2008 took a lot of my time during that spring and summer, but it was worth all the effort.

After the reunion events were over, Arden and my cousin's husband Paul Fagan went golfing at the Ballyliffin Golf Club. Nick went along to ride in the golf cart. He wanted to ride with Paul instead of his dad. Paul made a U-turn to leave the hole they had played and head down the fairway to the next one. Nick wasn't really holding on. As Paul made the turn, Nick lost his balance and made a graceful fall out of the cart, tumbling onto the grass.

Paul was horrified. Afraid that Nick was injured, he quickly turned around and drove over to where Nick was lying face down in the grass, rhythmically jerking. Arden had seen the fall and ran over. They both arrived at Nick's side simultaneously. His eyes were shut, his skin color was ashen, and he was jerking. Arden and Paul were afraid that the trauma of falling out of the moving golf cart had brought on a seizure. Arden gently turned Nick over, only to discover that he wasn't seizing at all, he was laughing so hard that he wasn't breathing properly.

When he finally caught his breath, he said to Paul, "You falled me out. Dad, Paul falled me out." And he went on laughing. It has become a classic Nick story told with gusto far and wide.

That fall, Nick began attending the Bridge of Promise adult day program, which had been organized by our friend Sally Coomer and her agency, Special Care. We hired a caregiver from the agency to drive Nick to the program, which freed up that time for Arden and me to focus on other things such as our work commitments and chores like grocery shopping. Nick required a lot of supervision during the program but he reveled in socializing with the other young adults. They worked on life skills through play, music, crafts and taking field trips.

Nick's stability when walking kept declining. He seemed to trip and fall more often, even on level ground. He fell more and more, especially whenever we needed him to hurry. We weren't sure what to do. Martha Jones had been providing respite for us on Tuesday nights for years. Martha often knew just what Nick needed. One Tuesday evening, she showed up with a used transport wheel-chair that she had purchased from Goodwill.

Although Arden and I hadn't wanted to admit that Nick needed the accommodation, it was a godsend. Even daily living tasks that Nick had already mastered grew inconsistent. He'd remember how to put on his socks one morning with great success, and the next day he'd act as if he had never done it before. It was very difficult to witness the regression in skills that Nick had initially fought so hard to gain.

Nick's sleeping pattern continued to be a source of concern, especially because lack of sleep can trigger seizures. He woke up many nights a week, crying out until we got up and rushed into his room to calm him down. He couldn't ever explain what the problem was, so we would hug him and reassure him that all is well. Eventually he'd fall back asleep.

In the fall of 2008, Arden planned a weeklong Elk hunting trip to Colorado. I decided to take Nick over to Ireland. With the daunting task of going through security, managing the bags and watching out for Nick, I decided it would be easier to use a wheelchair to get us to the gate.

Everything was going smoothly, and I was feeling pretty proud of myself for thinking ahead. We had arrived at the airport with enough time to move to the gate at a leisurely pace. I explained to the wheelchair attendant what would be helpful going through the security checkpoint, and all was well. I put our carryon bags onto the belt to go through the X-ray, took off Nick's shoes and my own, and headed through the scanner. After I had been cleared, I waited on the other side for the attendant to bring Nick through, just as I had every other time we'd traveled.

A large Transportation Security Administration (TSA) uniformed man briskly walked over to me and in a stern, voice loudly announced, "You need to collect your belongings and move along."

Startled, I explained, "I told the officer on the other side of the barricade that my son was special needs and would need my assistance to get through the checkpoint. She said that would be okay, and to wait for him on the other side."

The officer rolled his eyes. "All right, but don't interfere."

I held my tongue because I knew that if I caused any trouble for the TSA they could prohibit us from flying. The female TSA officer brought Nick through and was signaling me to join her.

"Return to your post." The male officer commanded her.

Talking directly to Nick he said, "You'll need to stand up so that I can clear the chair."

Nick sat there silent, blinking quickly. He didn't know what to do.

"My son is not able to do what you are asking."

The officer turned quickly toward me and said, "Ma'am, I told you not to interfere. You will need to wait over there."

Turning back to Nick, he said even more sharply, "Sir, you need to cooperate with us if you want to travel today."

That got Nick's attention. "Mom, I go on the airplane, right?"

I tried to calm him.

"Nick, we need to get you cleared through security and then we will go to the gate."

"Ma'am, unless your son cooperates, he will not be traveling."

I was very upset, but I didn't argue with him. Quietly I said, "He will need assistance to stand up. Would you allow me to help him, or will you do that?"

"You are not allowed to touch him. Although you have been cleared, he has not."

"Will you assist him to stand? Someone needs to move the wheelchair foot pedals and help him up."

The officer did move the pedals out of the way.

Because he was upset, it was difficult for Nick to follow the officer's directions.

"Nick, you need to stand there with your hands out to side."

"You help me, Mom?"

"Mommy can't help you. Please try to keep your hands up to the sides."

He tried his best, but he has difficulty balancing with his hands out to the sides. I was afraid he was going to fall.

"You now need to remove your belt from your pants."

It is an elastic sports belt with a plastic buckle that we use to hold up his oversized jeans so that we could easily remove them when needed for toileting.

"Sir, my son doesn't have the fine motor skills required to undo the belt and remove it."

"There is nothing wrong with your son. You should quit treating him like he's disabled."

I was shocked.

I wish I could give you a piece of my mind. I want Nick and I to be able to fly today. You're a jerk. You don't know what my life has been like for the last twenty-eight years and you tell me that there's nothing wrong with my son.

"Sir, my son is mentally retarded and has cerebral palsy since birth. He is twenty-eight years old, and as his mother I know what my son is capable of doing and not capable of doing. The belt is holding up his pants; and even if he managed to take off the belt, his pants would fall down and he would be exposed in this public place."

The guard laughed. "Obviously, your son would hold up his pants with one hand if they are that oversized."

"He doesn't have the capacity hold up his pants."

I could barely breathe.

"Ma'am, you need to calm down. There is nothing wrong with your son and you both need to cooperate or you will not be traveling."

That was it. I took a long deep breath.

"You need to call your supervisor," looking the officer straight in the eye.

"You're violating the Americans with Disabilities Act and I need to report your actions."

"I have done nothing wrong."

I repeated, "You need to call your supervisor. You're violating the Americans with Disabilities Act and I need to report your actions."

He looked around as if he was worried about who might hear. He didn't call anyone over, but I noticed one of the officers behind the screening machine talking on his two-way radio.

For the third time, and in an even louder voice, I repeated, "You need to call your supervisor. You're violating the Americans with Disabilities Act and I need to report your actions."

A calm voice behind me said, "What seems to be the trouble here?"

The officer in front of me started to speak but his supervisor cut him off. "I need to hear from this lady first."

I explained the whole thing, including the fact that Nick flew on airplanes almost once a month and that we had never had any trouble before.

"I am appalled at this officer's actions. I am sorry that this has happened to you and your son."

The other officer tried to walk off, but his supervisor told him to wait there.

"Another of my officers noticed that your son was being mistreated, and reported the situation on the radio to me. I will personally screen your son."

He noticed that Nick was swaying a bit from being on his feet for so long. "Can you help your son back into his wheelchair? This officer clearly needs more training on how to assist individuals with special needs, and I personally will make sure that this incident is written up."

He was very kind to Nick, and within just a few minutes we were on our way to our gate.

As we were leaving, I heard the supervisor say to the officer, "What were you thinking? If you ever do that again, you'll be dismissed immediately."

I decided that day that I would take a firmer proactive stand advocating for Nick when we traveled. I knew the law, but I had allowed a bully to abuse his power. Now, I make it a point to talk to each person we approach about Nick's capabilities and ask them what they can do to help us with the screening process. I am calm but firm when communicating with the security personnel. This has worked very well.

Chapter Forty-Eight

In 2007, Arden, Karen and I created a candy business based on the Rocky Road Caramel Popcorn recipe that Karen had previously developed. We called it KK's Gourmet and we sent out samples to everyone we could think of, both business and personal contacts. We created a professional commercial kitchen in our home by remodeling our second kitchen. Nick worked with us. His job was to watch the popcorn poppers and tell us when the kernels had stopped popping, so that our employees could turn off the machines and avoid burning the popcorn. He was also in charge of the music. We had an old jukebox full of forty-five records that he loved to play, so he would select the playlist. When the last of the six songs were just about finished, he would run over to the machine and select six others. It was fun to work together.

The national economy took a nosedive in October 2008. It has even been called a crash. Our major corporate customers for our popcorn decided that they weren't going to be able to send out holiday gifts. Revenue was down so we didn't hire the seasonal holiday employees.

One afternoon, Karen and I were making popcorn in the candy kitchen while Nick was manning the jukebox. He had been particularly defiant for a couple of days and I was frustrated with him like any other kid, he wasn't listening to me, and I was upset, just like any other mom. The difference was that he was acting like a five-year-old in a twenty-nine-year-old body.

He was bored and wanted to go upstairs to his room but since he was so unsteady walking around, he wasn't allowed to navigate the stairs by himself. I told him that I would help him go upstairs in ten minutes, when I could take a break from our manufacturing process.

Nick didn't like that answer. He got up and quickly headed for the stairs.

I yelled at him to stop, and told him sit back down. He turned and reluctantly sat down.

With a voice full of frustration, he asked, "Why you do this to me?"

I looked at him, shook my head, and didn't answer.

He could tell I was upset. "Mommy, I love you."

I was so tired and frustrated I yelled back at him, "Do you really, Nick? Do you really love me? Sometimes, I don't think that you love me at all by the way you act toward me."

Shocked, he sat there for a few seconds. Then he stood up and raced over to the jukebox, punched in three numbers, hurried back to his chair and sat down.

Looking straight into my eyes, something he rarely did, he said, "You hear this, Mommy, you hear this."

A song began. "Look into my eyes, you will see what you mean to me." He chose Bryan Adam's song, "Everything I Do, I Do It for You."

As the last notes faded, I sobbed, still looking into my son's eyes.

Softly I said, "I hear it, Nick. I understand. I love you too."

He nodded, and the tears ran down my cheeks.

I just experienced the one thing that I have been wanting since his birth. I communicated with my son, heart to heart, soul touching soul, with no misunderstanding. He didn't articulate his feelings with words, but the message came through loud and clear.

I was grateful that we were able to financially provide Nick with whatever he needed at the time. However, I was concerned about some possible time in the future when he might need some services that would be denied because he was not on the Waiver program.

Mary Kanter, our DDD Case Manager, reapplied for the Waiver on our behalf. Again, we were turned down. Lack of funding was the reason. It didn't seem right. Because of a clerical error made by a previous case manager when he was six years old, Nick was being denied access to certain services to which he was otherwise entitled.

In addition to this problem with Nick's services funding, we learned that we were being forced by our state legislature to be signed up as independent providers with DDD to be paid for our caregiving hours. Currently we were employees of Special Care Agency, the licensed care provider agency owned by our friend Sally Coomer. Even Sally couldn't have her care provider hours for her daughter managed by her own agency. She had to sign up as an independent provider with DDD as well, in order to be paid for her care hours for Becky. It was ridiculous, but there was nothing any of us could do about it.

Nick wanted his thirtieth birthday party in Ireland at the home of my cousin who owns a lovely nineteen-room B&B between Carndonagh and Malin. My mom and many of our friends came from the States.

The party was magical. We had singing and dancing and great *craic*, Gaelic for good time.

The guests included not only our visitors from the US, but many local family and relations, neighbors, our friends from the O'Dochartaigh Reunion committee and the LDS Church in Derry.

Nick walked around from group to group with my help and frequent rests. He introduced people to one another.

It was a great night. We got back home in the wee hours of the morning with a very tired but happy young man.

As we were putting him to bed, he hugged me and said, "Thank you, Mom. I love my birthday party."

"It was wonderful. I loved it too. So many people who love you were there.

He drifted off to sleep with a big smile.

We were invited to a party honoring our friend Paddy Bogside Doherty in Derry City, Northern Ireland. Paddy had been awarded an honorary doctorate from Magee University because of his legendary civil rights work in Northern Ireland. As is the tradition in Ireland, a sing song had started.

Nick wanted to sing too. Arden and I tried to quiet him, but Paddy said, "Let the man sing!"

Nick chose "The Town I Loved So Well." It was written by composer and musician, Phil Coulter, a famous son of Derry City himself. A long song with many verses, it tells the story of the difficult time during The Troubles and the immutable spirit of the local Irish.

Paddy pulled up a chair across from Nick. All of a sudden, the room went quiet. Everyone paid complete attention. I was worried that Nick would get nervous or shy, so Arden knelt down beside him in case he needed any help.

He didn't. He sang the whole song, in full voice, with a stunning smile on his face, looking straight at Paddy the whole time. Neither Arden nor I would have been any help; we were both sitting there with tears streaming down our faces. We couldn't have sung a note.

Paddy exclaimed, "This clearly disabled Yank just sang our song to us."

Another voice rang out, "I don't think I know all the words!"

Amongst the sustained applause for Nick's rendition of their local anthem, Paddy stood up with tears in his own eyes and embraced Nick.

I heard him whisper in Nick's ear, "Thank you, son, thank you."

Paddy mentioned that night with great fondness whenever we visited him over the ensuing years.

PART TEN

Dancing Slowly

Chapter Forty-Nine

Nick is most comfortable when things are the same. That was difficult to do on our epic road trip of 2016, but we tried to eat at the same restaurant chains and stay in the same hotel chains. One afternoon as Arden and Nick headed to the bathroom in McDonald's, Nick stopped and looked at the disabled sticker on the door.

"The handicapped door?"

"Yes, Nick, just for you."

"I handicapped? Why I handicapped?"

"We can talk about it later in the car with mom, right now we need to get you into the bathroom."

Once we were back on the road, Arden mentioned Nick's question.

Placing my hand on Nick's shoulder, I asked, "Do you mind being called handicapped?"

"No."

"Do you know why you are handicapped?"

"Because Heavenly Father make me."

Again, we experienced his profound wisdom. I wish I was just as accepting of my handicaps. I know that this term is not currently politically correct. I use it here because it is what Nick uses to talk about himself.

It was more complicated to travel with Nick than it had been in prior years. Slowly, as his capabilities deteriorated, his accommodating equipment increased. We now constantly have a transport wheelchair available and use a bath lift daily to assist him in the bathroom. Some of the typical road trip places we didn't stop and get out of the car, for logistical reasons.

In Memphis, at Graceland, we just drove through the parking lot listening to the Elvis station, and in Nashville we drove around the city streets at night for a couple of hours. With the windows rolled down, we heard all the variety of music spilling out of the bars creating a cacophony of sound.

Driving back to the hotel, Nick exclaimed, "I have a concert in Nashville."

It had been a concert. A private concert.

We stayed for a week in Park City visiting with a few of our kids and grandkids while they were on vacation there. The time-share complex had a giant accessible pool and Nick vigorously played games in the water with the others.

One evening, we headed over to the pool after dinner. Arden took Nick into the restroom before going into the pool. I was waiting just outside so I could help get Nick into the water when Arden yelled out.

"Nick's seizing. He has fallen forward in the stall."

"Do you need me to come in there and help you."

"No, there is a kind man here that has helped me get Nick back into his wheelchair. We'll be right out."

"Do you have his backpack in there?"

"No, I left it in the condo."

Arden appeared in the doorway of the restroom holding Nick in his chair.

"How often have the cluster's been?"

"About every three minutes. Let's get him quickly back to the condo so we can start the rescue meds."

We both pushed the wheelchair back toward the condo, each of us holding onto a side of Nick so that he wouldn't pitch forward onto the ground. We laid him down on his bed and started his meds, used the magnet for the Vagus Nerve Stimulator (VNS), and began our usual seizure routine.

"This freaked me out, Arden!"

"Me too. He has never had a seizure this late in the evening time before."

"Arden, every day, for all of these years, I have always felt relieved when we got past ten or eleven in the morning seizure free. That meant we were clear for the day. Now we have a new normal, and I don't like it."

"I know, we will now need to look for seizure activity all day long, not just the mornings."

Even our grandkids were affected by Nick's seizure. Eight-year-old Cassidy asked me, "Why does Nick have a seizure every time we have a family reunion?"

I tried to explain to her that Nick had seizures a lot of times; it wasn't just when we were together.

Dr. Doherty told us he believed that the prolonged exposure to high altitude triggered Nick's seizure. We are sad that we won't be able to take him to higher altitudes anymore.

Chapter Fifty

Martha Jones had been watching Nick one night a week for over ten years to give Arden and I some respite. For many years we said that it would be magnificent if she could be Nick's full-time caregiver. In August 2010 she said that she was ready to make a change. She left her day job at Special Care Agency and came to work for us full time. Martha is a five-foot nothing powerhouse. She is such an extraordinary person and Nick loves her very much. Within a week she had our house and our schedule in shape. It's a great blessing to our family to have extraordinary people like Martha in our lives.

One afternoon, Nick started seizing. By 6:00 p.m., after talking to Dr. Glass multiple times and following our seizure medicine protocols, we transported him by ambulance to Evergreen Hospital in Kirkland. Nick experienced his last seizure in the ambulance, but the Emergency Room staff decided to keep him for observation until after 11:00 p.m.

On the way home, Arden looked at Nick sleeping in the back and then at me.

"Have you noticed how often Nick has seizures around his birthday in August. Dr. Glass adjusts his prescriptions and we go merrily along for six to eight months until Nick seizes again."

"I have noticed that. I hope that he stays in that pattern."

Unfortunately, Nick starting having cluster seizures every few days. We had an additional complication—he vomited in the midst of the seizures, every five minutes or so.

Arden, Martha, and I took turns sitting by his bedside.

One morning Martha asked, "Eva, do you think the oral rescue medicines we are giving him are actually being ingested since he keeps vomiting."

"I don't know. I think so. The seizures usually stop after a few hours along with the vomiting. So I think that the medicines are working."

"I noticed that he has the dry heaves coming and going for about twenty minutes. Do you think those are seizures too? When he is done, he falls asleep for hours just like when he has had a grand mal seizure."

"I asked Dr. Glass about that, Martha, and he isn't sure that they are seizures, but we are using the rescue meds as if they are."

We were talking to Dr. Glass almost every day. It took over four weeks to get Nick's seizure medicines to the correct blood levels to stop the cluster seizures and the vomiting. It was the longest thirty-two days of our lives.

Nick spent most of those days in his bedroom. Even on Sundays, he wanted to stay in bed and not go to church. Some days he would waken as his normal happy self, and then all of a sudden, around midday, he'd grow quiet, less interactive. Suddenly he'd be unable to walk on his own and he would tell us that his feet were asleep. He'd be very tired and want to lay down. We spent most of those days fearful that either the seizure episodes would start or, if they had already begun, afraid that they wouldn't stop.

At the beginning of October, even though Nick's seizures hadn't calmed down yet, Arden sent me over to Ireland for ten days. We are both very aware of each other and notice when the other one is getting overwhelmed. We have learned to be generous and supportive of each other. It has been a great blessing to us that we haven't fallen apart at the same time.

Arden and I do miss each other while on those solo trips, but we understand that caregiving can be exhausting and stressful, and it is valuable to have other life experiences for balance. It helps to give us perspective, rejuvenate our spirits and then when we return home we are prepared to reengage and pick up where we left off.

After being on high alert for a month, it was so strange to be alone in the quiet of our home in Donegal. I went on long walks, visited with friends and family, made simple meals, and took long showers. I did whatever I felt like doing every day for ten days. In the middle of my trip, I flew to Liverpool to visit my cousin in North Wales for a few days. My trip was both healing and centering. The trip refilled my physical and emotional reservoirs, so that I was able to jump back into the maelstrom of my life.

Dr. Glass told us that he wanted Nick evaluated at Swedish Hospital with a week-long video-EEG to try to discover what was going on with him since his seizure activity had escalated and was uncontrolled.

I made arrangements to stay with Nick in the hospital. After we checked in, EEG leads were hooked up to Nick's head. An around-the-clock video was taken of him in his hospital bed to analyze electronically and visually what was happening to Nick. Dr. Michael Doherty, the epileptologist who administered the test, started Nick on melatonin daily at bedtime in the hope that better sleep might reduce Nick's seizures.

Dr. Doherty came in to talk to us when Nick was ready to be discharged. There was no conclusive evidence as to why Nick's seizures had changed in frequency and severity. He believed Nick had sleep apnea, which can increase seizures if left untreated. He recommended an overnight sleep study. He also suggested that we follow up with Dr. Glass but said that he would be happy to see Nick too.

We talked it over with Dr. Glass and decided that it was a good time to change doctors. Dr. Doherty had a very caring attitude and we all liked him. His connection with Swedish Epilepsy Center was key. It was a poignant decision for us, and we have continued consulting with Dr. Glass on an annual basis, but from November 2010, Dr. Doherty has been making the treatment decisions.

Nick and I stayed at the hospital's "hotel room" for the sleep study. I got him into his pajamas and they put electrodes on his head just like during an EEG. Nick was used to sleeping on his side in a very dark room. The room wasn't completely dark and they wanted him to lie on his back. I wanted him to sleep at least a little while so all of our effort wouldn't be in vain. He kept talking to me. I didn't feel like either of us had slept at all, but I guess he slept enough for them to get their data, because he was diagnosed with sleep apnea.

We have many friends with C-PAPs, Constant Positive Air Pressure machines. It can be difficult to fall asleep with a strong wind blowing in your face. We were relieved when the sleep doctor ordered an A-PAP, an Automatic Positive Air Pressure machine. These machines start out at a lower pressure when you're falling asleep and automatically titrate to the pressure required by your body during sleep to keep a positive airway.

When Nick was being fitted for his mask, I noticed that it looked similar to the masks worn by naval aviators. Since Nick's favorite movie is *Top Gun* and he loves Maverick, I had an idea.

"Nick, you are getting a *Top Gun* mask. You will wear it each night when you sleep, just like Maverick wears when he is flying airplanes."

The technician picked up on my idea and said, "Here is your *Top Gun* mask, Nick. I need to make sure that it will fit just like Mavericks mask fits him."

"Can I carry it to the car, Mom?"

On the way home, he kept saying, "I got a *Top Gun* mask, just like Maverick."

"Yes, Nick, you do. You need to wear it all night, okay?"

"Okay, Mom. I got a *Top Gun* mask."

We got him into bed with the machine set up and the mask in place and then realized that he couldn't talk very well to say his prayers. So, we took it all off him, he prayed, and we got him set up again. We turned off the light, said good night and shut the door.

Arden and I stood on the other side of the door, straining to hear if anything was going on that needed our intervention. The machine was very quiet and all seemed well with Nick, so we peeked in one more time and went to bed ourselves. Nick had not been sleeping through the night for a couple of years. Looking back, he probably was being woken up by his sleep apnea. We were all sleep deprived.

Dr. Doherty had instructed us to be very exacting in the times that we administered Nick's medicine and consistent with bedtime. That first night with the A-PAP machine we put him into bed just before 10:00 p.m. and we woke up at 8:00 a.m. with no nighttime disturbance. Upon waking, my first thought was intense. *It is already daylight. He never woke us up. What if something bad has happened to Nick?*

Frightened, I told Arden that we needed to go into his room together. Slowly we opened the door, only to hear Nick quietly breathing in and out through his mask. He had slept through the entire night. It was a miracle. He still loves his *Top Gun* mask and still sleeps all night.

Nick's seizure outbreaks continued to be a grave concern. Dr. Doherty decided to do a lumbar puncture to rule out other possible reasons for the seizures. Any medical procedure can be scary, but when you add in physical and mental disabilities for the patient, they're nerve wracking. A lumbar puncture required him to lie on his side without moving, while the needle was inserted into his spine between the lumbar vertebrae to remove a sample of cerebrospinal fluid. I was concerned that he wouldn't be able to follow the directions necessary to complete the procedure.

Nick was cooperative and held very still. He seemed to understand that this was a very serious procedure and we all hoped we would get some answers. We did learn that Nick didn't have any of the serious conditions the doctors were afraid he might have, but the tests didn't show why his seizures were suddenly so hard to control.

Chapter Fifty-One

Nick had a follow-up appointment in the sleep clinic after two months. Our only concern was the open sores on his nose and face. We had taken pictures to document this. The doctor was appalled. He said that the sores were pressure sores because Nick's mask was too tight. It had not been fitted correctly. He explained that there were many mask types and that as long as there were no air leaks, the mask was sufficiently tight. It didn't need to be so tight that he developed pressure sores.

I felt horrible. Many mornings when we got him up, we noticed reddened skin around his eyes and on his nose, but the skin usually faded to his normal color by mid-morning. We didn't know there was something wrong. I really hate it when Nick suffers because I don't understand something.

When we got home from the appointment, Arden talked to the supervisor of the woman who had fit Nick's mask.

"Mr. Gremmert, I am so sorry."

"I told your employee that the mask was extremely tight on Nick's face, but she insisted that it was correct. Her mis-fitting caused Nick months of pain and suffering because he couldn't articulate that it wasn't comfortable. Over time his skin was compromised and my son experienced the trauma of pressure sores."

We have not had a recurrence since Nick's mask has been fitted correctly.

During our October 2011 appointment with Dr. Doherty, he recommended genetic testing for Nick. He prescribed a blood test for the MTHFR mutation. Methylenetetrahydrofolate reductase (MTHFR) is an enzyme that is encoded by the MTHFR gene.

Mutations in this gene are associated with MTHFR deficiency, which may result in intellectual disability, psychosis, weakness, ataxia, spasticity, and homocystinuria due to elevated blood levels of homocystine.

Nick tested positive for the mutation and began taking methylfolate, a folic acid, to help combat complications, specifically the heart-related ones. An MTHFR mutation is associated with poor methylation and enzyme production. MTHFR mutations affect every person differently, sometimes contributing to hardly any noticeable symptoms at all, while other times leading to serious, long-term health problems.

My mom became unable to care for herself suddenly after New Year's Day. We took her to the hospital, where she was diagnosed with cancer. It was of an undetermined origin and had ravaged her body. She never went back home. It was tax season. My sister Rosie and Arden attended the various doctor and treatment appointments. I visited with her in-between client appointments. Those hours were precious to both of us. She was grateful to see me. I was trying to capture all the visiting time possible, as if I could store up time, saving it for when she was no longer here. Mom died just four short months after her diagnosis.

Martha was an unbelievable support through that difficult time. The main caregiver for Nick, she also took care of the rest of us. She worked 8:30 a.m. to 4:30 p.m. all week and still stayed late on Tuesdays so that Arden and I had our date night. There were lots of things each week for her to do, depending, of course, on how well Nick was doing. Monday, they did chores at home and went grocery shopping. Tuesday, it was lunch at Ixtapa, our favorite restaurant in Carnation, and the preschool music class that Nick loved. Wednesday was story time at the library. Nick chose his reading books for the week. On Thursdays our friend and yoga teacher, Kelley Rush, came and taught a private yoga class. We moved the dining room table and chairs off to the side and put yoga mats on the floor. Anyone at our home on Thursday mornings was invited join the class. Nick loves yoga, and sometimes he is even a bit competitive during the various poses. That is not very yogic, but we sure have fun. We purchased a stationary recumbent exercise bike for Nick. This is especially useful on those days when he can't walk very well.

With all the new treatments and intervention, Nick's seizures dramatically decreased. When Dr. Doherty gave Nick the okay to resume airline travel in 2012, we took him at his word. Over the next three months, we flew on five trips.

Arden and I took Nick and Martha to Ireland for a three-week trip.

In November, our family gathered in Louisville for my granddaughter Lacey's baptism. Nick's wings were no longer clipped.

As our family grew, we began holding our own family reunions. It takes a lot of organizing to arrange for four separate busy households to get together somewhere for a brief vacation. Each family has their own interests and individual criteria of what would make a successful reunion. We had to consider not only Nick's accessibility needs, but also local activities that would interest everyone. Even with these challenges, we have created enjoyable, memorable trips over the years.

Our kids decided that for 2013, we would go to Lake Chelan, a popular vacation spot in eastern Washington. Arden and I had never been there before. Karen had found a large vacation rental home that met all our needs; it even had a heated pool. We experienced a glorious time with everyone in the same house. We swam, took lots of pictures, ate spectacular food and laughed a lot. Nick didn't want to leave when it was time to go. For a long time, he kept asking us if we were going back.

I have found during the tough times in my life, when it is difficult to get through the current challenges, that having these precious memories of great times really helps me. They give me perspective concerning the balance of life. We all have challenges that will stretch us to the maximum and we also have intense moments of joy that bless our lives. Experiencing the bitter makes the sweet even sweeter.

In September 2013, Arden and I planned a trip to visit with my cousin in Grand Cayman. Upon landing, we automatically turned on our phones. We both noticed that from the time our flight had left the States and we had turned off our phones, they had blown up with text messages and voice mails from all of our kids. We were very worried, but the flight attendant was telling everyone that phones had to remain turned off until we cleared Customs, so we didn't call any of the kids.

Arden decided to go into the restroom and use his phone. He wanted to find out what was happening. Nick had started seizing just as our flight left Charlotte, North Carolina. They hadn't stopped yet, and Troy and Derek were enroute to help her. Karen was gathering up her kids to go out there too. Arden came back out of the restroom and told me what was going on. It was our worst nightmare. We were so far away. We felt so helpless.

The kids and Martha urged us to stay, while Arden and I both felt we should return home. Since we were flying stand-by, Arden returned to the restroom to ask Ryan about the possibility of listing us on a flight out of Grand Cayman that day. Ryan said that we needed to clear Customs no matter what we decided to do about going home. He said he would investigate the flights and we should call him when we were through Customs.

Arden believes that we were only standing in that line another ten minutes before we were through, but I feel it was much longer. In any case, it was certainly a horrible time. There we were, hoping to have a wonderful romantic weeklong break from our daily lives in a glorious tropical paradise with dear friends. Instead, we were stuck in a dreary room inching slowly forward, all the while worrying about our sweet Nick suffering in his bedroom in Carnation. Everyone around us in line was excited and happy, looking forward to their vacation, while Arden attempted to comfort me. I just couldn't stop crying. One or both of us had always been with Nick before when he had seizures.

Finally, it was our turn at the counter. We successfully answered the Customs officer's questions and were on our way through the door out into the sunshine.

Arden dialed Ryan as we made our way over to my cousin's car. I explained the situation to my cousin. Most of the time our kids don't tell us what to do, but I could tell that Ryan was being persistent. He believed that we should stay and have our vacation. Initially Arden and I were both resistant to that plan. Ryan explained that we wouldn't be home until the next day anyway, the medical crisis would be over, and Nick was in very competent hands with people that loved him. He mentioned that the flights weren't very open and it wasn't certain that we would get home the next day. Arden kept saying, "I don't know...I just don't know, Ryan."

We had flight benefits on an airline that didn't fly every day to and from Grand Cayman. It would be at least two days before we could possibly get a flight back to the US.

Then out of the corner of my eye, I noticed that my cousin had put our bags into his car. He had reached the same conclusion as Ryan. We told Ryan that we were staying at least for the next few days and got into the car.

We talked to everyone back home once we got to the apartment. Nick had stopped seizing and was finally asleep. Martha sounded frazzled, but the other kids were helping her. Arden and I decided that we were going to enjoy ourselves. It would be a shame to have this chance and not take advantage of this great opportunity for the week. We Skyped with Nick once he woke up and that was very comforting to me. It was a relief to see how our kids rallied to help care for their brother. The experience showed that he will be well cared for if and when something happens to us.

The next April, Arden, Nick, and I went to Ireland for two weeks for a family wedding. While we were on our trip, Martha had a planned surgery. She expected to be fully recovered by the time we got home. We were looking forward to that.

Martha had worked full-time for us for almost four years. She really did take care of Arden and I while she was caring for Nick. We were all devastated when the doctor told her that she couldn't physically continue caregiving as a job.

When you have a family member with special needs, it is very easy to rely on the caregivers for more than just the physical care they provide. Martha is like my sister.

A few months after she recovered, she decided that she could still come on Tuesdays for our "date night." We had to adjust a few things to make it work. We fed Nick dinner and had him upstairs ready to watch game shows with Martha.

It wasn't ideal, but it worked out. Nick and Martha got to spend time together while Arden and I got a break. Nick often asks her, "Why you not work here, Marfa?"

To which, Martha replies, "I have to work for Special Care Agency now, Nick."

Exasperated, Nick always says, "That Special Care Agency," as if the situation was the Agency's fault.

Our family encouraged us to take another trip together, but Arden and I still hadn't recovered from the horrific experience we had when we landed in Grand Cayman the previous year. We just couldn't imagine going through that again. Besides Martha wasn't able to give us overnight respite anymore.

Chapter Fifty-Two

I was surprised how awkward it was to have Nick out in public, in a wheelchair. Arden and I had taken him on multiple long trips. The most difficult time we had was in the United States. I guess I was spoiled by the treatment that we had received in Europe and I erroneously expected the same at home.

I was shocked at the lack of accommodation not only in accessibility but also from other people. Sometimes people were not helpful or kind. They would cross in front of us while we were walking straight ahead and then yell at me because I "ran the wheelchair into their legs." When I tried to explain that they had walked in front of us the retort was, "You should watch out and be more careful."

It was happening all the time, so I began to walk in front of the wheelchair with Arden and Nick close on my heels. Like the old-time town crier, I called out, "Wheelchair coming through!" I got some dirty looks, but at least no one was yelling at us.

At some point during 2014, Nick gained the ability to sometimes tell us that he was having seizures. One morning he said he didn't want to go to church. He put up one arm, as if he was having a partial seizure, and said, "Look, I having a seizure. Not I go to church."

It wasn't a seizure. I said he was going to church. I watched him carefully as we dressed him that day. I rode to church facing him in the back seat while Arden drove, so that I wouldn't miss it if anything was happening.

We got him in his wheelchair, and I walked backward in front of him into the building. Just as we entered the foyer, he had a hand flip. (That is what we call it, when he is seated and one or both of his arms fly up involuntarily and uncontrollably.) It was a seizure. By the time we wheeled him over to the couch he'd had another one, and a whole-body twitch. Somehow, he had understood that he was going to have seizures that morning. I felt horrible for not believing him when he tried to tell me.

Martha was very worried about us. She kept mentioning that we still hadn't hired anyone to replace her. My response was always the same: "We just can't find anyone who can replace you. You're one of a kind."

She would murmur and tell me not to be silly. I think that she was a little frustrated because she knew that she was right. We did need someone.

In November, Martha bravely brought up the subject again.

"I know a fabulous caregiver by the name of Debi Teter."

"I think I know her. Wasn't she the live-in caregiver for that woman in town with special needs who recently passed away?"

"That's her."

"She has always been kind to those she is caring for. I'd be interested in interviewing her."

"I'll set up the interview and come along to facilitate and answer questions."

"That'll be a good idea since you know all of us so well."

Arden and I both were impressed with Deb. She was a dedicated, hardworking and experienced caregiver. We wondered how she would handle our Nick. When we brought him downstairs to introduce them, Nick grabbed her hand and gave her a sloppy, slobbery kiss on the back of it.

I watched and waited. *How will she react?*

Debi laughed, grabbed a paper towel to wipe her hand, and said, "Nick, you don't need to do that, do you? Now give me a nice kiss," as she stuck her hand back out toward him.

He carefully kissed her hand, no mess. I was relieved. She had exhibited just the right level of firmness, coupled with compassion, and had thrown in some humor. We hired her.

Within just a few weeks, Deb became a valued employee and was quickly becoming a dear friend. Sometimes in life you meet someone that you instantly click with. That was Deb and me. It seemed that every day we found something else that we could share with each other. It's not like we had hours and hours to talk; these gems were discovered during brief interchanges in the middle of the work day. We had similar ideas on most everything and shared stories from one another's lives.

At the end of January 2015, while visiting us for dinner, Arden's father had a massive heart attack. It was very traumatic and scary, especially when the paramedics took him by ambulance to the hospital. Arden and his mom followed while I stayed home with Nick. I sat with him on the couch and talked to him about his grandpa.

"Nick, Grandpa is very sick and we will go visit him in the hospital when he feels a little better."

With a sincere forcefulness that I rarely saw in my son, he looked me right in the eyes and said firmly, "Mom, Grandpa dying. He go to heaven to be with Jesus."

I knew that it was true. I didn't need to prepare Nick for anything; he was preparing us for the rapidly approaching inevitable event.

Although my father-in-law never regained consciousness, he waited long enough for all of his kids to get to the hospital and say goodbye.

The next day, we gathered around his bed as he drew his last breath.

Within seconds, Nick said, "Grandpa's gone to heaven."

Nick was right; his grandfather was gone. We stayed for a while, hugging and crying and even laughing.

As we wheeled Nick out of the hospital room, he turned back to where his grandpa's body was lying on the bed and said, "Goodbye, Grandpa, see you later, have a good time in heaven."

We all laughed as the tears streamed down our faces. Nick knew better than any of us what had just happened.

Chapter Fifty-Three

The next time we saw Dr. Doherty for our semiannual visit he asked the usual questions and then said, "I want to discuss your objections to Nick getting a VNS."

A VNS is a surgically implanted Vagus Nerve Stimulator. Arden and I must have had the "deer in the headlights" look on our faces.

The doctor turned to me first. "Eva, what are you specifically concerned about?"

"My main concern is the risk that comes with having surgery. Having Nick undergo anesthesia has always been a fearful thing for me. It can have such a disastrous effect on him because of potential drug interaction."

The doctor turned to Arden.

"I am concerned because there is no guarantee of any benefit to having the VNS."

"Arden, the technology has advanced dramatically since I first mentioned it over four years ago in October of 2010. I want you both to understand that Nick's escalating seizures are a greater risk to his continued well-being than the VNS surgery."

With that knowledge, Arden and I decided Nick should have the procedure, and it was scheduled for the end of the summer, several months away.

One Tuesday night, Arden and I went out to dinner for date night. We had just gotten our food when my phone rang. Martha sounded breathless, which put me on high alert.

"I've called 911—"

I immediately interrupted her. "What happened, is he seizing?"

"No, he's not having seizures—"

I interrupted again. "So what's happening then?"

Poor woman, it would have been much easier if I had just let her talk.

"Nick has fallen backward and split open the back of his head on the edge of a piece of furniture in his bedroom. He never lost consciousness, but he needs stitches. The EMTs are already here, and they have called the ambulance to transport him to the hospital."

"We are leaving immediately. Have the ambulance wait for me so I can accompany Nick to the hospital."

We got the food packed up to go, paid our bill, and drove home. That twenty-five-minute drive seemed to take forever. We pulled into our driveway, where a crowd had gathered. It included two fire trucks, the ambulance, and a couple of other emergency vehicles, all with lights flashing and their personnel standing around the back of the ambulance. A few of our concerned neighbors were also there. The firemen had just gotten Nick down the stairs and into the ambulance. I hugged Martha and went around to the side door to get in. The driver asked me to ride up front, but I insisted that I needed to be with Nick.

Nick heard me and turned his head toward me. "Mom, I fell."

"Nick, you are okay, we will get you fixed up at the hospital." I hugged him and said, "Mommy will be right back."

I grabbed his backpack full of his medical information from Martha, hugged her again, and got my purse from the car, just as Arden brought my phone charger from the house. Since we had been to the hospital many times with Nick, it was just like a well-rehearsed ballet. We knew what to do to make the whole trip smoother.

According to the technician that irrigated the wound in the Emergency Room, it was an "awesome" cut. Arden and I didn't think that it was so awesome, but it *was* a clean straight line that sutured well. Nick didn't seem bothered by it; he just kept telling us that he fell. I realized that he didn't know what had happened to him, so I asked if he wanted me to take a picture of his head so he could see his cut.

When we showed him the picture, he was very somber. Tilting his head slightly, he said, "I have a cut."

That was it. From then on, he said, "I have a cut," not "I fell." Seeing the photograph of the back of his head helped him process what had happened. This incident further reinforced our commitment to always be near him.

In June, we had another semiannual Arden Gremmert family reunion. This time Karen had found a cute house with a separate small cottage in Seabrooke at the Washington beaches. The men in the family decided to go deep sea fishing. Arden decided to stay back with the rest of us.

Nick started seizing shortly after he woke up that morning. I was grateful that Arden was there. No one panicked. The smaller grandchildren either stood patiently watching while a seizure was happening or played quietly upstairs as the adults were engaged in caring for Nick. Once the seizing stopped and Nick was asleep, the little boys played with their toys on the floor next to the couch were Nick was sleeping. They wanted to be able to check on him to make sure he was okay. It was so cute. The desire to care for Nick had moved down to another generation.

One Friday in August, Deb mentioned that she was very tired. She was coughing a lot and we both thought that she might have a cold. She called on Sunday evening to say that she had pneumonia and wouldn't be at work for a few days. She was taking an antibiotic and hoped to be feeling better by the end of the week.

She still wasn't well enough to come to work on Nick's birthday on Wednesday, so we took him to her house so that she could wish him happy birthday. She had ordered a couple of airplanes for his birthday present. Nick loved them.

The next day, I took Deb to a follow-up doctor's appointment. She had not responded to the prescription, so the doctor prescribed another antibiotic and referred her to a lung specialist.

There was a huge hole without Deb's presence at our house. Arden and I managed everything okay, but the feeling of support Deb provided was missing and we all felt a bit lost.

A couple of weeks passed. Debi was in and out of the hospital. They hadn't discovered the source of the infection, and now she had fluid around her heart too. Nick's VNS implant surgery was approaching. He wanted to see Deb before he went into the hospital, but she wasn't up to visitors so we talked to her on the phone.

Chapter Fifty-Four

The Sunday before Nick's surgery we called a family fast. In the LDS faith, we believe that combining fasting and prayer is a powerful way to petition God. As we abstain from food and water for the duration of two meals, our entire being has the opportunity to focus more clearly on spiritual things and on our connection with God. It's a great comfort to feel others participating in a fast with a common supplication to Heaven. Our common prayer was for a successful surgery, and that the VNS would make a significant difference in Nick's health.

In my morning prayers the day of the surgery, I had the distinct impression that I should look for miracles that day. It gave me a purpose in the midst of my anxiety.

The first miracle I noted was that Nick woke up easily and wasn't having seizures. As we drove into Seattle during the morning rush hour, the traffic was heavy but not stopped. Blessing number 2. We arrived at Swedish Hospital about fifteen minutes early and easily found a parking place. Number 3.

The staff was kind and caring toward both Nick and me. The gal who printed Nick's hospital wristband came out from behind the desk to put it on him. She asked him which wrist he wanted it on, and made sure it wasn't too tight. She was so tender with him. Number 4.

As we made our way to the Outpatient Surgery department, I was concerned how we would meet up with Karen on such a large hospital campus. She was coming to the hospital to support us and was running a few minutes later than she had hoped. She told me not to worry about it, she would find us. Just as we got to the crossroads at the main hallway where we were to turn to head toward

Outpatient Surgery, Nick spotted Karen coming from the West parking garage. Number 5.

We hugged, and I told Karen about my task of looking for miracles. I told her that I was counting them, and meeting her was number 5.

Karen laughed. "Mom, I think that you'll find that the number of miracles today will be too many to number. Just notice them and feel the gratitude in your heart."

She was right, and my heart swelled with gratitude.

When we got to Outpatient Surgery waiting room, there were signs posted that said only one visitor was allowed with the patient in the presurgery room. Karen said that she would wait with Arden while I went with Nick to get him ready. That sounded like a good idea, but I had hoped that we would all be able to be with him.

When the nurse arrived to take Nick back to prep him for surgery, she looked a little surprised at his entourage.

I said, "We recognize the policy of one visitor with a patient, but could my husband Arden come back with me to help change Nick into the hospital gown? Dressing him is often a two-person job."

"That will be okay. Here is the open room."

The area around the bed inside the curtains was very tight and it was awkward for us to get Nick dressed in the space provided. The nurse came by twice to make sure that everything was okay. It must have looked funny for the curtains to be moving so much as Arden and I worked together to get Nick completely undressed and re-clothed in the hospital garb.

Nick's loud exclamation, "Why you do this to me?" when we took off his underwear, probably didn't help the situation.

Finally, we were done and he was lying calmly in the bed under the blankets. Arden and I were sweating. Since they would be transporting him in the hospital bed, I had piled all of the stuff into his wheelchair. Nick kept asking us what was happening, and Arden was quietly trying to calm him and explain what we were doing. A new nurse tripped over the wheelchair when she came into the curtained area. She asked us if she could take the wheelchair out into the hallway. We weren't comfortable with that; Nick's backpack contained all his seizure medicines and my purse was also hanging on the wheelchair.

I asked, "Can I take it out to our daughter in the waiting room?"

She looked surprised. "You have another family member here?"

"Since I am staying with Nick until he is ready to go into the surgery room, Karen came along to sit with her dad. She is our support person."

"Will you excuse me a minute, I'll be right back."

Five minutes later, she came back with Karen.

"We have a separate room for you all to use that will be more private and probably more comfortable for Nick. Please follow me."

There was enough room there for all of us. We were so grateful. Karen had been right; I couldn't count the number of miracles that day, they were compounding one upon another.

During our pre-op meeting with the surgeon, Dr. Gwinn, I requested that I be allowed to accompany Nick until the anesthetic was working and he was asleep, and also be allowed into the recovery room before he awoke. Dr. Gwinn explained that the decision was completely up to the nurses who ran the pre- and post-surgery unit. With that in mind, I humbly approached the head nurse with my request.

"Sometimes Nick's seizures seem to be brought on by anxiety and we want him to be as comfortable as possible. I know that is your goal too. I have accompanied Nick many times for a variety of procedures, including his lumbar puncture a few years earlier in this same hospital. I respect the other patient's privacy, as well as the need to stay out of the way of the hospital staff so they can do their jobs. My goal is to help keep Nick as calm as possible. I know this isn't your usual procedure like it is at Children's Hospital, but mentally Nick is just like a five-year-old, and it would be calming to him if you let me accompany him."

"Mrs. Gremmert, we'll allow you to go with Nick down to the pre-op area, even though it is unusual. And we'll call your cell phone when he's coming into the recovery room and you can join him there. We expect you to do what you have said you would."

"I assure you that my only desire is to help with the successful completion of this procedure for my son."

Another miracle. I was relieved.

Dr. Gwinn's surgical assistant came in to make sure that all was prepared.

"We will be taking Nick down in a few minutes and you can wait in the waiting room or the main lobby. Please check in with the attendants in the lobby so that they know you are there. There's a new monitor that will track Nick's progress through the morning. He's assigned a patient number, and the monitor shows where that patient is by their number."

"Dr. Gwinn had told me that if the nurses agreed, I could accompany Nick until he was asleep before the procedure and then I could go to the recovery room to be there when he awoke. I talked to the head nurse and she has made those arrangements."

"Mrs. Gremmert I'm not aware of that accommodation."

"Well, as you know, anxiety can bring on seizures and since we are here to insert the VNS to help control seizures, it doesn't make sense to bring an episode on now."

"I do agree with you, I just need to go check with someone."

Again, we waited. It seemed like a long time, but it was probably only a few minutes.

We got the okay from everyone for me to accompany Nick. Another miracle.

Nick and I said goodbye to Arden and Karen and began the journey to the surgery rooms. Nick wanted to hold my hand as we walked along. He kept asking the same questions and I gave him the same answers. I was glad I was with him. I wasn't sure where we ended up with all the twists and turns in the hallways, but eventually we arrived somewhere in the hospital basement.

A good-natured compassionate nurse introduced herself. She was going to be with Nick from this presurgery room, through the procedure, and into the post-operative area. That was a comfort to me.

She asked the usual questions to Nick. "What's your name, what's your birthday, what are you having done today?"

He did a good job answering and I filled in when his answer wasn't complete.

The nurse told Nick that she had a daughter just like him that was one year younger. That was a surprise. Here was a mother who could completely understand what I was going through. Truly a peer. I began to cry. She put her arm on my shoulder to comfort me and I said, "I'm not sad, it's just a comfort to know that you have this special experience that makes you uniquely qualified to care for my son while I won't be with him."

She smiled. "I understand. You can stay here until he's asleep, and I'll make sure that the post-operative staff call you when we're done." Another miracle.

She and I talked for a while as she got Nick ready, then the anesthesiologist came in to examine Nick. He explained what he would be doing to care for Nick and answered my questions. Then he pronounced Nick ready and began to move the bed. I didn't understand that he was preparing to head for the surgery room.

The nurse said, "Mrs. Gremmert, didn't you want Nick to be asleep before he left you?"

Startled, I said, "Yes, Dr. Gwinn said that you would begin administering the anesthetic before Nick went into the room."

The doctor stopped and said, "That isn't our usual procedure, but I can do that. Let me go and get the meds."

I was so grateful that the nurse was looking out for me as well as my son. Another miracle.

Nick became drowsy immediately after receiving the meds. I kissed him and watched them wheel him through the double doors.

Another pleasant nurse arrived to take me up to the main lobby waiting room. She showed me where I would return to when they called me. She would be in charge of Nick post-op, and I was grateful that she took the time to show me where to go.

Arden had texted me that they were in the cafeteria sitting in a booth waiting for the food area to open. I sat with them for a few minutes and explained all the awe-inspiring things that had occurred since Nick and I had left them. We marveled at all that had happened. I was hungry, and as I walked past the breakfast area, I had the impression that I should go to the hot food line. The only person standing at that counter was a man in a white lab coat. Consumed in my own thoughts about Nick and what was happening to him, I stood a little way back from the man, until I heard his voice. It was familiar. I stepped a little closer and looked at his face. I knew him.

"Steve?" I said. It was the father of one of my former skating students. I'd had more interaction with his wife during the time I taught their daughter, but I had met him many times at the rink and at competitions. He had always been a kind, soft-spoken man.

I knew that he was a doctor, and that he worked at Swedish. I had forgotten until that moment that he was a neuropathologist with a special interest in brain tumors and epilepsy. During the time that I knew the family, we had talked about Nick's seizures and the treatments we were using. Talking to him again in the cafeteria was so comforting. Not only did he know us, he was familiar with Dr. Gwinn and the procedure Nick was having.

He gave Dr. Gwinn's whole team a glowing recommendation and told me that Nick couldn't be in better hands. Running into him wasn't a coincidence. It was a huge miracle and I was comforted.

After we returned to the lobby waiting room, I looked at the Facebook post we had made that morning about Nick's surgery. There are always hundreds of "likes" and comments whenever we post something about Nick. He's loved by so many people. This particular day, it was humbling to read the many comments wishing him well, expressing love and telling us that people were praying for us. We really needed those prayers, and we felt supported to know that so many people across the world were thinking about our Nick.

My cell phone rang. It was time for me to join Nick. I made my way down the elevator and through the maze of hallways. He was still asleep when I got to his bedside but his brow was furrowed, and he was moaning and thrashing a bit.

I put my hand on his leg and whispered, "Nicky, Mommy is here."

He immediately calmed and was breathing normally.

The nurse said, "That's better. I'm glad you're here."

I was too. Nick's recovery was quick, and very soon we were upstairs with Arden and Karen, waiting to be discharged. We texted everyone that it had been a success and we headed home. He had to heal from the surgery for a month and then Dr. Doherty would turn the device on during a subsequent appointment.

Chapter Fifty-Five

A week later, we traveled to Salt Lake City for another annual doTERRA convention. Deb couldn't come on the trip with us; she was too ill. We visited her in the hospital before we went to Utah. Nick told her that he missed her and she should get well.

She said, "I'm trying to do that, Nick, I really am trying."

It was so strange that she was so sick and the doctors couldn't find the reason. It had been over three weeks since she had gone to the doctor the first time.

I called Deb's daughter Lisa repeatedly from Utah to get progress reports. Lisa worked in a hospital in Puyallup and had decided to move her mom there, in hopes of getting some diagnostic results.

Nick loved everything about the convention—all the people, the excitement, and the enthusiasm of the presenters. We stayed in a hotel across the street from the convention center, and that was much easier than the previous year.

After we got home, we tried to see Deb, but Lisa said that she was very tired and not seeing visitors. She was saving her strength to get well.

Sunday afternoon, Nick and I had returned from church, had lunch and were settled in to watch the pregame show for the Seahawks versus the Packers game on TV when Deb's daughter Lisa called. She was crying.

"The doctors said that she doesn't have much time…if you and Nick want to say goodbye, you'd better hurry."

Nick was a little resistant to moving after settling in to watch football until I told him that Deb was going to heaven, and we needed to hurry to say goodbye to her. While I had him in the bathroom before we left, I called Martha and Karen and asked if they would join me, since Arden was out of town.

Picking both of them up added about fifteen minutes to the trip to Good Samaritan Hospital in Puyallup, but I felt we would get there in time. It was a very surreal experience as I pushed Nick's wheelchair into the room. Deb was surrounded by four women I had never met before. Martha knew the family and went over to speak to Debi's sisters as Lisa greeted us and introduced herself. I told her that I was very sorry and we cried together.

Nick was trying to scoot his wheelchair closer to the hospital bed and I said, "Oh, I'm sorry, Nick. Let me help you."

I excused myself from Lisa and moved Nick to the side of the bed. I could tell that Debi was near the end. Her breathing was labored and she appeared unconscious.

Just as I was explaining to Nick that Deb was sleeping and we needed to talk softly to her, he reached out his hand and placed it on her arm. He said, "Hi, Debi, I here."

Her whole body turned slightly toward him. Her eyes didn't open but it was obvious that she was aware of Nick's presence. Then it was odd; he kept his hand on her arm but he turned his head to the left toward the corner of the room, away from Deb lying there in the bed. He began talking to her, telling her what he had done that day.

I told him to look at Deb and not at the corner. He emphatically said, "No, I talking to her."

Then I realized that he might be seeing something the rest of us weren't. Perhaps her spirit had left her body and she was standing in the corner. Nick was definitely sure that he was talking to her.

He then said, "I done. Mom, your turn."

I wheeled him back and stepped forward. *What can I say to my dear friend at this moment? She is leaving, and I can't imagine my life without her in it.*

I leaned down, hugged her, told her that I loved her, that I would miss her, and that she had made such a difference in our lives. We had met just ten months before but we had known each other well and loved each other deeply.

Nick touched my back and said, "Let's go."

I wheeled him toward the door as both Karen and Martha took their turns to say goodbye. As we were preparing to leave, Nick said, "Wait."

Turning back toward the bed he said, "Have a fun time in heaven, Debi. See you soon."

I was worried that he was confused. I tried to explain as we went to the car that when people go to heaven, they don't come back. I couldn't tell if he understood or not.

The drive back home was somber. We took turns telling Debi stories and talking about how wonderful she was. I dropped Martha and Karen home and turned on the radio to distract my thoughts. When we were about fifteen minutes from home, I heard my cell phone chime with a text. I pulled the car over in a parking lot, turned off the radio, and picked up my phone.

A two-word text was on my phone. "She's gone."

I began to sob. I put the phone down.

"Mommy, Debi is all better. She's in heaven with Jesus."

"Nick, I know that. I am just really sad."

He sat there quietly. After a few minutes, I drove the rest of the way home. I wished that Arden was there. I really wanted some comfort and I believed that I needed to be strong for Nick.

When we got home, I gathered up Nick's backpack and my purse and assisted Nick up the stairs. He waited as I struggled to get the front door open and turn off the security alarm. I was putting all the bags down as he stepped across the threshold and suddenly stopped.

I was just about to tell him to come in and shut the door when he excitedly said, "Oh, hi, Debi," as he looked straight into the room.

I turned in the direction Nick as staring. Although I didn't see anything, I knew my friend was there.

"I don't know how these things work, Debi, but if you can be assigned as one of Nick's guardian angels, I think that would be superb. We will miss you."

I knew that she had heard me, and I received a very special comfort that evening.

I believe that Debi visited Nick a few times over the next few days.

A couple of days later, Nick told me, "Mom, Debi said she couldn't come take care of me anymore, and she is okay."

I laughed and said that she wouldn't be able to bathe him or dress him or fix his food without her body, but that she could still visit him.

This type of experience was not new to Nick. He had made a special friend at Riverton Heights his first year of public school. The boy's name was Guy. Guy was a sweet little man who had a heart condition that is prevalent with Down Syndrome. Guy would always greet Nicky in the morning with a bright "Hi, Gicky" (he couldn't pronounce the N). Guy passed away a few years later. For years afterward, Nicky would randomly tell us, "Guy, say hi, Gicky." And we believe that Guy was still checking up on his friend Gicky.

Chapter Fifty-Six

Deb's daughter Lisa kept in contact with us as she prepared for her mother's memorial service. It helped me to have something to do. I missed Deb badly. Every day there were reminders in our home of things that she had done, drawers that she had organized, and caregiving procedures that she had implemented. I was very grateful that she had been in our lives. I just wished that it had been longer.

The morning of the memorial service, I was working on some tax files in the office and Arden had been raking some leaves outside. The service was scheduled for 1:00 PM, so we planned to leave about twelve forty-five. At about twelve fifteen, Arden came inside to get ready. I was surprised when he came into my office rather than going to take a shower. He was restless, pacing, and then he laid down on the floor.

"What is wrong?"

"I don't feel good."

He quickly got up off the floor and said, "That feels worse."

I finally looked up from my papers. He was rubbing his chest and was sweating. I went over to him.

"Please tell me what's happening, sweetheart."

"I don't know. I can't catch my breath. I'm a little nauseous. I feel this pressure..."

He rubbed his open palm over his chest, partway down his left arm and then back up to his jaw.

"You have just shown me the six classic signs of a heart attack. I am calling 911. You need to lie down."

I turned to the phone and started to dial, only to see him leaving the room.

"Where are you going?"

"I'm going downstairs to wait for the medics."

I hung up the phone without completing the call. I was so conflicted.

Nick's in his room and I can't leave him unattended because of the risk of falling if he tries to move around unassisted. Arden's having a heart attack. His dad died of a heart attack just a few months ago. What if Arden suddenly collapses as his father did.

"Nick, you need to stay in your room. Promise me you won't get up until I came back upstairs."

He didn't respond and I again yelled at him as I followed Arden downstairs, "Nick, promise me. It's really important. Promise me you'll stay there."

"Okay, Mom," floated down the stairs as I turned the corner and headed for the living room.

Arden was trying to lay down on the couch. He was in obvious pain.

"You need to lay on the floor near the door where I can see you when I called 911. They will have questions and I will need to observe you to answer them."

I dialed the number. The operator was tremendous. She was calm when I didn't feel calm. With very matter-of-fact questions she guided me through her information-gathering process. Emergency medical professionals have always been a great support to us every time we've needed them.

Arden wanted to get up to unlock the door for the EMTs but the 911 operator said that he needed to stay on the floor. She suggested that I put the phone down and unlock the door.

Arden said that the pain was diminishing, which was good news.

The operator stayed on the phone with me until the EMTs arrived. Meanwhile I had sent a text to our nearest neighbors, saying that Arden was having a heart attack and I had already called 911. I asked if one of them could come over to help. She replied that her husband Christian was coming right over. He arrived before the aid car did.

"What can I do?"

"Please go upstairs and be with Nick until we know what was going to happen. Make sure that he stays seated."

A few minutes later, the EMTs arrived. They did their evaluation and quickly determined that Arden needed to go to the hospital. I don't know how much time had passed. I felt separated from the experience, as if I was watching a movie as they loaded my husband on the gurney, took him out the door, and put him in the back of the ambulance. I told him that I would follow along after I got Nick ready to go. I knew that Arden was in good hands but as the ambulance drove out of the driveway, but I wondered if I would see him again, and how would I cope with caring for Nick on my own.

Christian was sensational. I couldn't seem to decide what to do next.

"Can I drive you guys to the hospital?"

"Yes, that'd be a good idea."

"What do we need to do to get ready?"

"I'll take Nick to the bathroom. While he is in there, I'll gather a few things that we'll need, like the cell phone chargers, as well as Nick's wheelchair and backpack."

I finished packing up everything but Nick still wasn't done.

"Do your kids know about Arden yet?"

I hadn't thought about that. Grateful for the reminder, I called the kids. Ryan lived on the East Coast, Derek was hunting in northeastern Washington State and Karen and her family were camping up north. No one was close by. It was hard to say the words, and I wanted to reassure them that their dad would be okay even though I didn't know that myself. I told them that I would keep them in the loop. I finished gathering everything and finally Nick was done. We were on our way.

By the time we arrived at the hospital, Arden looked much better. They had already started tests and had given him needed medication. Arden's two brothers were with him in the emergency room. Our family and friends rallied and even though it took a lot of coordinating, I was able to stay with Arden at the hospital for the next two days while he was there. Nick was with me during the daytime. In the evening, I drove him home, got him ready for bed, tucked him in, and then drove back to the hospital while someone stayed at the house with Nick until he woke up in the morning.

Arden had a mild heart attack and the cardiologist decided to place a stent into the left descending heart artery with the blockage. The procedure was very successful, and Arden came home on Monday. I noticed earlier that morning when we were leaving the hospital, that I was wheezing a little. I have asthma, so I used my inhaler and kept on going.

The next morning, I was still struggling to breathe.

The inhaler isn't helping. I need to go to the hospital to get a nebulizer breathing treatment. I shouldn't drive myself to the hospital. I need someone to take me and I also need someone to sit with Arden and Nick while I'm gone. Arden shouldn't be alone so soon after his heart attack and he can't take care of Nick yet. We need lots of help, where am I going to find it?

I made a few phone calls and got it all arranged and a girlfriend took me back to the hospital in Bellevue for my breathing treatment.

Another friend came and picked me up a few hours later to go back home.

I am still out of breath just walking out to the car. I had three hours of treatment and I need to be back home. I should be okay. I will sit here and try to literally catch my breath. It seems a bit better.

On the way home, I was worse again. I should have had my friend take me back to Urgent Care, but I didn't. Soon there wouldn't be anyone at home with Arden and Nick, so I continued home.

I felt awful. I tried to eat some dinner but I couldn't breathe in between bites. I didn't want to concern Arden, so I went upstairs to our bedroom. I tried to lay down on the bed but literally couldn't breathe in at all.

I sat back up and drew in a little bit of air. *I'll blow into my Peak Flow meter to test my breathing. The output didn't register on the scale at all. I think this meter is broken.*

Arden came into the room and asked what was happening. I could only get one word out at a time and explained as best I could. I asked him to check the Peak Flow meter to see if it was working.

When he blew over three hundred on the meter scale I knew I was in trouble. It was not broken.

We called Derek to take me back to the Urgent Care. Martha came over to sit with me for a few hours while I was hooked back up to the hospital's nebulizer.

The nurses asked, "Have you been under any stress lately?"

I laughed.

I was hooked up to the breathing machine for over seven hours until my bronchi finally relaxed enough so I could breathe without the nebulizer running.

Since I was there after the shift change, the doctor who released me from the hospital felt that she needed to review all of my notes before she let me go. I was a little frustrated at the delay and I'd had a lot of albuterol so I was more than a little bit excitable, too.

She pulled her rolling chair directly in front of me and said, "Mrs. Gremmert, you have had a serious asthma attack. I want to help you prevent this from happening again. I myself have asthma, so I understand the condition, both as a patient and as a doctor. Please let me do my job. I promise we'll come up with a solution."

That calmed me down. I was willing to listen.

Over the next hour, she was able to get me a portable nebulizer to take home with medication. She explained each of the different treatment protocols and how they differed: when to use the inhalers, and when to use the nebulizers. She also explained that if I ever got to the point that I needed to take a breath in between my words when I was trying to talk, I had waited too long and I needed to get to an emergency room ASAP.

She counseled me that I needed to take better care of myself. It would take time for my bronchi and lungs to heal but if I followed her instructions, eventually my asthma would subside and I would be healthier.

She was right. It took about eight months before I felt like the inflammation and airway irritability were back to more normal levels. I told my friends that Arden's heart attack had taken my breath away.

Chapter Fifty-Seven

Arden's cardiologist told him that he had no restrictions on travel so we were able to take our planned trip to Ireland in November, just a few weeks after his heart attack.

We had planned to stop in Paris for three days before heading back home at the end of our trip. They had undergone a terrorist attack on Friday 13 while we were still in Ireland; 130 victims were killed in the shootings and bombings. It was horrific.

We decided to go ahead with our plans, even though the airline was willing to change our itinerary. Nick really wanted to go to Paris.

The desk clerk at the hotel asked Nick what he wanted to see.

"I see two things. One, Eiffel Tower. Two, Mona Lisa."

Turning to me, the clerk asked, "Are you looking for a tour to see the sights. I can offer a personal cab that you can hire for as many hours as you want. He will go exactly where you want to go. The driver will wait for you at the various venues and later bring you back to the hotel."

It sounded terrific. We went to the Eiffel Tower first. I stayed with Nick as Arden went closer to take pictures. It was raining and there were lots of stairs that would have been hard to navigate. Nick saw a vendor with small key chain replicas of the tower and I bought him one.

He kept looking at his key chain and at the real tower, saying over and over, "I see Eiffel Tower, I see Eiffel Tower."

I'm not sure where he learned about the tower but it certainly seemed to be on his bucket list. Arden returned from his photo odyssey and we returned to the van.

After we were all buckled in and ready to go, Nick said, "Oh and I forgot, Arden, you need Hard Rock Café pins."

Arden is an avid Hard Rock Café fan and has a very large collection of pins. We had not even thought about finding the Paris Hard Rock but Nick remembered. The cab driver said that it was on the way, and we parked down the street while Arden dashed into the store.

We also got to fulfill one of Arden's dreams—we rode around the Arc de Triomphe in a cab, very fast, multiple times. It was just as crazy as it is depicted in the films we had seen and truly as memorable. We drove past the Louvre and showed Nick where we would be going the next day. We got out of the cab at Notre Dame.

The cab driver said, "I will look for you after an hour. Go to the front of the line and ask where the access for disabled persons is."

It was a bit awkward as the line was very long to get in, but when I asked, they motioned us to come right in. So we did.

We went through the large carved doors of the famous western facade and purchased a tourist guide at the table there. The building is truly a work of art. It was astonishing inside. We were walking slowing pushing Nick's wheelchair up one side of the church and had progressed about half way when a security guard approached us. In a heavy French accent, he tried to tell us that if we wanted to view the various chapels, we should go to the stone stairs leading up there and press a button. Someone would come and help us.

Eventually, we made our way to the stairs and saw the button. We let Nick push it and we waited. I couldn't see a lift anywhere, but I did notice that in the middle of the stairs there was a distinctive cut line down through each stair. I showed it to Arden and we wondered what it was. When the guard arrived, he turned a key and pushed a button on a stand. Then, all of a sudden, the ancient carved steps began moving down and flattened out. It was an ingeniously engineered hidden lift.

Arden walked up the adjacent three stairs and I rode with Nick. After wheeling him onto the lift, a short metal strip rose up behind the wheelchair as a safety guard to keep Nick from rolling backward. It was pretty cool. Nick loved the short ride. We wandered around looking at all the artifacts, stained glass windows and chapels dedicated to different saints. It was truly breathtaking and we were very happy we had stopped there.

I wanted to see the Basilique du Sacre-Coeur de Montmartre. The cab driver took us to the top of the city. He suggested that we not try and take Nick in because of the large number of stairs. Nick and Arden stayed by the cab, looking out over the staggering vista of Paris. By then it was beginning to become dark and the City of Lights was dressing herself to put on a show. It was stunning.

The next morning, after breakfast, we took a cab back into the city to go to the Louvre. First stop was the Mona Lisa. The museum can be confusing to most visitors, and with Nick's wheelchair, we needed to find the elevators, so we just kept asking for help to find our way. We went into the room that houses the Mona Lisa. I still don't know why seeing the painting was so significant to Nick. He had been in art classes in both junior high and high school, but I don't remember him mentioning the painting before we told him that we were going to Paris. I was surprised that he even knew that the Mona Lisa was in Paris.

We stood in line waiting our turn to be up at the front rope-line. Nick couldn't really see anything in the room while we were in line because of the crowd around him. He kept asking where the Mona Lisa was. It really is a tiny painting. Finally, we were at the front and a security guard approached Arden. I was worried that he would say that we needed to move Nick along. I couldn't have been more wrong. We don't speak French, so we didn't know what he was saying to Arden. But when he moved the crowd control rope divider back and motioned for Arden to come in toward the painting, it was obvious that he was letting Nick get a closer look.

I started to walk forward too, and he put the rope in front of me and said something. I understood the word no. So I stayed back. Nick sat within a few feet from the most famous painting in the world. For about fifteen minutes he looked at the painting while his dad was talking to him. Again, I had underestimated my son. He did have an appreciation for art. It obviously was important to him. I had no idea.

Finally, he said, "I done, what next?"

Arden turned him around and the guard opened the rope for them to rejoin me.

We spent another couple of hours in the museum. A couple of the elevators weren't working, so we had a museum employee guiding us through the bowels of the museum to get to elevators that were working so we could visit the various exhibits. I felt that the museum staff was very kind and accommodating.

That day at the Louvre was also Thanksgiving Day 2015 back in the US. We found a charming little restaurant around the corner from the Louvre and ordered roasted chicken with potatoes for dinner. We felt like we had a lot to be thankful for and it was a great Thanksgiving feast. Outside the restaurant was a taxi stand, and it was very convenient to grab a cab and head back to the hotel.

Our flight home the next day was uneventful. Nick loved it of course, and we were very grateful for our grand little adventure in Paris.

PART ELEVEN

Is This the Last Dance?

Chapter Fifty-Eight

None of us know when the last dance with our loved ones will happen. After Dr. Doherty talked to us about SUDEP and then a few weeks later, we almost lost Nick from seizures, I experienced a paradigm shift. For over thirty-eight years I have been consciously aware that because of LGS, Nick has an increased risk of unexpected premature death. This hangs over me every day. When the seizures don't stop, when he oversleeps in the mornings, when he is sick with a normal illness, when he… The fear is constant.

A friend's son did pass away unexpectedly from SUDEP. He had LGS. He was twelve. I cried for her and her family. I sent her messages of support. I prayed for her. I wondered what I would be doing each day as the time passed, if I were in her shoes. The funeral was over and everyone went back to their own lives, but her life was completely changed by that experience.

I have experienced losing close friends and family members. I understand that grief, but SUDEP is different. It is the loss of a family member, a child, and someone who is completely dependent on you. It is also a loss of one's job, responsibilities and daily duties. It is even the loss of a portion of one's personal identity as a caregiver and an advocate. There is the potential for guilt and shame. "Could I have done anything more for my child? Was there something I didn't do?"

The basic routine of our everyday lives would immediately change. Loss of any kind is profound and when the day comes that I am walking down that path, I hope that I will remember the joyful moments and I will laugh in the midst of my tears.

Since I don't know exactly what I will do when this occurs, I have committed to suspend judgment of others as they are walking through the dark days of their grief. We need to grab hold of every opportunity and fully experience it. That is exactly what we did in 2016.

Our own beds felt great once we were back home from our epic six-week road trip. Although we hadn't seen everyone we loved, we got to visit with many who had moved away or lived elsewhere. We only had a few days of seizures and Nick really loved seeing his friends again. It was truly an excellent opportunity.

Chapter Fifty-Nine

Nick had two birthday parties that year. One in Heppner, at Uncle Gene's during the rodeo weekend, the other one a few days later at home with the family. He loves everything about birthdays. The presents, the cake, ice cream, and candles, everyone singing "Happy Birthday" to him—all of it.

For me, August 19 is a difficult day every year. I know that he's happy and that he's loved. However, on that one day of the year, I can't seem to stop myself thinking about what others his same age are doing, and I am sad. It's my own little pity party. I used to feel guilty. But I've decided that my feelings are real, and I sometimes I feel sad and disappointed. Most of the time, I don't. I always make the day exciting for Nick and then I go cry in private. The next morning, I'm all better and I move on.

Dr. Doherty counsel to us still was to travel with Nick while we were able to, so we booked our usual fall trip to Ireland.

We awoke one particular morning in Carndonagh to a very cheerful Nick. It's inspiring to hear him singing songs with Arden as the day begins.

Suddenly, Nick asked, "I have a drop seizure?"

"I haven't seen a seizure. When was it? Was it yesterday?"

"I don't know…maybe…I think today."

Arden again told him that he hadn't seen any seizures. I found myself holding my breath. I was thinking that maybe Nick had experienced a bad dream. I was just about to ask Nick if it could have been a dream, when I heard a loud crashing thud. Once you have heard it, you always remember the sound of an unconscious body hitting the floor.

"Arden, was that a seizure?"

"Yes, a drop seizure, just on the first stair."

I let out my held breath.

"Are you okay? Do you need help?"

"We are both okay. I was able to lower him onto the landing as he went down."

This is why we try to always have our hands on him when he's up and moving. We never know when a seizure will happen.

I went down the stairs and stepped over Nick and Arden, sprawled on the stair landing. As I was moved past, Arden was speaking softly.

"Nick, you had a seizure. Mom is going to get the rolling office chair so we can move you into your bedroom and help you lie down."

Arden and I are very familiar with the steps to the seizure management dance. Get him safe and comfortable, grab the rescue seizure medicine from Nick's bag to start the protocol, begin taking detailed notes of when and what is happening, administer the magnet to the VNS device, call the doctor, keep careful watch of Nick for any indication of further seizures. Repeat the steps until the seizures either stop or we have to call the ambulance and go to the hospital.

Thankfully this particular seizure episode lasted only thirty minutes. After an hour of no seizures, Nick fell asleep for about four hours, and Arden and I could breathe again. Some days the seizures last over three hours. We feel very lucky when they're less.

I watched Arden tenderly caring for Nick through that long morning.

He's always been a tremendous example of loving kindness to me. We've had our share of disagreements and frustration over the years, but he's usually the first one to apologize and forgive the hurt. Throughout our forty years together, his remarkable example of how to love others has inspired changes in me. I've learned about service and compassion by being loved by Arden. After forty years together, we are a good team.

This stressful situation that day created another opportunity for us to bond even closer as we devotedly served our son together. Everyone has challenges in their life. The key is to look for the good moments and then hold on to those memories. I believe that we could have easily handled everything else if Nick didn't have seizures. My journey has been to find things to be thankful for within the experiences of uncontrolled seizures. This has been difficult, but here is my short list:

People, often strangers, are kind to us and offer to help.

Arden and I are closer as a couple as we work together to care for Nick during those extreme moments.

I have met and grown to love other parents who have experienced the same issues with LGS and other disabilities.

I have compassion for others as they support their family members with a rare and debilitating disease.

Those hard days have shown me with pinpoint focus what is truly paramount in my life.

Epilogue
Will We Dance in the Future?

Life's experiences are often unexpected. The expected often doesn't happen. It is essential to find joy in the journey. I have known that and yet every so often I relearn it. We have met so many wonderful people because we have Nick in our life. We have experienced such extreme stress because we have Nick in our life. The highs are sweet and the lows can be terrifying. We thought in 2016 that our time with Nick was nearly over. I have no idea what the future holds for us.

I do know that Arden and I have developed the strength to stand in the middle of the storm and look for the calm that we know will always eventually come.

I do know that since that meeting with Dr. Doherty in December of 2015, following Arden's heart attack, every moment that we have with our loved ones is precious. The memories are strung together like a precious pearl necklace shimmering in the light of awareness.

We find joy every day. Every minute if we can. Sometimes we forget when the situation is particularly trying or we are exhausted. Then some moment of emotional sunshine bursts forth and we remember.

Recently we were at a party. People were dancing and Nick was moving to the music in his wheelchair.

"I dancing."

"Nick, I wish I could dance with you again."

Sometimes I will take the brakes off his wheelchair and we "dance," but that is not what I meant.

"Okay, Mom. I okay, we dance, okay?"

"Really, Nick, you feel strong enough to get up and dance?"

"I okay, help me, okay?"

He put his spinner on the wheelchair seat.

Nick knows how to twirl me under his arm and move his feet back and forth to the rhythm of the music. His smile melted my heart. We danced through most of the song. Suddenly he stopped.

"I sit down now. Okay, Mom? I done dancing."

I helped him back into his wheelchair. He picked up his spinner and watched it going around and around. We had danced and it filled our hearts with joy. I hope that it isn't the last one. If truly was, I will remember it always. Quoting Nick, "I okay."

This is what I wish everyone reading this book could find and experience. May we all find the strength and the hope that we need, and the joy we desire. I know it will come.

Glossary of Terms

Apraxic: Apraxia of Speech; Apraxia is a motor speech disorder that makes it hard for children to speak. It can take a lot of work to learn to say sounds and words better.

ARC: Was called Advocates for Retarded Citizens now The ARC of King County. Founded in 1936, the ARC of King County advocates for the rights of children and adults with intellectual and developmental disabilities to live, work, and play in the community, improving the quality of life for all of us.

Cerebral Palsy: CP; Developmental Delay, Static Encephalopathy. While Cerebral Palsy is a blanket term commonly referred to as "CP" and described by loss or impairment of motor function, Cerebral Palsy is actually caused by brain damage. The brain damage is caused by brain injury or abnormal development of the brain that occurs while a child's brain is still developing— before birth, during birth, or immediately after birth.

Cerebral Palsy affects body movement, muscle control, muscle coordination, muscle tone, reflex, posture, and balance. It can also impact fine motor skills, gross motor skills, and oral motor functioning.

Developmental Delay and Static Encephalopathy are other common terms used to describe permanent or unchanging brain damage. The effects on development depend on the part of the brain involved and on the severity of the damage.

COHMC and COH: Children's Orthopaedic Hospital and Medical Center in Seattle, WA.

LDS: A common abbreviation referring to the Church of Jesus Christ of Latter-Day Saints and its members.

Lennox-Gastaut Syndrome: LGS is a form of severe epilepsy that begins in childhood. It is characterized by multiple types of frequent seizures and intellectual disability.

Postictal: The postictal state is the altered state of consciousness after an epileptic seizure. It usually lasts between five and thirty minutes, but sometimes longer in the case of larger or more severe seizures, and is characterized by drowsiness, confusion, nausea, hypertension, headache, or migraine, and other disorienting symptoms.

Seizures: *Tonic Clonic or Grand Mal*. This type of seizure (also called a convulsion) is what most people think of when they hear the word "seizure." An older term for this type of seizure is "grand mal." As implied by the name, they combine the characteristics of tonic and clonic seizures. Tonic means stiffening, and clonic means rhythmical jerking.

Absence or Petit Mal: An absence seizure (formerly classified as *petit mal*), is a very uncommon seizure that begins suddenly and occurs without any warning signs.

People experiencing absence seizures typically appear to stare without moving. Usually lasting less than fifteen seconds, absence seizures can occur many times a day and may be mistaken for daydreaming. While the patient may not remember what happened during the seizure, they'll typically return to being instantly alert as soon as the seizure is finished.

Focal or Partial: Focal seizures (also called partial seizures and localized seizures) are seizures which affect initially only one hemisphere of the brain. The brain is divided into two hemispheres, each consisting of four lobes—the frontal, temporal, parietal, and occipital lobes.

Atonic or Drop: Muscle "tone" is the muscle's normal tension. "Atonic" (a-TON-ik) means "without tone." In an atonic seizure, muscles suddenly become limp. Part of all of the body may become limp. The eyelids may droop, the head may nod or drop forward, and the person may drop things. If standing, the person often falls to the ground. These seizures typically last less than fifteen seconds. People may get injured when they fall.

Head protection, such as a helmet or other protective gear, may be needed. These seizures are also called "drop attacks" or "drop seizures."

Cluster: Seizure clusters are seizures that start and stop, but occur in groups one right after another. They are more commonly seen in children with certain epilepsy syndromes such as Lennox Gastaut Syndrome (LGS) and can look different depending on the child.

SUDEP: Sudden Unexplained Death in Epilepsy is defined as the sudden and unexpected, nontraumatic, and nondrowning death of a person with epilepsy, without a toxicological or anatomical cause of death detected during the postmortem examination.

About the Author

Eva Doherty Gremmert is a talented, published author, a successful business woman, a sought-after public speaker and a professional genealogist.

In January 2017, Eva began a blog on her website, www.evagremmert.com. These posts are short vignettes of her current life experiences and lessons learned from parenting Nick, her son with special needs. She writes for *Patient Worthy*, an online magazine and has published an article on the *Tenacity to Triumph* Blog. Through her writing and presentations, Eva actively creates a platform to better support and educate parents. Video presentations can be viewed in the Schedule section of her website and on YouTube.

Her first work of fiction, "A Cottage in Donegal. *Mary Doherty's Story*," was self-published in 2011 and is available in print and Kindle versions. The audiobook is scheduled to be released in 2019. It is an entertaining and evocative read, written from Mary's perspective. Eva has researched and published five books on her family history and hosts two major genealogy research websites.

Eva owns a tax preparation and business development firm, founded in 1981. She's volunteered with many non-profits over the years.

She and her husband, Arden, have been married for 42 years. They divide their time between their homes in Carnation, WA and Carndonagh, Co. Donegal, Ireland. They have raised four amazing children and have eleven beautiful grandchildren.

CPSIA information can be obtained
at www.ICGtesting.com
Printed in the USA
BVHW030422091019
560429BV00033B/88/P